Praise for *The Win-Win Wealth Strategy*

"Tom Wheelwright is an expert at making complex financial concepts simple. He walks you through each investment in a way that's easy to understand — and easy to implement in your own plan. If you're serious about building wealth, *The Win-Win Wealth Strategy* needs to go on your must-read list immediately."

— **Anik Singal**,
Founder and CEO of Lurn.com

"Everyone deserves the opportunity to build wealth for themselves and their communities. *The Win-Win Wealth Strategy* levels the playing field by unveiling the worldwide tax code secrets that the rich already know. If you have the heart of an entrepreneur, it's time you learn these secrets, too."

— **Marco Antonio Regil**

"The tax code can either be a minefield or a treasure map. Most tax strategists focus on keeping you from harm. Tom Wheelwright shows you how to follow the tax code to get richer. In what is sure to be another best-seller, Tom's *The Win-Win Wealth Strategy* reveals not just one or two, but *seven* strategic investments the tax code rewards investors for making…and the why and how to make them work for you."

— **Russel Gray**,
Co-host of The Real Estate Guys Radio Show

"In *The Win-Win Wealth Strategy*, passionate CPA Tom Wheelwright opens a world of tax savings…figuratively and literally. You'll not only learn a ton, but you'll also glean actionable steps to immediately put the tax code on your side. Don't read this book to save taxes. . .read this book to become wealthy."

— **Robert Helms**,
Co-host of The Real Estate Guys Radio Show

"*The Win-Win Wealth Strategy* is perfect for anyone interested in a new way of thinking about wealth. I wish I'd had this book when I first started working. It would have saved me A LOT of money."

— **Buck Joffrey**,
Founder, WealthFormula.com

"Anyone who thinks tax incentives are immoral will change their mind after reading this book. The truth is: Tax incentives work. This book explains why they work for the government and, most importantly, how they can work for you."

— **Josh Lannon**,
Co-Founder and CEO, Warriors Heart

"Tom Wheelwright is the master teacher when it comes to taxes. In this book, investors will experience an important and valuable shift in context — from viewing government tax policies as a wealth killer to viewing them as a wealth enabler. *The Win-Win Wealth Strategy* is a game changer for investors!"

— **Andy Tanner**,
Best-selling Author of *401(k)aos*, Founder, Tanner Training

THE WIN-WIN WEALTH STRATEGY

FOREWORD BY **ROBERT T. KIYOSAKI**

Author of International Bestseller *Rich Dad, Poor Dad*

THE WIN-WIN WEALTH STRATEGY

7 Investments the Government Will Pay You to Make

TOM WHEELWRIGHT, CPA

WILEY

Published by John Wiley & Sons, Inc., Hoboken, New Jersey.
Published simultaneously in Canada.

For general information on our other products and services or for technical support, please contact our Customer Care Department within the United States at (800) 762-2974, outside the United States at (317) 572-3993 or fax (317) 572-4002.

Wiley publishes in a variety of print and electronic formats and by print-on-demand. Some material included with standard print versions of this book may not be included in e-books or in print-on-demand. If this book refers to media such as a CD or DVD that is not included in the version you purchased, you may download this material at http://booksupport.wiley.com. For more information about Wiley products, visit www.wiley.com.

Library of Congress Cataloging-in-Publication Data:

Names: Wheelwright, Tom, author.
Title: The win-win wealth strategy : 7 investments the government will pay you to make / Tom Wheelwright.
Description: Hoboken, New Jersey : Wiley, [2022] | Includes index.
Identifiers: LCCN 2022013696 (print) | LCCN 2022013697 (ebook) | ISBN 9781119911548 (cloth) | ISBN 9781119911555 (adobe pdf) | ISBN 9781119911562 (epub)
Subjects: LCSH: Investments. | Finance, Personal. | Wealth.
Classification: LCC HG4521 .W4725 2022 (print) | LCC HG4521 (ebook) | DDC 332.6—dc23/eng/20220504
LC record available at https://lccn.loc.gov/2022013696
LC ebook record available at https://lccn.loc.gov/2022013697

Cover Art: Tree: © Getty Images | Leonello Calvetti
Bills: © Shutterstock: Paul Fleet
Cover Design: Paul McCarthy

SKY10034152_051922

For my sons, Max and Sam

I dedicate this book to you with the hope that you continue your financial education so that you may achieve your dreams.

Also by Tom Wheelwright...Tax-Free Wealth
WealthAbility CTAs
Stay Connected with Tom Social Media details

Contents

Foreword xi

Preface xv

Acknowledgments xvii

Introduction 1

Chapter 1 Partnering with the Government 3

Chapter 2 Investment #1: Business 13

Chapter 3 Investment #2: Technology | Research and Development 43

Chapter 4 Investment #3: Real Estate 59

Chapter 5 Investment #4: Energy 83

Chapter 6 Investment #5: Agriculture 97

Chapter 7 Investment #6: Insurance 111

Chapter 8 Investment #7: Retirement Savings 129

Chapter 9 Conclusion 151

Bonus Chapter How to Get the Government to Pay for Your Ferrari 155

Endnotes 163

About the Author 225

Index 227

Foreword

by Robert Kiyosaki

Most people hate taxes. . .

but not Tom Wheelwright.

That's why he is my personal tax advisor and CPA. Tom's love for the subject of taxes is why I trust him to understand every incentive in the Tax Code — and use them to reduce my taxes while increasing my wealth. Tom's love of taxes is why he knows more about taxes than most people — most other CPAs, certainly, and (I suspect) most government bureaucrats who work for the IRS, America's Internal Revenue Service.

Most people pay taxes first. . .

but not Tom Wheelwright.

The primary reason so many employees struggle, living "paycheck to paycheck," is because the taxman always gets paid first. As an employee, I remember opening my paychecks and noticing the taxman had been there before me. As an employee, the taxman always gets paid first.

Most entrepreneurs pay the most taxes. . .

but not Tom Wheelwright or his clients.

Small business entrepreneurs pay a higher percentage in taxes than employees, and most small entrepreneurs don't reserve enough of their profits to cover their taxes.

My rich dad's CASHFLOW Quadrant, pictured below, explains the differences between employees and small business entrepreneurs when it comes to taxes:

TAX PERCENTAGES PAID PER QUADRANT

E stands for employee

S stands for self-employed, specialists, such as doctors and lawyers, and small business entrepreneurs.

B stands for Big Business with 500 employees or more

I stands for ***Inside*** Investor.

These tax percentages, defined by quadrant, are pretty consistent throughout most of the Western, capitalist world.

Most **E**s and **S**s invest from the "outside." They invest in "public investments" such as stocks, bonds, mutual funds, and ETFs. Investors in the **I** quadrant invest in "private investments" available only to insiders.

Tom's first book, from the Rich Dad Advisor Series titled *Tax-Free Wealth*, is essential reading and study if you want to make more money and pay less in taxes, even no taxes. . .legally.

Interestingly, according to Tom, the biggest tax cheats are small business owners in the **S** quadrant. If I were paying 60% in tax, I could understand. But you do not have to be a tax cheat if you read Tom's books and my Rich Dad books.

The reason so many millions of people are tax slaves is because they followed my poor dad's advice:

> *"Go to school, get a job, work hard, pay taxes, buy a house, get out of debt, and invest for the long term in a well-diversified portfolio of stocks, bonds, mutual funds, and ETFs."*

People who have these words of advice imbedded in their brain become the tax slaves of the government. They are silent partners with the government. They simply allow the government to take a percentage of every dollar they earn.

As my rich dad used to say:

> *"If you think education is expensive. . .try ignorance."*

Is Tom Wheelwright's tax advice legal?

It is. In fact, emphatically so. Not only is Tom's tax advice legal, it's also advice that mirrors what the tax law and lawmakers anticipated when they created the incentives in the Tax Code — do what the government wants done and receive tax benefits in exchange.

Tom teaches that "**B**s and **I**s do not need to cheat in order to pay less in taxes." Tom teaches, "Tax laws are government incentives for **B**s and **I**s to assist the government by doing what the government wants and needs done. For example, the U.S. government offers tax incentives to real estate investors and oil investors. The government needs energy and housing, hence offers 'tax-incentives' for taxpayers who invest from the **B** and **I** quadrants. **B**s and **I**s are active partners with the government."

Tom's books are filled with many "tax facts" for pro-active entrepreneurs and investors on how to reduce taxes while creating wealth. If you are a patriot and want to do what the government wants done — creating jobs, housing, energy, and food — Tom's books are essential reading.

Does Tom's tax advice apply outside the United States? Yes. Tom and I travel the world teaching. In every country we visit, the people we teach learn that their country offers similar tax incentives to investors on the **B**- and **I**-side of the quadrant.

Regardless of the country in which you pay your taxes, Tom always recommends that you seek professional advice for your country's tax laws. His books are guides that will empower you to ask better and more sophisticated questions of your personal tax advisor.

If your personal tax advisor does not know or understand your questions, it might be time for you to seek new, smarter advisors.

In every country we teach in, there are always some people who come up to Tom and say:

"You can't do that here."

I've learned not to argue with idiots. Those who are locked into a mindset and can't appreciate other points of view aren't worth arguing with. Words of wisdom from over 100 years ago. . .from the great American writer Mark Twain, concur: *"No amount of evidence will ever convince an idiot."*

Rather than argue with idiots in front of thousands of people, Tom just respectfully nods his head silently. . .and moves on to the next person.

Tom was following another bit of wisdom from Mark Twain:

"Never argue with a fool. . .onlookers may not know the difference."

If you are ready to earn more money and pay less taxes, legally, Tom can teach you how to use tax incentives to your advantage and this book is for you.

Because some people see the inevitability of two things: death and taxes.

. . .but not Tom Wheelwright.

Robert Kiyosaki
Entrepreneur, Investor and Author
of the international bestseller *Rich Dad Poor Dad*

Preface

On September 26, 2016, in a nationally televised debate between the two major party candidates for U.S. President, Hillary Clinton accused Donald Trump of not paying taxes. In response, Donald Trump famously said, "That's because I'm smart." On September 27, 2020, almost exactly four years later, *The New York Times* printed a story claiming that President Trump had not paid taxes in 10 out of 15 years. In two of those years, he only paid $750 in taxes. People were outraged, but President Trump is not alone in paying next to nothing in taxes. In fact, it's common for the rich.

For years, the richest people and companies in the world have paid little to nothing in taxes. Amazon, one of the largest companies in the world, paid nothing in federal income tax for 2017 or 2018 despite reporting pre-tax income of $3.8 billion and $11.2 billion,[1] respectively. In fact, they received refunds of $137 million in 2017 and $129 million in 2018! In 2019, they only paid $162 million[2] of federal income tax despite reporting pre-tax income of $13.9 billion. Through the end of 2020, Tesla, the leader in the electric car revolution, has never paid U.S. Federal income tax, despite a valuation as one of the largest companies in the world.[3]

This begs two questions. First, is it legal to pay little to nothing in taxes? Second, if it is legal, how can it be so? Are the rich simply finding inadvertent loopholes? Are lobbyists paying off the politicians for these tax benefits?

It turns out that these tax benefits are actually incentives—intentional policy decisions designed to encourage investments. All developed countries with income tax laws provide similar incentives, and knowledgeable business owners and investors, like former President Trump, Amazon, and Tesla, use these incentives to reduce or eliminate their taxes *legally*.

This book analyzes these tax policies from a practical perspective. This will not be an academic analysis. I do have a Bachelor of Arts in

Accounting and a Masters of Professional Accounting with an emphasis in tax, and I was an adjunct professor in the Masters of Tax program at Arizona State University for 14 years, and spent three years in the National Tax Department of Ernst & Young. But I've spent most of my career as an advisor to companies and individuals related to their tax obligations and wealth creation. In short, I help people and companies pay little to nothing in taxes. And that's as practical as it gets.

As I wrote in my first book, *Tax-Free Wealth*, governments have long used the tax laws to incentivize certain behaviors. Using the tax laws in this way has come under severe scrutiny by many, including the European Union, Senator Bernie Sanders, Senator Ted Cruz, and others. The arguments against using the tax code as incentives generally range from including a broad-based flat tax or a global minimum tax to ensuring wealthy individuals and companies pay at least some tax. Ironically, some of the most vocal critics, including President Joe Biden, continue using the tax laws as incentives. Many of those who complain about the current tax structure just want to change which activities are incentivized, such as moving from primarily economic incentives to environmental and social incentives. They really don't want to eliminate tax incentives. There is a reason for this: tax incentives work. And governments get as much out of tax incentives as the wealthy who take advantage of them.

Human nature hasn't changed. People will rail against others (read: *the rich*) getting tax incentives but get even more up in arms when their own incentives are yanked away. Just look at the uproar over Americans losing their deduction for state income taxes. (The Democrats in the U.S. Congress, while excoriating the rich and their tax breaks, continue to fight to restore this deduction.)[4] I've never met anyone who enjoys paying taxes. And very few governments are willing to give up the power and control that come with high marginal tax rates and correspondingly large tax incentives.

This book will teach you that the tax law is the best roadmap to wealth ever devised. This is *not* a book about tax loopholes for the rich. It's about the investments and activities the government wants you to engage in and the tax incentives they provide in exchange. My goal is to raise the level of consciousness and literacy around the biggest expense to individuals and corporations, *and* the largest source of revenue to most governments — income tax.

Acknowledgments

Special thanks to Michael Edden, who conducted massive amounts of research producing tables for 15 different countries. My thanks as well go to Mona Gambetta who made sure this was not a work of fiction.

Introduction

U.S. President John Kennedy proposed the first substantial investment tax credit in 1961. The goal was to spur investment in manufacturing equipment during a U.S. economic downturn. Since then, the use of investment credits and other tax incentives have exploded within the United States as well as in most other developed countries.

Even before investment tax credits, there were business incentives. While individual taxpayers historically receive very few deductions to offset their taxable income, businesses have long deducted their business expenses to offset their income. This is because income tax for businesses, in most countries, is based on *net* rather than *gross* income.

Gross income taxes, like sales taxes, are based on the total amount received, whether or not the taxpayer makes a profit. These taxes are typically passed on to the customer. Net income taxes are assessed only against the company's profits and therefore, become a company expense. A company's profit is defined by the tax law, rather than by generally accepted accounting principles.

Sometimes, tax incentives directly offset a tax liability, such as the investment tax credit or child-care credit. Child-care credits enacted in 2021 in the United States provided up to $3,600 of direct tax offsets to the income tax of parents. The result for a family of four would be a direct income tax reduction of up to $7,200. Other incentives indirectly offset taxes through deductions against taxable income. Examples are depreciation and research and development (R&D) deductions, which reduce the income that's subject to tax. At a 30% tax rate, a $1,000 deduction would reduce a person's taxes by $300. In addition to economic incentives, most countries also use tax incentives to encourage certain types of social behavior (e.g., adoption and education credits), environmental protection (e.g., conservation easements and carbon credits), energy production (e.g., fossil fuel and renewable energy deductions and credits), and international commerce (e.g., foreign tax credits).

Governments provide these incentives not only to boost the economy and other programs they support, but also to control the way their economy grows, including sector growth (e.g., agricultural or mining) and the size of the company impacted. For example, in their treatise on research and development tax incentives, The Organization for Economic Co-operation and Development, an intergovernmental collective of 38 countries founded to stimulate economic progress and global trade, specifically said, "The direct funding of industry research — through supports or subsidies — has the advantage of allowing governments to retain control over the nature of R&D conducted."[1]

Along the way, the Internal Revenue Service, Her Majesty's Revenue and Customs, Canada Revenue Agency, Australian Tax Office, and other tax authorities around the world have established tax laws that are a roadmap for reducing taxes (sometimes to zero) and building vast amounts of wealth. The wealthy have long used these laws to grow and protect their wealth. You can, too. In fact, with proper education, anyone — rich or poor, young or old — can use this same roadmap to build and protect their own wealth while using their investment funds to finance government-supported programs.

And that's what this book is all about.

Chapter 1

Partnering with the Government

"Play by the rules but be ferocious."

—Phil Knight

My first full-time job was with Ernst & Whinney (today Ernst & Young) in its Salt Lake City office. With a master's degree from the University of Texas in hand, I soon learned that even in accounting firms, there were office politics. I was an extremely ambitious young accountant, and if there were office politics in play, then I was going to win. I didn't like office politics or make the rules of the game, but everyone was in the game, whether they wanted to play, or not.

I remember telling my manager at the time, "If I have to play the game, I might as well win it." Within two years, I joined the firm's prestigious National Tax Department in Washington, DC. Thousands had applied, but they only selected five of us to play. I had played the game well and won.

The game of taxes

The game of taxes is like my career at Ernst & Young. While nobody really chooses to "play" the tax game or has much if any control over the rules of the game, we *are* in the game. It's all about how we'll play the game and whether we will win or lose. Since we must play the game, we can choose what kind of player we'll be. Will we be a bench player or an amateur like most taxpayers, or will we be professionals and dominate the field like the rich?

Another way to look at the relationship between taxpayers and the government is as partners. Like it or not, we are all partners with our government. We share a portion of our income in return for services provided. Every time we receive a paycheck, the government takes a portion in taxes. While it's not really a voluntary partnership, it is one nonetheless. There is a famous scene from the sitcom *Friends* where the character Rachel receives her first paycheck. "Isn't this exciting?" she says. "I earned this! I wiped tables for it, I steamed milk for it, and it was totally . . . not worth it. Who's FICA? Why's he getting all my money?"[1]

The government doesn't really care what kind of partner we are. As a silent partner, we pay our full taxes at the highest rate possible, typically up to 40 percent or more. As an active partner, while doing what the government wants us to do, we can pay very little tax and build massive amounts of wealth at the same time. The government is very keen on encouraging investment in government-favored activities through tax breaks in exchange for us taking the risk of the investment.

To win the game of taxes while participating in socially beneficial activities, you must understand the rules of the game. While some may bend the rules, any professional athlete knows that the best way to be successful on the field is to understand the rules completely and discipline yourself enough to play the game to the best of your ability within the rules.

Few people understand the rules of the tax game. Even the rich don't necessarily understand them. They simply have advisors who do — advisors who know the Tax Code inside and out. They do what these advisors tell them, and they win. The average taxpayers cannot afford such advisors. They must learn the game on their own, and because of this, they start out at a disadvantage. The government, who creates the tax game, also makes the rules, and knows them well. They have the advantage of a huge team of agents defending the rules and practically unlimited resources to enforce them.

The object of the game of taxes

If you want to win the game of taxes, you need to understand the object of the game. The object is not merely to reduce taxes. **It's to build wealth that will never be taxed.**

By the end of this book, you will clearly understand that building wealth is not something frowned upon by the government. In fact, the government encourages wealth building so long as the wealth is used for government-sponsored activities. The best path to building generational, tax-free wealth is understanding how to best partner with the government. Believe it or not, the government *wants* us to be rich. They know that much of what they want done is best accomplished by taxpayers, not by them. They provide incentives to taxpayers to invest where they want the investments to be made and to accomplish what they want done.

Rules of the Game

1. We are all partners with the government.
2. Understand the rules completely and be disciplined enough to play the game to the best of your ability within the rules.
3. The object is not merely to reduce taxes, it's to build wealth that will never be taxed.

The five goals of every government

Every government has five primary goals:

1. **Keep the peace.** This is not just a function of legal systems, police, and traffic lights. The best way to keep the peace is to prevent uprisings. Uprisings are rooted in people feeling disenfranchised and not being able to meet their basic needs, such as food, clothing, and shelter.[2] One way to provide for these basic needs is through government handouts. The challenge with direct handouts is that it's a little like eating a candy bar. It satisfies you for a short while but eventually we want another candy bar . . . leading to an addiction to sugar and poor health.

   Democratic governments historically have stayed away from direct subsidies (with the notable exception of the pandemic subsidies) and have instead encouraged people to get jobs to earn enough to take care of their basic needs, plus surplus for a rainy day. They accomplish this through the private market, encouraging private industry to create enough jobs at high enough wages so people can work to sustain themselves and their families. These jobs are created by three primary sectors: government, large companies (500 employees or more), and small businesses (under 500 employees). In the United States, large and small businesses provide 82 percent of the jobs while the government only provides around 18 percent.[3] Most other countries also rely heavily on the private sector for job creation.[4] Figure 1.1 below shows job classifications in countries around the world.[5]

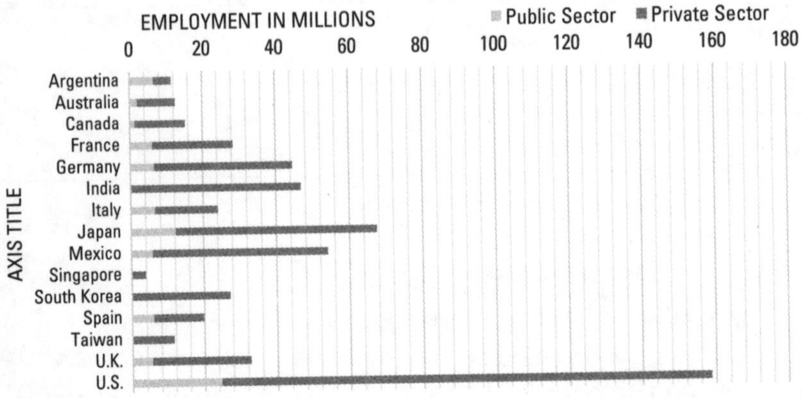

FIGURE 1.1

Government jobs are the least efficient way to provide jobs, as a dollar of cost only produces a dollar of results. Private industry produces many jobs at a much lower cost to the government. The benefit to the government for providing incentives to industries is that it costs much less than direct employment.

2. **Protect the people.** One of the primary objectives of most governments is national defense, and this doesn't apply only to military spending. Energy production is another key to a good defense and a strong economy. The United States has long maintained a policy of creating energy independence, only recently achieving it. Japan purportedly attacked Pearl Harbor because the United States cut off its oil supplies,[6] and

there is strong evidence that Germany lost World War II in large part because of a lack of oil.[7]

Other aspects of defense include agricultural production and cyber-security. In 2020, the cyberattack through the Orion software showed just how seriously governments must treat the national security defenses through technology.[8] Subsequently, there have been frequent security breaches that have affected energy transmission.[9] There have also been suspicions of security breaches through the Chinese company Huawei, leading Canada and the United States to ban the use of Huawei products.[10,11] Cyber-security has become a primary effort of governments to defend infrastructure and national defense secrets.[12]

3. **Feed the people.** "Let them eat cake" is not an effective way to maintain civilian peace and harmony, as Marie Antoinette discovered. The Arab Spring in the early 2010s was largely attributed to a low standard of living among the masses.[13] A lack of food and basic necessities is widely believed to have led to the civil wars in Yemen, Syria, Iraq, and Libya.[14] The rise of Adolf Hitler's National Socialists came with the devaluation of the Reichsmark and the subsequent hunger and inability for people to have their basic needs met. More recently, the call for Universal Basic Income by both then-presidential candidate Andrew Yang[15] and by U.S. Vice President Kamala Harris,[16] along with the earned income credit, the call for increased minimum wages,[17] and the child tax credits in the January 2021 stimulus bill enacted by the U.S. Congress[18] have all been efforts to ensure the basic needs of the poor and lower middle class are adequately met.
4. **Shelter the people.** Governments learned long ago that private markets do a better job of providing housing than public projects. Poland, Russia, the Czech Republic, and other former Soviet countries still feel the effects of public housing projects. The same is true for parts of the United States in cities like New York and Detroit as well as in the southern suburbs of Paris, France.[19] Encouraging the private markets to create housing has long proven to produce a better result,

both for the government and for the tenants, while providing passive income opportunities for investors.

5. **Educate the people.** The primary difference between a first-world country and a third-world country is often the level of education available to their people.[20] Countries with strong middle classes tend to overall be stronger financially.[21] Strong middle classes are a result of successful public education available at all levels of income and to all classes of society. The ability to move up in society has long fueled strong, peaceful economies.[22]

5 Goals of Every Government	
1.	Keep the Peace
2.	Protect the People
3.	Feed the People
4.	Shelter the People
5.	Educate the People

Tax incentives play a major role in each of these government goals. Tax laws:

- Incentivize business creation, which creates jobs
- Stoke energy and technology production, both of which increase economic performance and protect the nation
- Encourage agricultural investments, which feed people and provides a level of national security
- Increase construction and management of housing, providing shelter for people
- Encourage people to obtain higher levels of education

Governments know that if they don't use tax incentives, these goals may not be accomplished.[23,24] Local governments use tax incentives to encourage investment in struggling communities and to provide high-paying jobs. Federal governments use tax incentives to encourage development of technology, food, and energy. And the rich enjoy these incentives because they do what the government wants them to do.

Seven categories of investment incentivized by tax laws

Governments use tax laws to encourage seven primary types of investments. Investing in any of them can lower your taxes and increase your wealth. And each of them promotes one or more of the government goals of education, shelter, food, defense, and peace while producing other benefits simultaneously.

The Seven Primary Investments	
1.	Business
2.	Technology | Research & Development
3.	Real Estate
4.	Energy
5.	Agriculture
6.	Insurance
7.	Retirement

Contrary to popular belief, tax incentives are not merely gifts to the rich to help them reduce their taxes. Neither are they loopholes — because a *loophole* is an unintended consequence of a rule or law. And these incentives are intentional. Government attorneys and accountants spend thousands of hours evaluating each incentive and its impact to the government, the taxpayers, and the population at large. Most of these incentives are not the result of government graft or favors to political friends. Rather, they represent a genuine attempt at leveraging private enterprise to accomplish what the government wants done.

STOP
&
THINK
Local & Federal Governments leverage private enterprises to accomplish their goals.

Could the government undertake these projects on its own? Of course. It could hire contractors to build public housing, drill oil wells, install solar panel farms, hire farmers to produce crops, and build an entire arm of the government just to drive technological breakthroughs. But they don't want to — primarily because when they do it on their own, it's a bad investment.

Instead, the government wants to leverage its funds. Taking on investment internally would mean spending one dollar and at best in return, receiving one dollar's worth of housing, energy, crops, or technology. Through tax incentives, however, the government can spend one dollar on a tax credit and in return private builders will spend nine of their own dollars. In this scenario, the government ends up with $10 worth of housing at a cost of $1. That's pretty smart actually.

Whether or not you believe tax incentives work and whether or not you believe tax incentives are appropriate, the fact remains that all modern governments use tax laws to incentivize desired behaviors. Since most people would rather not pay taxes,[25] a small government incentive can produce a major result. When combined with the leverage that comes from debt, the current incentives in tax laws are so great that people in a high tax bracket could effectively receive tax benefits sufficient to pay for their Ferrari, Porsche, Tesla, or any other car they wanted to buy. At the end of this book, there is a bonus chapter where I illustrate how this is possible. It's not that the government wants us to buy fancy cars; it's just that understanding the rules and how to play the game sets us up for great wealth creation. Whether you want to spend your wealth on a luxury car is up to you. The rich do this all the time, and so can you — once you understand the rules of the game. This book will teach them to you by exploring the seven investments that the government wants us to make.

Chapter 1: Key Points

1. We are all partners with our government. We choose to be silent or active partners.
2. To understand the game of taxes, you need to understand how to actively partner with the government.
3. The goal of every government is to: Keep the peace, Protect the People, Feed the people, Shelter the People, and Educate the People
4. Governments use tax incentives to meet their goals.
5. Governments incentivize seven primary investments: Business, Research & Development, Real Estate, Energy, Agriculture, Insurance, and Retirement.

Chapter 2

Investment #1: Business

"Making money is art and working is art and good business is the best art."

—Andy Warhol

"It's OK to have your eggs in one basket as long as you control what happens to that basket."

—Elon Musk

"The entrepreneur always searches for change, responds to it, and exploits it as an opportunity"

—Peter Drucker

Government purposes: job creation, innovation, production, and trade

On February 1, 1995, shortly after leaving Price Waterhouse, I decided to start my own CPA firm. Even though I was the sole employee and only had two clients at the time, I clearly remember telling friends and family that I had two goals for this firm. The first was to create a CPA firm that could provide the highest level of tax advice to entrepreneurs, a group I felt were underserved by the CPA profession. The second was to create a place where people would love coming to work.

Three years later, I had a partner and a staff of 10 people. I met a former colleague at a tax conference, and he asked about my new business. He was amazed when I told him I had 10 employees.

"How did you grow so fast?" he asked.

"I never wanted to be small. It was always my intention to build a company that employed lots of people," I said. Over the years, our staff grew to as many as 50 employees in three offices across the United States. I was creating jobs.

Today, I run four companies, a CPA firm called Wheelwright Manahan, a commercial real estate company called Playworx, a software development company called PLA Software, and an education company called WealthAbility®. At each of these companies, as I stated before, one of my primary goals was to create a place where people loved coming to work. While it didn't happen overnight or without a lot of help, I can happily say that every team member within all four companies loves coming to work. And our clients reap the benefits that this positive energy and attitude deliver.

Creating well-paid, interesting jobs is one of the joys of being an entrepreneur. During the pandemic, my partners and I did everything we could to ensure that our employees continued to have jobs and get paid. While we had to reduce salaries for a short time, we did keep everyone employed and eventually restored all the pay we had withheld to stay in business. Fortunately, we had help from the government, both in the form of PPP loans and, more importantly, in the form of tax incentives. Without this help, at least one of our businesses could have been in serious trouble.

Tax incentives that give businesses an advantage

I've enjoyed many tax incentives as a result of owning and operating my businesses. These incentives range from deducting expenses and assets to accounting methods, net operating losses, and more.

The most common incentive that comes to mind for most people is that any money I put back into my business is deductible against the income from my business. Unlike employees, if every dollar I spend is intended to produce even more dollars, the government doesn't tax me. This is true in every country I have visited.[1]

Countries in Which Reinvesting Money Back into the Business is Tax Deductible		
	Yes	No
Argentina	✓	
Australia	✓	
Canada	✓	
France	✓	
Germany	✓	
India	✓	
Italy	✓	
Japan	✓	
Mexico	✓	
Singapore	✓	
South Korea	✓	
Spain	✓	
Taiwan	✓	
United Kingdom	✓	
United States	✓	

All countries that fund their government primarily through income taxes allow deductions against income for expenses that further the objectives of the business. This includes payroll and employee benefits, rent, office supplies, and almost every other expense that furthers the objectives of the business. This is why the income tax is referred to as a tax on "net" income. The tax is on income net of the expenses that produces that income. In essence, the government is sharing the cost of the expense through deductions.

STOP
&
THINK
The government is sharing the cost of the expense through deductions.

Deductions

There are four tests that must be met for a business expense to be deductible (see Figure 2.1).

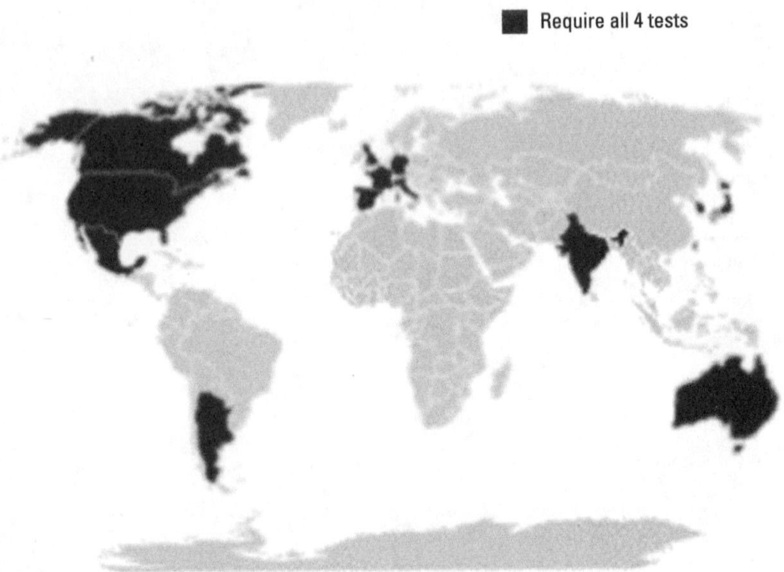

Figure 2.1

1. **Business Purpose** – the expense must be made with the business in mind. This prevents personal expenses from offsetting business income. For example, a nice dinner with a potential client has a business purpose. Dinner with your family normally does not.
2. **Ordinary** – another term for ordinary is typical. The expense must be typical, in amount and in frequency, for the industry and size of business involved. Dinner at a local restaurant is ordinary. Flying to Paris for dinner probably is not.
3. **Necessary** – the expense must be important to the business for either growth, profitability, or market share. Just because the expense is typical for other businesses in your industry

doesn't mean you should spend the money in your business. Going back to our flying-to-Paris example, it could be a deduction for a travel agency but not for your online marketing company.

4. **Documented** – all countries require a level of documentation to prove the deduction has a business purpose, is ordinary, and is necessary. If you have imaginary documentation, you get an imaginary deduction.[2]

4 Tests to Deduct Expense	
1.	Business Purpose
2.	Ordinary
3.	Necessary
4.	Documented

Countries in Which Documentation is Required to Take a Deduction	Yes	No
Argentina	✓	
Australia	✓	
Canada	✓	
France	✓	
Germany	✓	
India	✓	
Italy	✓	
Japan	✓	
Mexico	✓	
Singapore	✓	
South Korea	✓	
Spain	✓	
Taiwan	✓	
United Kingdom	✓	
United States	✓	

By requiring business expenses to have a business purpose and be ordinary and necessary, the government is effectively encouraging businesses and their owners to spend money wisely and in ways that drive economic growth and development. After all, the government is a partner in the business, reaping the rewards of success and sharing in the cost of failure. All successful business owners recognize this one truth — the purpose of an expense is to create income.

Ordinary Income/Expenses			
Income	Income from Sales		$ 100,000
Expense	Salary	$ 20,000	
	Rents	$ 5,000	
	Depreciation	$ 10,000	
	Total Expenses		$ 35,000
	Total Net Income		$ 65,000

Salary - Employees are used to increase sales

Rents - A building is needed to facilitate sales

Depreciation - Assets are needed to create products

In some countries, interest expense is also deductible when the funds are used to further business purposes (see Figure 2.2).[3]

FIGURE 2.2

This encourages businesses to borrow from banks and other financiers to grow their business, which promotes borrowing and expanding the money supply. Many countries allow a deduction for distributions to shareholders or some other mechanism to avoid double taxation as a way of encouraging investment or promoting paying dividends to shareholders.[4]

Single vs. Double Taxation

	Single	Double	Notes
Argentina		✓	
Australia	✓		
Canada	✓		
France	✓		Partial Deduction if specific requirements are met
Germany	✓		Partial Deduction if specific requirements are met
India		✓	
Italy	✓		Partial Deduction if specific requirements are met
Japan	✓		Partial Deduction if specific requirements are met
Mexico	✓		
Singapore	✓		Not taxable to the investor
South Korea	✓		Dividend received deductions (DRD) are available if certain requirements are met
Spain		✓	Dividends income received by a Spanish company from a foreign company are taxable at a reduced rate if specific requirements are met.
Taiwan		✓	
United Kingdom	✓		
United States		✓	

Those countries that don't allow a deduction for distributions typically do allow businesses to form so as to avoid double taxation (i.e., through flow-through entities).[5]

Countries that Offer Flow-Through Entities to Avoid Double Taxation		
	Yes	No
Argentina	✓	
Australia	✓	
Canada	✓	
France	✓	
Germany	✓	
India	✓	
Italy	✓	
Japan	✓	
Mexico	✓	
Singapore	✓	
South Korea	✓	
Spain	✓	
Taiwan	✓	
United Kingdom	✓	
United States	✓	

While deductions for businesses vary from country to country, the goal is always the same: to encourage business growth, which generates jobs and economic expansion. And as a business owner, it pays to know what you can deduct.

STOP
&
THINK
To encourage business growth, which generates jobs and economic expansion.

Capital Expenditures

Deductions are not limited to current expenses. In the United States, the United Kingdom, Canada, and many other countries, businesses can deduct the cost of assets used in the business.

Countries That Allow For Immediate Capital Expenditures		
	Allowable	Unallowable
Argentina		✓
Australia	✓	
Canada	✓	
France		✓
Germany		✓
India		✓
Italy		✓
Japan		✓
Mexico		✓
Singapore		✓
South Korea		✓
Spain		✓
Taiwan		✓
United Kingdom	✓	
United States	✓	

For example, if a business purchases new manufacturing equipment, the cost of the equipment is deductible in the year it is purchased even though the equipment may produce revenue over many years. In the United States, even used equipment purchases are allowed as a deduction.

Successful business owners quickly realize that, like an expense, the purpose of an asset is to produce income. The only difference between an asset and an expense is the length of time the expenditure produces income. While expenses produce income over a short time period, assets produce income over a much longer time period, typically multiple years.

By allowing an immediate deduction for equipment and other assets, the government encourages long-term investment and thus frees up cash that would otherwise go to taxes to help expand business operations. This creates more jobs and a better economy.

Lower tax rates

In most countries, entrepreneurs enjoy a lower tax rate for business income than for personal income and, in many cases, a lower tax rate for small businesses than for large businesses (see Figures 2.3[6] and 2.4[7]).

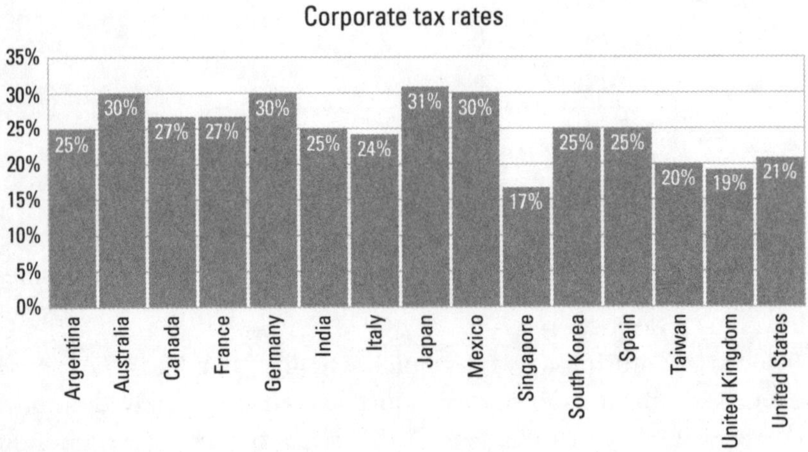

Figure 2.3

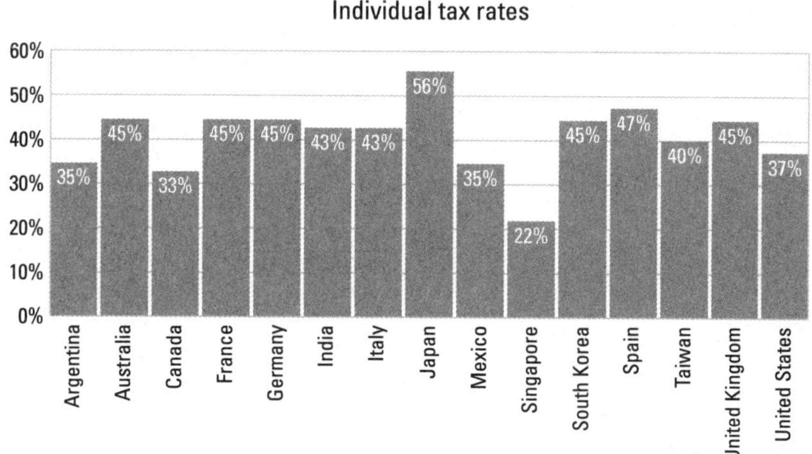

FIGURE 2.4

This makes business income a preferred source of income and is an additional incentive to owning a business rather than working as an employee.

ACCOUNTING METHODS

A business has more control over the timing of the tax paid by its owners than an individual taxpayer. As long as the business continues to reinvest income, no tax is paid. If the income is not distributed, only the business is taxed, not the owners — and at a much lower rate than other types of income.

If the business owners choose, they can form the company as a *pass-through* business entity and, in doing that, the income is only taxed to the owners and not to the business itself. In some countries, pass-through income is taxed at a lower rate than non-business income. In the United States, an owner can reinvest all business income in the business, pay no tax, and sell the business with no tax burden.[8]

As the chart below illustrates, pass-through income is taxed at a lower rate than non-business income in several countries around the world.[9]

Is Pass-Through Income is Taxed at a Lower Rate than Nonbusiness Income			
	Yes	No	Notes
Argentina		✓	
Australia	✓		Small Business Income Tax offset allows for a reduction in taxes you pay by up to $1,000 each year.
Canada	✓		Potential Canada Revenue Agency Abatement of 10% & an additional SDB reduction of tax on the first $500,000 of income.
France		✓	
Germany		✓	
India		✓	
Italy		✓	
Japan		✓	
Mexico		✓	
Singapore		✓	
South Korea	✓		A special deduction on corporate taxes is available for SMEs when they are engaged in a qualified business. The tax deduction ratio ranges from 5% to 30%, depending on corporate location, size, business types, etc., with a cap of KRW 100 million. This incentive is applied to taxable income arising in the tax years that end before 31 December 2022.
Spain		✓	
Taiwan	✓		First TWD 120,000 is tax exempt.
United Kingdom		✓	
United States	✓		Section 199A deduction allows for a deduction of qualified business income deduction for up to 20% of qualified income.

In addition, in some other countries, business owners pay little or no tax on the sale of the business.[10,11]

Are there Exclusions Related to the Gain from the Sale of Small Business Stock			
	Yes	No	Notes
Argentina		✓	
Australia	✓		Certain sellers of shares (not including companies and non-residents) may be able to discount the taxable amount of capital gains by up to 50%. Smaller businesses may be entitled to further discounts in some circumstances. However, a sale of assets by the company results in tax at the corporate level and potentially extra tax at the shareholder level.
Canada	✓		Disposal of qualified small business corporation shares (QSBCS) are eligible for the lifetime capital gains exemption.
France	✓		Capital gains on the sale of a qualifying participation owned for more than two years are tax exempt except for a 12% portion of the capital gain.
Germany		✓	
India		✓	
Italy		✓	
Japan		✓	
Mexico		✓	
Singapore	✓		Gains from the sale of a property, shares. and financial instruments in Singapore are generally not taxable.
South Korea		✓	
Spain		✓	
Taiwan		✓	
United Kingdom	✓		The sale of shares in a company where the seller has a "substantial holding" in that company (broadly, at least 10% of the ordinary shares in that company and of the income available for distribution and assets available for distribution in a winding up of the company) will be exempt from corporation tax on capital gains and any capital loss will not be an allowable loss.
United States	✓		Section 1202 Partial exclusion for gain from certain small business stock.

Businesses can also choose when to pay tax on business income. There are two primary methods a business can use for paying tax. It can pay tax when the income is earned (accrual method) or when the cash is received (cash method). Under the accrual method, income is taxed when the services are rendered or the products delivered to the customer, even if the customer doesn't pay until several days (or months) later.

Likewise, an owner may deduct expenses before it pays for them, so long as there is a fixed obligation to pay the expense and any services or products have been received.

Under the cash method, income is only taxed when the cash is received, and expenses are only deducted when the cash is spent. In many countries, only smaller businesses are allowed to use the cash method of accounting.[12]

Countries that Allow Cash Method			
	Yes	No	Notes
Argentina	✓		Available for Construction only
Australia	✓		Available for Businesses with an aggregated turn-over of less than $10 million
Canada	✓		Farmers, fishers, and self-employed commission agents only
France		✓	
Germany		✓	
India	✓		All non-corporate entities may keep books on a cash-based accounting system. However, the central government may give notice of accounting standards to be followed by any particular class of taxpayer or with respect to any particular class of income.
Italy		✓	
Japan		✓	
Mexico	✓		Method available for civil entities that render professional services (e.g, law and accounting firms) and low-income entities.
Singapore	✓		Available to small businesses whose annual sales do not exceed $1 million

Countries that Allow Cash Method (Continued)			
	Yes	No	Notes
South Korea		✓	
Spain		✓	
Taiwan		✓	
United Kingdom	✓		Available for a small self-employed business, for example, sole trader or partnership, have a turnover of £150,000 or less a year and if you have more than one business, you must use cash basis for all your businesses. The combined turnover from your businesses must be less than £150,000.
United States	✓		Under IRC Section 448, small businesses with a $25 million or less and three-year average of gross receipts (small-business taxpayer exception) are permitted to use the cash method of accounting.

There are also other accounting methods that are available solely to businesses. For example, incentives that allow a business to report income after it's been received, such as subscription revenue and revenue from long-term contracts.[13]

If a business uses one method of accounting and later decides to use a different method, it can usually change its method and "catch up" all the tax benefits in a single year. For example, in the United States, a business can choose to use the accrual method. Later, if its income is under $26 million, it can change to the cash method. In the year it changes to the cash method, the business can "catch up" on the benefits of the cash method all in one year.

As an example, suppose a business is using the accrual method and at the end of the year notices that it has $400,000 of accounts receivable and only $50,000 of accounts payable. The business has paid tax on the difference between the receivables and payables of $350,000 even though it hasn't yet received the money from the customers owing the $400,000. The business can choose ("elect") to change to the cash method and deduct $350,000 from its income in the year of change. As you can imagine, that is a significant tax savings.[14]

NET OPERATING LOSSES

In addition to the incentives of different accounting methods is the incentive of the net operating loss. In most countries, a business can use losses from one year to offset income from another year.[15]

Countries that Allow Loss Carryforward		
	Yes	No
Argentina	✓	
Australia	✓	
Canada	✓	
France	✓	
Germany	✓	
India	✓	
Italy	✓	
Japan	✓	
Mexico	✓	
Singapore	✓	
South Korea	✓	
Spain	✓	
Taiwan	✓	
United Kingdom	✓	
United States	✓	

The advantage to the business is that while it may start out with large losses funded by the owners and lenders, income from later years can be offset with these losses until the losses are recouped. As mentioned earlier in the book, both Amazon and Tesla have made effective use of the net operating loss rules to pay very little tax in later years.[16,17]

The combination of net operating losses and diverse accounting methods allow businesses great flexibility in choosing when and how income is taxed. In addition, businesses can choose their fiscal year. While individuals normally file taxes on a calendar year basis, reporting income received during that calendar year, a business can choose any 12-month period for recognizing income. This gives businesses additional flexibility they may need because of their cash flow, sales cycles, or simply to postpone income into a later taxable year.

Two Primary Methods for Paying Tax	
Accrual Method	Cash Method
When income is earned	When cash is received
Net Operating Losses	
A business can use losses from one year to offset income from another year	

Policy considerations that fuel business tax incentives

On a global scale, business tax incentives are the most widely used incentives. Governments create incentives for people to start businesses, further incentives to grow the business, and even more incentives to create an international business. The following charts indicate just how prevalent these incentives are around the world for starting a business, hiring employees, and expanding internationally. . .private-sector investment that benefits governments by both generating tax revenue and creating jobs.[18,19,20]

Incentives to Start a Business			
	Yes	No	Notes
Argentina	✓		Potential tax exemption on profits, notional income, & personal wealth. Exportation is exempt from VAT & excise taxes. Reduction of CIT for small business, up to 60%
Australia	✓		Refundable tax offsets ranging from 16.5%–40% for certain expenditures in specific industries. Tax credits for Junior Minerals Exploration Incentives. Accelerated deductions for capital expenditures on exploration and extraction of petroleum and minerals
Canada	✓		Specific investments related to the following industries: Research & Development, manufacturing & processing, liquefied natural gas, environmental sustainability, and file, media, and computer animation.

(Continued)

Incentives to Start a Business (Continued)			
	Yes	No	Notes
France	✓		Research & Development credits & tax exemptions for certain sector businesses; Regional assistance zones & Rural regeneration zone exemptions, Financial assistance via loans (PCE - Start up loan of €7,000) .
Germany	✓		Research & Development credits; grants to cover costs of hiring employees.
India	✓		Tax holiday from 5 to 10 years with up to 100% of the initial years for the following industries: Commercial productions or refining of mineral oils, processing fruits & vegetables, storages & transportation of grains, and hospital operations. Deduction of capital expenditure is allowed at 100% in initial years for several business sectors, however, several conditions must be met to take this deduction
Italy	✓		Up to 50% in tax credits for certain new capital assets; incentives in government funding for purchasing new machinery, plants, equipment, as well as digital technology & software. Incentives in investments in innovative start-ups.
Japan	✓		Investment in innovative corporations special income deduction. 30% special depreciation or 15% tax credit for businesses that invest in infrastructure for 5G technology. Special tax treatment for investment in specific equipment. 20% income deduction for investment in a National Strategic Special Area
Mexico	✓		Tax credits for investing in movie production, theater production, and transportation of goods or passengers. Full deduction of investments in renewable or efficient energy sources.
Singapore	✓		Investment allowance tax exemption on profits (up to 100%) of the capital expenditure incurred for qualifying projects
South Korea	✓		Small & medium enterprises (SMEs) can receive a special deduction from 5%–30% depending on the corporation location, size, and business type

Incentives to Start a Business (Continued)			
	Yes	No	Notes
Spain	✓		Small and medium-sized companies are eligible for tax relief, such as accelerated depreciation/ amortization and potential bad debt provision treatment.
Taiwan	✓		Free-Trade-Zones can apply for income tax exemption on income from sales of goods.
United Kingdom	✓		Accelerated capital allowances on certain assets; Annual investment allowance deduction on qualifying expenditures
United States	✓		General Business credits, Qualified Business Income deduction, accelerated depreciation & amortization

Incentives to Hire Employees			
	Yes	No	Notes
Argentina	✓		Fiscal credit of up to 70% of social security contributions paid by the employer with respect to employees dedicated to the Promoted Activities, which can be applied to the payment of certain taxes with a potential increase for new hires in special interest groups.
Australia	✓		Wage subsidy for trainees & apprentices for certain businesses. JobMaker Hiring Credit.
Canada	✓		Canada Employment Credit equal to 15% of the lesser of $1,245 or the employee's salary.
France	✓		Reduction in payroll charges paid by employers to finance the French social security system.
Germany		✓	Employers can apply for a grant to employ people who are unable to find a job due to personal reasons (for example, because of disability or long-term unemployment). An employer can claim up to 50% of the employee's salary for up to 12 months. Some circumstances may increase the deduction and timeline.
India	✓		Eligible for deduction of 30% of additional wages paid to new regular workers in a factory for a period of three years wherein the workers are employed for not less than 240 days in a year (150 days in case of apparel, footwear, and leather industry).

(Continued)

Incentives to Hire Employees (Continued)			
	Yes	No	Notes
Italy	✓		Tax credit on Training expenses, up to 50% of eligible expenses for small business.
Japan	✓		Employee-related tax credits related to revitalization of local areas.
Mexico	✓		Tax credit of up to 25% of the income tax corresponding to the salary paid to workers with certain types of disabilities.
Singapore	✓		Wage credit for senior employees, persons with disabilities. Additional wage credit scheme.
South Korea	✓		The STTCL provides for a tax incentive for increasing the number of full-time employees from the preceding year, with certain limits. The tax credit will not apply to companies engaged in businesses falling under the category of consumption-oriented services.
Spain	✓		Wage credits are specific to industry and region.
Taiwan	✓		Small and medium enterprises (SMEs) can deduct up to 130% of their annual gross salary payments for additional hired domestic workers.
United Kingdom	✓		Incentive payments for hiring apprentices.
United States	✓		Employment credits of up to 25% of the qualified first-year wages for employees employed at least 120 hours but fewer than 400 hours. 40% of qualified wages for employees employed for over 400 hours. Limited to $2,400 per employee.

International Tax Incentives			
	Yes	No	Notes
Argentina	✓		Foreign-source income tax credit (credit is limited), can be carried forward for five years.
Australia	✓		Tax exemptions for certain venture capital sector investments held for more than 12 months.
Canada	✓		Income or profits taxes paid to foreign governments generally are eligible for credit against a taxpayer's Canadian income taxes payable.

International Tax Incentives (Continued)			
	Yes	No	Notes
France		✓	No specific foreign incentives, however tax incentives & development subsidies for underdeveloped areas.
Germany	✓		Foreign-source income tax credit (credit is limited).
India	✓		Export profit from a new undertaking, satisfying prescribed conditions and set up in an SEZ, is eligible for tax exemption of 100% for the first five years, from the year in which manufacturing commences, followed by a partial tax exemption of 50% for the next five years.
Italy	✓		Foreign tax credits for income taxed-abroad. Credit can be carried back or forward, and limitations of the credit are applied separately to income from each country that produces foreign sourced income.
Japan	✓		Tax credit of up to 35% for foreign taxes paid.
Mexico	✓		Foreign-source income tax credit (credit is limited).
Singapore	✓		A double tax deduction scheme for internationalization allows companies expanding overseas to claim a double deduction for eligible expenses for specified market expansion and investment development activities.
South Korea	✓		Foreign tax credit for taxes paid to foreign governments. Limited to income taxes paid in Korea. If there is excess credit, it can be carried forward 10 years.
Spain	✓		Spain offers special foreign income relief for both economic and juridicial double taxation.
Taiwan	✓		Credit for foreign taxes paid on foreign sourced income. This is limited to the taxes derived from the foreign sourced income.
United Kingdom	✓		Credit for foreign taxes paid on foreign sourced income.
United States	✓		Credit for foreign taxes paid on foreign sourced income.

One goal of government is to drive business activity, and there are multiple policy considerations for doing that.

Job creation

The primary policy consideration is job creation. Governments have a choice between creating government jobs or encouraging private individuals to create jobs. As I've cited earlier, the cost of creating a government job is a 1:1 ratio, i.e., it costs $1 of government funds for every $1 of wages paid to a government worker. It costs governments much less to encourage job creation in the private sector.

In addition, government jobs only create taxable income from government funds. This is parasitical. The government pays for the job and then taxes that labor. In contrast, private job creation not only creates taxes from the labor but also taxes on the business profits.

STOP
&
THINK
When private businesses create jobs, the government not only receives taxes from employees, but also from the business profits.

Economy

The second policy consideration is growing the economy — which also fuels more job creation. Consider that a single worker typically produces 40 to 60 hours of effort in an average work week. A business that employs 100 people can produce 4,000 to 6,000 hours of effort in the same work week. In addition, businesses use other types of leverage, such as machinery, equipment, and technology, to magnify the work produced in those hours. And private-industry labor has long been shown to produce more output per hour than government labor.[21] The result is that a small incentive from the government (e.g., deductibility of expenses) results in more jobs, a better economy, and more tax revenue to the government.

How this government strategy pays off

Let's use a simple example of a home-based business to see how the government strategy of tax incentives for businesses pays off for the taxpayer and the government. The government allows a deduction for the investment in the furniture, equipment, and supplies of the business. It also grants a deduction for the cost of the portion of the home used in the business (home office deduction). Taxpayers invests their own money and, assuming a 33 percent tax rate, the government shares 33 percent (roughly one-third) of the cost and the taxpayer pays the remaining 67 percent. The fact that the taxpayer already owned the house and the car now used in the business is irrelevant. The taxpayer is still repositioning the use of the house and car to the business, in which the government is now a partner.

Down the road, the business begins to earn income. The government receives its 33 percent share of the income — and does so for the life of the business. There is no option for the taxpayer to buy out the government's position in the business. As the business grows, it adds employees. Now, the government also receives a share of the wages — taxable income — paid to the employees. In addition, the government gets the benefit of an employed and productive citizenry. When the taxpayer sells the business, the government also gets a share of the proceeds in the form of capital gains taxes, all of this at a cost of 33 percent of the expenses of the business. Any investor would be thrilled with this return on investment (ROI). Let's take a look at the numbers.

Suppose the taxpayer invests $10,000. The government pays back the investor $3,300 in the form of tax deductions against other income of the taxpayer. The government never pays another dime yet enjoys long-term benefits. The business grows and reinvests its earnings back into the business. The government still has no additional outlay. It simply postpones receiving any payouts or incoming tax revenue. By year three, the business produces net income of $50,000. The government receives its 33 percent share of the $50,000 by way of $16,500 in taxes. On an investment of $3,300, the government receives $16,500 in taxes in the third year. Even if the taxpayer invested another $20,000 over the three years, resulting in tax benefits of

$6,600, the government still would have invested less than $10,000 in the business ($3,300 plus $6,600). The return in the third year for the government is 67 percent of the initial return, and the government received all its capital back.

Government Gain on Tax Deferral		
Initial Investment		$ 10,000
Tax benefit	33%	$ 3,300
Taxpayer Additional investment over three years		$ 20,000
Additional Tax Benefit	33%	$ 6,600
Total Tax Benefit (Government Investment)		$ 9,900
Growth after three years		$ 50,000
Tax Rate	33%	
Tax on growth		**$ 16,500**
Original Government Investment		$ 9,900
Tax after three years		$ 16,500
Gain from deferred Tax		$ 6,600
Rate of return on investment ($6,600/$9,900)		67%

After year three, the government's return becomes infinite. It has no money in the deal — and continues to receive 33 percent of the income. Suppose in year five the business adds two employees with combined wages of $100,000 and the business still nets $50,000 after all deductions. The government receives $16,500 in taxes from the business and another $20,000 or more (assuming an average tax rate of 20 percent) on the wages paid to the employees, for a total of $36,500 on an investment in which the government has no net investment. Every investor on earth would love this deal, especially considering the government does little to earn this money. It simply provides courts and roads for the business to operate. (Police and fire protection, as well as schools to educate future employees, are typically funded by local property taxes.)

The chart below recaps the math:

Government Gain After 5 Years			
Annual Net Revenue after 5 years		$	50,000
Tax on Net Revenue	33%	$	**16,500**
New Employees taxable salaries		$	100,000
Tax Rate on Wages	20%		
Tax on wages		$	**20,000**
Total tax collected in years 5 forward		$	**36,500**

How the taxpayer strategy pays off

While the government gets a good deal out of this partnership, so does the business owner and taxpayer. Business tax incentives are available to every individual who decides to use them. They are not limited to big companies, technology start-ups, or other deep-pocket ventures. If you have ever considered starting a business, consider the difference in tax benefits between a having a job and owning a business. It's significant.

First, consider the deductions. If you are an employee, chances are you do not receive deductions for having a meal with a co-worker even if you talk about business. A business owner does. Nor do you receive a deduction for your home office so you can work remotely (especially during a pandemic). A business owner does. And, unless you're a business owner, you don't receive a deduction for driving your car for business purposes, taking education that furthers your career, or traveling to improve your job prospects. A business owner gets a deduction for all of these: same expenses, but different tax consequences. (While some of these expenses may be reimbursed by an employer, the reality is that most employees do not get reimbursed or a deduction for their home office, their drive to work, or meals with other employees.)

Deductions Allowed		
Type of Deduction	Business Owner	Employee
Meal Expense	Yes	No
Home Office Expense	Yes	No
Vehicle Expense	Yes	No
Education Expense	Yes	No
Travel Expense	Yes	No

Then consider the opportunities business owners have for postponing your income by a year. Employees simply report their income when they receive it. Their only opportunity for deferring income is to load up their pension or profit-sharing plan. They don't get to choose their accounting method. They don't get to use losses from one year to offset income from another year. . .if, for example, they lost their job and had to dip into their savings. Business owners get to do all of this and can even choose between a fiscal year or a calendar year for reporting income.

But perhaps most important, tax incentives help fund an entrepreneur's business. Let's look at how.

Suppose you want to start an online business. You need a computer, furniture, an office, internet access, utilities, and supplies. You need a good computer, so you pay $3,000 for a top-of-the-line system with multiple screens. You spend another $1,000 for a desk and $500 for supplies, including a printer. You already have internet access in your home and an office space in your home. Your total outlay is $4,500.

To start, the government gives you a tax deduction for the entire $4,500. In addition, since you have a home office, a portion of your utilities, internet, maintenance, and the cost of your home is now deductible. Suppose your home office is 10 percent of your house and your house cost $500,000. Your utilities, internet, and maintenance are about $3,600, $600, and $1,200, respectively. You get a deduction of 10 percent, or $540 plus a depreciation deduction of $1,026.

Purchases			
Computer		$	3,000
Desk		$	1,000
Supplies		$	500
Total Expenses		**$**	**4,500**

Depreciation of Home for Home Office			
Value of Home		$	500,000
Allocation of Building	80%		
Total Building		$	400,000
Allocation for home office[22]	10%		
		$	40,000
Depreciable years for business asset[23]	39		
Total Yearly Depreciation expense		**$**	**1,026**

Apportionment of Expenses Related to Home Office			
Expenses			
Utilities		$	3,600
Internet		$	600
Maintenance		$	1,200
		$	5,400
Allocation for home office	10%		
Total Allocated Home office expense		**$**	**540**

Total Home Office Expenses Allocated to the Business		
Purchase expenses	$	4,500
Depreciation expense	$	1,026
Other apportioned expenses	$	540
Total home office expense deduction	**$**	**6,066**

In addition, your car is now deductible for any business use. Since you no longer have a commute (your commute is from your kitchen to your home office and back each day), the business use of your car could easily be 75 percent.

Auto Calculation for Business Example

Year 1	Normal commute per day	40 miles
	Commute days during the year	250
	Total commute days: 40x250	10,000
	Personal use miles	2,000
	Total Miles	12,000
Year 2	Start a business and eliminate commute	
	Business miles	6,000
	Personal use Miles	2,000
	Total Miles	8,000
	Percentage of miles used for business use 6,000/8,000	75%

Auto expenses are now 75% related to business purposes and are an expense to the business.

Let's assume your car cost $40,000, resulting in an annual depreciation deduction of about $6,000. Cars typically are depreciated over a period of five years, with some countries limiting the deduction to about $8,000 per year maximum under luxury car deduction rules.[24]

With a maximum deduction of $8,000 and a business use percentage of 75 percent, the annual deduction would be $8,000 x 75%, or $6,000. Maintenance and gas for your car could easily add up to another $4,000 per year.

Calculation for Business Auto Deduction		
Auto Purchase	$	40,000
Maximum Yearly Deduction for Auto	$	8,000
Business Use		75%
Total Deduction allocated	$	6,000
Maintenance & Gas expense ($4,000x75%)	$	3,000
Total Auto Expense Deduction	$	9,000

Your total deductions are the $4,500 initial outlay plus $1,566 for your home office plus $9,000 for your car, for a total of $15,066. Even in a tax bracket as low as 33 percent (federal plus local), these deductions are worth $4,972 — and more than the amount of your initial outlay for your business. You would have had the car, house, and utilities even without the business. In addition, you get the car and home office deductions in subsequent years as well, so in each subsequent year your taxes are reduced by over $3,000.

Total Deductions Attributed to Home Office		
Total home office expense deduction	$	6,066
Total Auto Expense deduction	$	9,000
Total Deductions	$	15,066

The government has paid for your entire business investment. All it wants in return is 33 percent of the profits. Not a bad deal since you didn't have to put in any of the money to start it. And any time you spend money for your business, the government pays 33 percent of the cost. How many people rush to a sale at a store because items are 20 percent off? The government gives you a much bigger discount, and you don't have to wait for a sale nor do you have to restrict yourself to last season's fashions or last year's car models.

This is a good deal for the business owner and the government. The business owners gets deductions for expenses they simply reposition from personal to business, such as their car and home office. The government and the taxpayer share the rewards of the business by a return of their initial investment and much more over the years. Fundamentally, this is a good deal for the taxpayer who's doing the work and the government that is sharing the costs.

Of the Internal Revenue Code's 6,000 pages, over 1,000 apply specifically to businesses and business tax incentives. No other incentive commands this much attention from the IRS or Congress. What's more, this is true in most countries. Governments around the world have tax incentives for business creation and operation. It's up to the individual business owner to fully use these incentives to do what the government wants done when it comes to the economy and jobs.

Chapter 2: Key Points

1. Partner with government: The government is sharing the cost of the expense through deductions.
2. There are four tests that must be met for a business expense to be deductible.
3. The purpose of an asset is to produce income.
4. The two primary methods a business can use for paying tax are accrual method and cash method.
5. Net operating losses is another way businesses can reduce taxes on business income.
6. Governments create tax incentives for people to start and operate businesses.

Chapter 3

Investment #2: Technology | Research and Development

"Failure is an option here. If things are not failing, you are not innovating enough."

—Elon Musk

"I'm interested in things that change the world or that affect the future and wondrous, new technology where you see it, and you're like, 'Wow, how did that even happen? How is that possible?"

—Elon Musk

"It's kind of fun to do the impossible."

—Walt Disney

Government purposes – healthcare, innovation, and national security

Technology and innovation have always fascinated me. Years ago, I sat down with my business partner, Rob, to discuss the future of the CPA profession. I saw three big opportunities. The first was creating a platform where tax preparers could choose tax returns to prepare in exchange for a flat fee. The preparers would not be employees of the CPA firm. Instead, they would be independent contractors who chose how much work they wanted, how fast they would do it, and how much they would charge for it. This is now a reality with multiple services offering just such a platform.

The second was technology that would allow 80 percent of tax planning to be completed via a computer. This would be a more difficult task, as artificial intelligence would be required to allow the computer to "learn" how to use the different opportunities in the tax law and apply them to a specific individual's situation to reduce their taxes, while still earning the same or more income. This technology is in the planning stages and will become a reality within a few short years.

The third opportunity was a platform to develop a comprehensive wealth and tax strategy. This platform would not only record an individual's strategy for building wealth and reducing taxes but would also give reminders of when to invest, find investments suitable for the strategy, and link with other team members, such as attorneys, accountants, and financial planners, to carry out the strategy. The minimum viable product (MVP) for this software is currently in use by members of the WealthAbility® Network and is called WealthAbility Roadmap™.

These technologies will help people build more wealth, achieve more dreams, and enable CPAs to do more analysis for their clients at a lower price. They will change the world, one person at a time.

Thomas Edison, Walt Disney, Steve Jobs, and Elon Musk all devoted (and, in Elon Musk's case, continues to devote) their lives to doing the impossible. From electric grids lighting the world to entire worlds of entertainment in hand-held computers masquerading as phones, electric cars, and spaceships, these technologies have completely transformed the world in a few short years.

The incentives that spur technological development

Research and development of new technologies and systems have long been a governmental priority in most countries. To encourage such innovation, which is often very costly and produces more failures than successes, governments provide tax incentives to anyone willing to put their time, money, and energy into technological improvements.

Deductions

Tax incentives for technology generally come in two forms: tax deductions and tax credits. While a normal business deduction is equal to $1 of deduction for every $1 spent, research and development deductions are often a multiple of the amount spent. In South Africa, the deduction is equal to 150 percent of the amount spent on research.[1] In Singapore, the deduction can be as high as 400 percent.[2,3]

Two Forms of Tax Incentives	
1.	Tax Credits
2.	Tax Deductions

R&D Deduction Percentages by Country	
Argentina	Up to 100% deduction in specific industries
Australia	R&D Credit Only
Canada	35% on qualified SR&ED expenditures of $3 million. May also be eligible to earn a non-refundable ITC at the basic rate of 15% on an amount over $3 million
France	R&D Credit Only
Germany	R&D Credit Only
India	Up to 100% deduction for R&D Expenses
Italy	0%
Japan	0%
Mexico	0%
Singapore	Up to 400% tax deductions can be claimed for R&D costs
South Korea	0%
Spain	0%
Taiwan	Can deduct qualifying R&D expenses of up to 200%
United Kingdom	Deduct an extra 130% of their qualifying costs from their yearly profit, as well as the normal 100% deduction, to make a total 230% deduction
United States	100% immediate deduction of research expenditures if no credit taken

This means that if the tax rate in South Africa is 40 percent, the deduction could be worth $60 for every $100 of expenditure. In Singapore with a tax rate of about 20%, the deduction could be worth about $80 for every $100 spent (400% of $100 = $400 deduction x 20% tax rate = $80).

CREDITS

Tax credits for research and development, in addition to tax deductions, are also popular. France gives businesses tax credits equal to the first two years of salary for an engineer with a PhD.[4] In the United States, in addition to a one-for-one deduction of research expenses, there is a federal tax credit of 10 percent, and many states have their own tax credits. For example, Arizona's is 20 percent.[5,6]

R&D Credit Percentages by Country	
Argentina	Up to 70% on specific expenses.
Australia	39%
Canada	Generally, a 15% non-refundable credit on SR&ED expenditures that can be applied against federal taxes payable.
France	5%–30%
Germany	25% of their R&D activities to a total maximum of EUR 500,000.
India	0%
Italy	10% - 20% Tax R&D Credit based on eligible costs incurred.
Japan	10% credit based on eligible costs incurred.
Mexico	30% equal to current-year R&D expenses in excess of the average R&D expenses incurred in the previous three years.
Singapore	0%
South Korea	5%–30% tax credit in relation to qualifying R&D expenditure.
Spain	25% of gross tax liability if the tax relief for R&D and technological innovation equals or is less than 10% of the tax due; else the cap is increased to 50% of the gross tax due.
Taiwan	R&D credits are available for up to 15% of qualified R&D expenses incurred with the maximum credit capped at 30% of tax payable in the year in which the expenses were incurred.
United Kingdom	13% RDEC tax credit.
United States	10% of qualified research expenditures.

R&D Credit Percentages by State	
Alabama	No credit
Alaska	18%
Arizona	20%
Arkansas	Up to 100% of tax liability
California	15%
Colorado	3%
Connecticut	20%
Delaware	Up to 100% of Delaware's apportioned share of the taxpayer's federal R&D Tax Credit
Florida	Up to 50% of the company's tax liability
Georgia	Up to 50% of the company's tax liability
Hawaii	Up to $5 million
Idado	5%
Illinois	6.5%
Indiana	15% on the first $1million of expenditures, 10% on the excess
Iowa	6.5%
Kansas	6.5%
Kentucky	5%
Louisiana	Up to 40%
Maine	100% on the first $25,000 in tax liability plus 75% of liability in excess of $25,000
Maryland	Up to 13%
Massachusetts	Up to 25%
Michigan	No credit
Minnesota	Up to 10%
Mississippi	No credit
Missouri	No credit
Montana	No credit
Nebraska	15% of federal credit
Nevada	No credit
New Hampshire	Lesser of 10% of the business organization's qualified manufacturing Research & Development expenditures or $50,000.

(Continued)

R&D Credit Percentages by State (Continued)	
New Jersey	10% of the excess of the qualified research expenses for the tax period over the base amount, plus 10% of basic research payments for the tax period.
New Mexico	The credit is equal to the sum of all gross receipts taxes and 50% of withholding taxes paid on behalf of employees and owners with no more than five percent ownership, that are due to the state.
New York	Up to 50% of their federal R&D credit.
North Carolina	No credit
North Dakota	25% on the first $100,000 of excess expenses in a tax year, 8% on excess expenses over $100,000.
Ohio	7%
Oklahoma	No credit
Oregon	No credit
Pennsylvania	Up to 20%
Rhode Island	Up to 22.5%
South Carolina	Up to 50% of taxpayer's tax liability
South Dakota	No credit
Tennesee	No credit
Texas	Up to 50% of taxpayer's tax Liability
Utah	The sum of 5% of a taxpayer's qualified spending that exceed the base amount, 5% of payments made to qualified organizations for basic research in Utah that exceed the base amount, & 7.5% of qualified research expenses for the taxable year.
Vermont	Credit is equal to 27% of the federal credit.
Virginia	Credit is equal to 15% of the first $300,000.
Washington	No credit
West Virginia	No credit
Wisconsin	Up to 10%
Wyoming	No credit

Tax credits are even better than deductions because every dollar of tax credit offsets a dollar of tax liability. In this case, the government pays for the research to the extent of the credit.

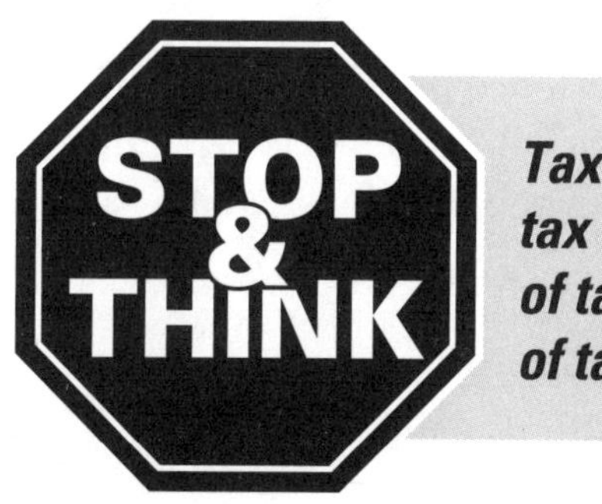

Tax credits are better than tax deductions. Every dollar of tax credit offsets a dollar of tax liability.

Requirements

It's not only new technological development that receives these tax benefits. What's rarely understood is that you can take deductions and credits for improvements in existing products or processes. Generally, an expenditure qualifies as a research expense if the following conditions are met:

1. **Business deduction** – the expense must meet the four tests of a business deduction outlined in Chapter Two before being considered for research tax benefits. Only research expenses conducted by an operating business are considered for tax benefits.

R&D as a Business Expense	Yes	No
Argentina	✓	
Australia	✓	
Canada	✓	
France	✓	
Germany	✓	
India	✓	
Italy	✓	
Japan	✓	
Mexico	✓	
Singapore	✓	
South Korea	✓	
Spain	✓	
Taiwan	✓	
United Kingdom	✓	
United States	✓	

2. **Technological** – the research needs to be based in scientific, engineering, or computer science principles (see Figure 3.1). These principles don't have to be new. The nature of the work must simply be engineering or scientific (physical, biological, or computer).

Scientific/Engineering Research Required		
	Yes	No
Argentina	✓	
Australia	✓	
Canada	✓	
France	✓	
Germany	✓	
India	✓	
Italy	✓	
Japan	✓	
Mexico	✓	
Singapore	✓	
South Korea	✓	
Spain	✓	
Taiwan	✓	
United Kingdom	✓	
United States	✓	

FIGURE 3.1

3. **New or Improved business component** – a business component is any product, process, computer software, technique, formula, or invention that is either held for sale or leased to a customer or used in the business. This is a rather broad definition. While product and software are well defined, a new business component includes new or improved processes, formulae, or techniques used within the business itself. In other words, it doesn't have to be a new product or process to the public; it's sufficient to be a new product or process to the business itself.
4. **Process of experimentation** – this is a process designed to evaluate one or more alternatives to achieve a result where

the achievement of that result is uncertain. Take software development as an example. Normally, beta tests are done to find out what isn't working properly in the software and how to improve it. This is a process of experimentation.

Policy considerations that fuel tax incentives for technological development

Multiple benefits come from a country promoting technological advancements. Let's start with defense, where many modern technologies are tested, perfected, and employed. Defense technologies are not limited to new weapons or direct defense equipment. The coronavirus pandemic, for instance, left many companies vulnerable to political, technological, and economic attacks. Governments didn't give incentives to invent a vaccine solely for the overall health and well-being of their citizens. The faster the vaccine was made available, the faster the country recovered from its vulnerability to these attacks.

Technological warfare

Technological warfare is one of the newest and most successful forms of warfare. Attacks on a country's security infrastructure through hacking, computer viruses, and other malware have proven to be extraordinarily disruptive. Take the attack (reportedly by Russia) on the United States in 2020 through the hack on SolarWinds. That attack infiltrated many U.S. government defense systems.[7] Or consider the requirement by China that all software and hardware built in China include a backdoor for the government to gain access.[8] This is the reason Huawei hardware has been banned by the United States, Canada, and several other countries.[9] Because of the rise of technological warfare, it's in a government's best interests to offer tax incentives to develop defenses against these kinds of attacks.

Agriculture and shelter

Technology also produces improvements to agriculture production. In the 1970s, there was a real concern about whether the rapidly increasing global population could be fed with existing agricultural technology. The rise of Monsanto and its recent technology allowed agricultural production to grow by leaps and bounds[10] (see Figure 3.2).[11]

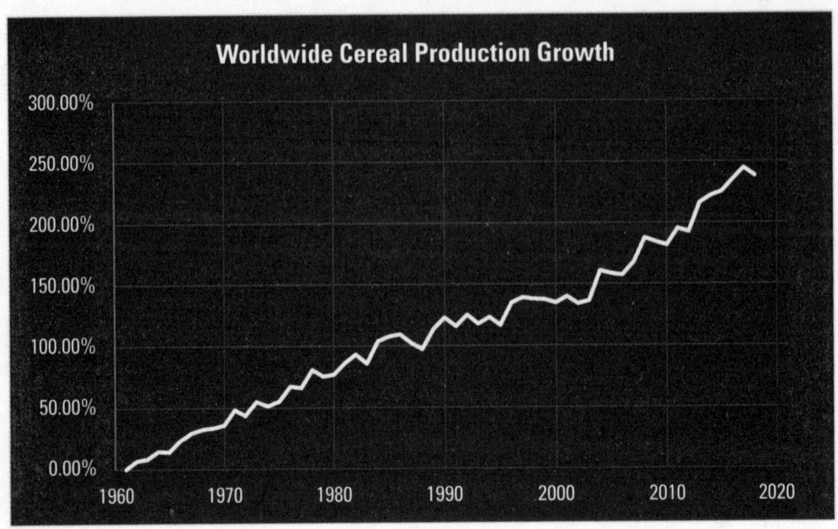

FIGURE 3.2

New building technology, such as the pod techniques developed in Asia and the United States,[12] are rapidly increasing the availability of housing and short-term rentals around the world.[13]

ENERGY

Oil and gas fracking, while controversial, made the United States energy independent for the first time in decades[14] (see Figure 3.3).[15]

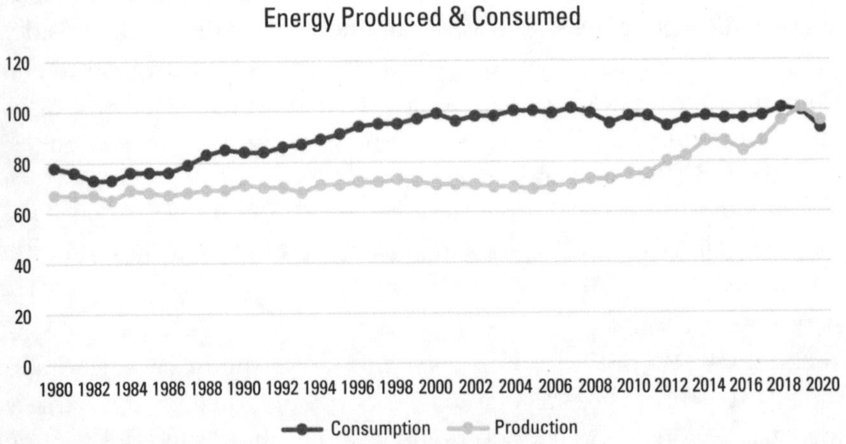

FIGURE 3.3

Solar, wind, and other renewable energy technologies contribute to both lowering energy costs for business and personal use and renewing the environment and stemming climate change.[16]

Health

New medications and vaccines, most notably the vaccines against COVID-19, are spurred by government incentives, many of which are through the tax laws. Healthcare has long been a primary goal of governments, as good health promotes a healthy economy and social well-being. In the coming years, innovative technologies will be required to prevent considerable damage to the planet's air and water ecosystems through climate change.[17] Smart entrepreneurs will take advantage of the wave of tax incentives for these types of research and development.

All these benefits and more are the reasons governments continue to promote technology development through tax incentives. While governments could spend trillions of dollars creating the technology itself, most have found the private sector produces technology faster than they can — and at a fraction of the cost. For instance, SpaceX has made monumental strides in rockets and space travel with no direct subsidies from the government and will likely make it to Mars long before NASA.[18]

How the government strategy pays off

The government's strategy is quite simple: provide a small incentive, such as a 10 percent tax credit, a 150 percent deduction, or a combination of these and in return reap the benefits of technological developments that require little funding from the government and produce enormous rewards. Let's use a simple project to create new software as an example.

Assuming the same tax bracket as the business example in Chapter Two, in the case of technology development, the government provides a 33 percent deduction incentive plus an additional 10 percent tax credit for a total of 43 percent. Suppose the technology costs $100,000 to develop. The government provides 43 percent of the cost of development ($43,000) and the taxpayer provides the remaining 57 percent ($57,000).

Technology Developments Incentives for the Government	
Cost to Develop Technology	$ 100,000
Government incentive ($100,000 × 43%)	$ 43,000
Taxpayer provides ($100,000 × 57%)	$ 57,000

Let's also assume there is no revenue in the first year, and in the second year, the business developing the technology breaks even. Then, in the third year, there is a $100,000 profit. The profit will be shared 33 percent by the government and 67 percent by the taxpayer. The government receives $33,000 on a $43,000 investment. Now let's say the business continues to produce income at a rate of $100,000 per year. This amounts to a 76.7 percent ROI for the government — each year!

Year 1 Income	$ –
Year 2 Income	Break Even
Year 3 Income	$ 100,000
Government Tax at 33%	($ 33,000)
Income After Tax	$ 67,000
Government Initial Investment	$ 43,000
Year 3+ Taxes Paid	$ 33,000
Government's Return on Investment	76.7%

Suppose after five years, the taxpayer sells the technology for $500,000, and the government receives $100,000 in the form of capital gains taxes. In all, the government received a $265,000 return on a $43,000 investment. That is a 616 percent ROI.

Technology is sold in Year 8	$ 500,000
Government Receives Capital Gains	($ 100,000)
Income after tax	$ 400,000
Government Initial Investment	$ 43,000
Total Taxes paid Years 4–8: Including Sale Capital Gains (5 × $33,000) + $100,000	**$ 265,000**
Government's Return on Investment	**616%**

And on top of this return, the government also receives a percentage of all the payroll paid to the taxpayer's employees via payroll taxes.

Every good investor knows that the operator's return is irrelevant. It's fine if the operator of the investment makes a lot of money. The only thing investors care about is their own return. So, while the taxpayer (i.e., the operator) in this case receives more than the government, it's because the taxpayer invested more of the money and put in 100 percent of the effort. The government simply received the benefits of its initial investment. Not all investments will pay off. The government and the taxpayer share this risk. Both have money at stake and have the potential for significant rewards. In addition to the financial rewards, the government benefits from the positive global ramifications of the recent technology and the increased employment.

How the taxpayer strategy pays off

Let's look at an example of how the government can pay for research and development of a new product or technology. In 2020, my company, WealthAbility®, spent roughly $400,000 developing new software for our business. The federal tax credits amounted to about 10 percent ($40,000). Arizona, where we are headquartered, has an additional credit equal to 20 percent ($80,000). The federal and the Arizona government allow a deduction for the cost of development less the credits, $360,000 for the federal deduction and $320,000 for the state deduction. The federal tax rate is 37 percent, and the state tax rate is 4.5 percent. Combined, the tax benefit of the deduction was $147,600 ($133,200 for Federal and $14,400 for state).

WealthAbility® Software Example		
Cost to Develop Software		$ 400,000
Federal Tax Credits - 10%	10%	$ 40,000
State Tax Credit (Arizona) - 20%	20%	$ 80,000
Total Federal & State Tax Credits		$ 120,000
Deductions from Federal Income		$ 360,000
Deductions from State Income		$ 320,000
Federal Tax Rate 37%		
Federal Tax Benefit of Deductions		$ 133,200
State Tax Rate 4.5%		
State Tax Benefit of Deductions		$ 14,400
Total Federal & State Tax Benefits		$ 147,600
Total Credits & Tax Benefits		**$ 267,600**
Software Development Costs		$ 400,000
Total Credits & Tax Benefits		$ 267,600
Percent of Tax Credits & Benefits to Total Software Costs		**67%**

The combination of the tax credits and tax benefits from the tax deduction amounted to $267,600, or 67 percent of the cost of the software development. Suppose we earn one million dollars from this software. We will only have to share 41.5 percent of this with the government even though the government contributed 67 percent of the cost. By being smart in using government tax incentives, we used government money to pay for a significant majority of our R&D costs, while more than recouping our money in the profits gained.

Have you improved a process or invented a new way of doing something that could qualify for a research and development tax incentive? Many business owners don't understand that the software they have created, the processes they have invented, and the products they have developed come with added tax benefits.[19] They see the benefits to their business, so they make the improvements. It's likely that many of these businesses are eligible for tax credits that, unfortunately, they are not taking advantage of. There are steps to determine if a business may have unused research tax benefits. The first step in determining that is to ask these questions. Has the business:

1. Created a new product, made improvements, or added new features to an existing product?
2. Modified an existing technology?
3. Integrated various databases or applications that don't normally communicate?
4. Added new features or modified or improved an existing product?
5. Improved response time of its software application?
6. Changed a process to reduce costs or to improve manufacturing capabilities or timing?
7. Incurred costs related to a process, project, or prototype that is incomplete because of unresolved technical problems?
8. Modified its product formulation?
9. Automated production?
10. Modified existing products or machines to new applications?

This is not an exhaustive list of items to assess, considering the possibility of qualifying for research and development tax benefits. If you have any questions about whether you qualify, it's best to consult with your tax advisor to determine whether you might be eligible for these benefits. While they may not apply to everything you improve, there is a good chance you are missing out on deductions or credits for your research and development activities.

Chapter 3: Key Points

1. Governments provide tax incentives to anyone willing to put their time, money, and energy into technology improvements.
2. Tax incentives for technology come in two forms – tax deductions and tax credits.
3. There are four requirements that must be met for the deduction to qualify as a research expense.
4. There are 10 questions to ask to determine if a business has unused research tax benefits.

Chapter 4

Investment #3: Real Estate

"The major fortunes in America have been made in land."

—John D. Rockefeller

"Ninety percent of all millionaires become so through owning real estate."

—Andrew Carnegie

"Home is the nicest word there is."

—Laura Ingalls Wilder

Government purposes – housing, commercial development, energy, technology, manufacturing, and jobs

I grew up in a nice, middle-class area in Salt Lake City, Utah, called the "East Bench" in a house on Yalecrest Avenue. This house was not the house where I was born. That house was one block away on Michigan Avenue. My parents owned the house on Michigan Avenue throughout my childhood and rented it out because they didn't like to sell real estate. Just a few blocks away, they also purchased two duplexes on Sunnyside Avenue, that included vacant land. My brother-in-law, Jim, grew a very nice vegetable garden on the land. Later, when I moved out and they no longer had children at home, they sold the houses on Yalecrest and Michigan and with the proceeds, built their retirement house on the vacant land on Sunnyside.

They kept the two duplexes, which by then they owned free and clear and lived on the rent from the duplexes (one of which they had turned into a triplex) for the rest of their lives. My dad was always puttering around the duplexes and making sure they were in good repair and that everything was in working order. They had a waiting list for tenants because they always kept the rent just below market so they never had a vacancy. One of the tenants lived there for close to 30 years; it was her home.

Later, after I became a CPA, I helped my mother with their tax returns and noticed the terrific tax benefits they received from both their business and their real estate. My mother had always told us that the two most important professionals in our lives would be our CPA and our insurance agent. Seeing the small amount of taxes they paid convinced me early on that real estate was one of the most tax-advantaged investments available.

	Two Most Important Professionals
1.	CPAs
2.	Insurance Agent

Incentives for real estate investment

Every country has tax incentives for real estate, and most of them only apply to investment real estate. The United States and a few other countries, however, do provide incentives for home ownership.[1,2]

	Tax Incentives for Home Ownership		
	Yes	No	Notes
Argentina	✓		Interest deduction
Australia	✓		First home buyers in New South Wales with exemptions from transfer duty on new and existing homes valued up to AUD 650,000 and sliding scale concessions for up to AUD 800,000.
Canada	✓		Tax credit
France	✓		Exemption of land tax for two years
Germany		✓	
India	✓		Interest deduction
Italy	✓		Interest deduction

Tax Incentives for Home Ownership (Continued)			
	Yes	No	Notes
Japan	✓		Deduction of 1% of remaining mortgage loan balance from income tax up to a maximum amount for 10 years.
Mexico	✓		Interest deduction
Singapore	✓		Interest deduction
South Korea	✓		Interest deduction
Spain	✓		Real estate tax deductions
Taiwan	✓		Interest deduction
United Kingdom	✓		First-time buyers purchasing their first home for up to GBP 300,000 are exempt from Stamp Duty Land Tax.
United States	✓		Interest deduction

While these incentives vary somewhat from country to country, they can easily be placed into a few simple categories — deductions, including depreciation, tax credits, low tax on cash sales, deferred tax on installment sales, and nontaxable sales of real estate when the money is reinvested in more real estate. And let's not forget the additional benefit of nontaxable debt as well as the potential benefit in the United States of eliminating the tax on the sale simply by holding the property until death.[3]

Tax Incentives for Real Estate	
1.	Deductions
2.	Depreciation
3.	Tax Credits
4.	Low tax on cash sales
5.	Deferred tax on installment sales
6.	Nontaxable sales of real estate
7.	Nontaxable debt
8.	Eliminating tax

Deductions

Like business, rental real estate is subject to deductions for any expense that meets the four tests: 1) business purpose, 2) ordinary,

3) necessary, and 4) documentation. This includes deductions for utilities, taxes, maintenance, and interest. In addition to these deductions, real estate gets a deduction that is reserved solely to the real estate industry, a depreciation deduction on appreciating assets.

That's right, even though a property may be appreciating in value, the owner typically receives a deduction for the wear and tear on the building, improvements, contents, and landscaping. Most countries only allow depreciation on new projects, while a few, like the United States, allow depreciation on used buildings as well.[4]

Depreciation/Capital Cost Allowance			
	Yes	No	Notes
Argentina	✓		
Australia	✓		
Canada	✓		
France	✓		
Germany	✓		
India	✓		
Italy	✓		
Japan	✓		
Mexico	✓		
Singapore	✓		Only allowed if a tax incentive (land intensification allowance) is applied for and granted.
South Korea	✓		
Spain	✓		
Taiwan	✓		
United Kingdom	✓		
United States	✓		

Normally, depreciation on real estate is taken over many years, considered the useful life of the building. The chart below details the useful life of several elements of a real estate investment in the United States.

Useful Life of a Rental Property in the United States	
Land	N/A
Residential Rental	27.5 years
Commercial Rental	39 years
Land Improvements	15 years
Personal Property	5–7 years

In the United States, up to 30 percent or more of the depreciation can be taken in the first year of ownership due to the bonus depreciation rules of the 2017 Tax Cuts and Jobs Act (TCJA).[5] Here is how that works.

The law allows for the cost of the building to be separated (the technical term is *segregated*) into its components.[6]

There are typically four basic components: land, building, land improvements, and the contents of the building (such as window and floor coverings, ceiling fans, cabinets, and other furniture). The land doesn't wear out, so there is no depreciation allowance on the land. The building wears out gradually, so it is depreciated over a longer period, typically from 15 to 40 years, depending on the country.

Four Basic Segregated Components	
1.	Land
2.	Building
3.	Land Improvements
4.	Contents of the Building

Here's how building depreciation is calculated around the world.[7]

Life of Buildings	
Argentina	50 years
Australia	25 or 40 years
Canada	4%–10% per year until fully depreciated
France	20–50 Years

(Continued)

Life of Buildings (Continued)	
Germany	33–50 years depending on the age of the building and other factors such as original ownership
India	5%–10% per year until fully depreciated
Italy	Depreciation rates range per Subpart. For Group 4, Subpart 4, building life is 18.18 Years
Japan	12–50 Years
Mexico	10–20 Years
Singapore	No claim for buildings unless a tax incentive (land intensification allowance) is applied for and granted.
South Korea	20–40 Years; or 15–50 if useful life election is elected and approved
Spain	68–100 Years
Taiwan	50 Years
United Kingdom	3% per year after April 1 2020
United States	27.5-39 Years

The land improvements, such as outdoor lighting, fencing, covered parking, and landscaping are allowed to be depreciated over a shorter time period, ranging from 5 to 50 years. Again, this varies from country to country as the chart below illustrates.[8]

Land Improvements	
Argentina	10–50 Years
Australia	5–40 Years, depending on the types of improvements made.
Canada	Landscaping is immediately deductible in the year incurred. Other land improvements deductions are based on type of asset to which they relate.
France	No deduction allowed
Germany	Eight Years for lighting, fitting, & fixtures; other land improvements may not qualify
India	Not eligible for depreciation unless the classification falls under any category mentioned in the Income Tax Rules, 1962.
Italy	No deduction allowed

Land Improvements (Continued)	
Japan	No deduction allowed
Mexico	No deduction allowed
Singapore	Land Improvements are not depreciable
South Korea	No deduction allowed
Spain	No deduction allowed
Taiwan	50 Years
United Kingdom	No deduction allowed
United States	15 Years

The contents of the building are depreciated over an even shorter time period, typically five to 10 years.[9]

Building Contents	
Argentina	3–10 Years
Australia	5–20 Years
Canada	30% first-year depreciation and 20% regular rate
France	5–10 Years
Germany	8–13 years
India	10% per year until fully depreciated
Italy	2.86–8.33 Years for Group 4, Subpart 4 building contents
Japan	2–20 Years
Mexico	10 Years
Singapore	3 Years
South Korea	5–20 Years depending on the industry
Spain	4–20 Years
Taiwan	50 Years
United Kingdom	18% per year WDA – main pool
United States	3, 5 , 7 Years

Under the 2017 tax law, referred to as the TCJA, land improvements and building contents can be fully depreciated in the year the building is acquired. This benefit is available even if the building is not new.[10]

Bonus Depreciation/Cost Allowance			
	Yes	No	Notes
Argentina	✓		Accelerated depreciation is specific to a few industries.
Australia	✓		Taxpayers who are carrying on business and who, together with certain connected or affiliated entities, have an aggregated turnover of less than AUD 5 billion for the year may be eligible to apply accelerated depreciation concessions for certain depreciating assets.
Canada	✓		Accelerated Investment Incentive provides an increased first year capital cost allowance for certain asset types.
France	✓		Bonus is allowed under specific tests.
Germany	✓		Special depreciation is deductible for tax purposes in certain limited circumstances (e.g, small businesses, ancient monuments, buildings in designated renovated city zones).
India	✓		Investment allowance for certain manufacturing assets up to 45% for certain assets under the 'plant and machinery' block on satisfaction of certain conditions.
Italy	✓		Bonus is allowed in certain sectors.
Japan		✓	After 1 April 2016, only the straight-line method will be permitted.
Mexico	✓		Specific industries are eligible for accelerated depreciation.
Singapore	✓		Specific assets are eligible for 100% 1st year depreciation. Additionally, the Land Intensification Allowance provides faster depreciation but is subject to approval.
South Korea		✓	No bonus or accelerated allowance.
Spain	✓		Allowable for Equipment & Machinery used in R&D.
Taiwan		✓	No bonus or accelerated allowance.
United Kingdom	✓		Bonus is allowed under specific tests.
United States	✓		Bonus is allowed.

Let's look at an example of how it works.

Suppose a commercial building is purchased for $1 million on January 1st. Let's also suppose that after performing a cost segregation study (typically done by a team of accountants and engineers), it's determined that of the $1 million, 20 percent (or $200,000) of the purchase price applies to the value of the land, 50 percent (or $500,000) of the purchase price applies to the building, 10 percent (or $100,000) of the purchase price applies to the land improvements, and 20 percent (or $200,000) of the purchase price applies to the contents of the building. Under the TCJA, the depreciation in the first year would include $0 for the land, $12,820 for the building and $300,000 for the land improvements and building contents.

Year 1 Tax Savings from Purchase of Building for Business Use		
Building Purchase (January 1st)		$ 1,000,000
Cost Segregation		
Land Value	20%	$ 200,000
Building Value	50%	$ 500,000
Land Improvement Value	10%	$ 100,000
Building Contents Value	20%	$ 200,000
TCJA Depreciation and Bonus Depreciation Values		
Land value	0%	$ –
Building Value – Subject to 39 Year Regular Depreciation	39 Years	$ 12,821
Land Improvement Value – Subject to 100% Bonus Depreciation	100%	$ 100,000
Building Contents Value – Subject to 100% Bonus Depreciation	100%	$ 200,000
Total Allowable Depreciation in Year 1		**$ 312,821**

In this case, more than 30 percent of the purchase price can be deducted against income in the first year of ownership. And this is true even if the building is financed by the bank. As a result, an investor could put down $200,000 on the building, borrow $800,000, and deduct over $300,000 in the first year, effectively deducting 150 percent of the investor's original investment in the first year. At a 40 percent tax rate (assuming the investor has income from other sources), the first-year deduction is worth $125,128 in lower taxes. Effectively, the bank is putting in $800,000, the government is putting in $125,000, and the investor is only putting in $75,000. And yet the investor get all of the depreciation 9 as shown later in this chapter) and most of the income as well.[11]

Tax Benefits and Realized Investment Amounts after Depreciation Deduction		
Original Building purchase Value		$ 1,000,000
Loan Amount		$ 800,000
Amount Invested		$ 200,000
Allowable Depreciation in Year 1		$ 312,821
Total Amount invested in Year 1		$ 200,000
Percentage of deductions to amount invested to purchase building		**156%**
Allowable Depreciation in Year 1		$ 312,821
Tax Rate	40%	
Tax benefit from First-year Deduction		**$ 125,128**
Amount invested		$ 200,000
Tax benefit from First-year Deduction		$ 125,128
Net investment by taxpayer after tax benefits from year 1 depreciation		**$ 74,872**

Tax Credits

Depreciation is the most obvious of the tax benefits for real estate, but it is far from the only tax benefit. Governments frequently target certain types of real estate development to stimulate development of certain high-priority projects. These targeted projects are typically incentivized through tax credits. Tax credits, of course, offset taxes dollar for dollar regardless of the investor's tax rate.

The United States uses tax credits to encourage construction and ownership of low-income housing, maintaining historical buildings, and providing access for the disabled. The low-income housing credit can be up to 70 percent of the cost of a new building over 10 years.[12] There is also a 20 percent credit for improvements to a certified historic structure that is either rented or used in a business and there is a 50 percent tax credit for small businesses that make improvements to their properties to allow improved access for disabled individuals. Most countries, in fact, have targeted credits for real estate their government wants built or improved.[13]

Real Estate Development Credits			
	Yes	No	Notes
Argentina		✓	
Australia		✓	
Canada	✓		Investment Tax Credits
France		✓	
Germany		✓	
India	✓		Development & Expansion Incentive
Italy		✓	
Japan	✓		National strategic zones
Mexico		✓	
Singapore	✓		Development & Expansion Incentive
South Korea	✓		Integrated Investment Tax Incentive System.
Spain		✓	
Taiwan	✓		Tax incentives for Urban Renewal & Development of Satellite towns
United Kingdom		✓	
United States	✓		

Tax benefits for selling real estate

Tax deductions and tax credits are just the tax benefits available while the property is developed or owned by the investor. In addition, there are multiple tax benefits for selling a property. These benefits can be categorized as 1) low-taxed transactions and 2) non-taxed transactions.

Capital gains rates

Almost every country in the world has a lower tax rate for capital gains than for ordinary income. Capital gains are simply gains earned from holding on to an investment for a long period of time, typically more than one year, though some countries have multiple rates for different holding periods.[14]

Capital Gains Rates by Country			
	Yes	No	Notes
Argentina	✓		15%
Australia		✓	Ordinary rate however, 50% gain reduction if asset is held for more than 12 months.
Canada		✓	Ordinary rates but only 50% of the gain is taxed.
France	✓		Up to 19% for Real Estate, 30% for securities.
Germany	✓		25%
India	✓		10%–20%
Italy	✓		26%
Japan	✓		20%–39%
Mexico	✓		Tax on capital gains is computed by dividing the amount of the gain by the number of years for which the individual held the property in question, up to a maximum of 20 years. The result is added to the individual's other gross income for the current year and is taxed at the current year marginal rate. The individual then has the option of having the remaining portion of the gain taxed at: (i) the average effective tax rate imposed on the individual's total taxable income for the current year or (ii) the average effective tax rate for the past five years including the current year.
Singapore		✓	0%
South Korea	✓		11%–33%
Spain	✓		19%–23%
Taiwan	✓		20%–45%
United Kingdom	✓		10%–28% depending on the capital asset
United States	✓		0%–28%

Ordinary income typically comes from the efforts of the taxpayer — think your paycheck. In the United States, capital gains rates start out at zero percent and top out at 28 percent. In the United Kingdom, India, and South Korea, country capital gains range from 11 to 33 percent.

Capital gains benefits aren't solely related to the gain from holding the property. A property that is improved can receive capital gain treatment. Even depreciation that was an ordinary deduction is sometimes recaptured (taxed) at a lower rate. In the United States, the maximum tax rate for recaptured depreciation on a building is 25 percent, as opposed to the maximum tax rate for the depreciation deduction of 37 percent. This 12 percent differential is significant. On the $1 million building in our earlier example, the depreciation on the building after 20 years would be over $250,000, which, at a 37 percent tax rate, would amount to a $92,500 tax benefit. And yet, when it's sold at the end of 20 years, the tax on the $250,000 of additional gain from depreciation recapture is only $62,500 ($250,000 x 25%), for a permanent tax savings of $30,000.

LIKE-KIND EXCHANGES

Some countries, like the United States, allow for a deferral or postponement of the gain from selling investment real estate if it is replaced with other real estate within a short period of time.[15]

	Like-Kind Exchange Allowed		
	Yes	No	Notes
Argentina	✓		Whenever a depreciable asset is sold and replaced, income derived from the sale transaction may be assigned to the new asset's cost, thereby resulting in a deferral in the recognition of built-in gains.
Australia		✓	Rollover Relief is only eligible on assets that were lost or destroyed.
Canada		✓	A taxpayer may defer gain on a sale by rolling into a replacement property, provided the existing property was stolen, expropriated by government, or destroyed, and/or used by the taxpayer to generate income (excluding rental income) from a business.
France		✓	You may be exempt from tax when selling a property if you did not own a main home the previous four years and you reinvest the proceeds into one.

(Continued)

	Like-Kind Exchange Allowed (Continued)		
	Yes	No	Notes
Germany	✓		German tax law provides a special tax-freereserve for profits from the sale of these assets (such as real property), which means that the realized proceeds of the sale, including the hidden reserves, can be used under certain circumstances in full to finance a new investment, thus protecting the liquidity position.
India	✓		Rollover benefit from capital gains tax is available when the taxpayer invests the net consideration received from the transfer of certain long-term capital assets into another property.
Italy		✓	A sale of a real estate property owned for more than five years is not subject to tax.
Japan	✓		Taxation from gains realized from properties may be deferred by reducing the value of the newly acquired asset by the amount of the gain through rollover relief.
Mexico	✓		Capital gains deferral upon contribution of real estate to Mexican Real Estate investment Trust.
Singapore	✓		Gains from the sale of property are not taxable unless the individual buys and sells property with a profit-seeking motive, or deemed to be trading in properties.
South Korea		✓	No Rollover Relief available.
Spain		✓	No Rollover Relief available.
Taiwan		✓	No Rollover Relief available.
United Kingdom	✓		Business Asset Rollover Relief: Buildings & Land are included for this program.
United States	✓		§1031 like-kind exchange.

Typically, the new property must cost more than the old one and all the proceeds from the sale must be reinvested. The benefit of a like-kind exchange is that you can continue to invest in more valuable real estate and potentially enjoy higher cash flow without having to pay any taxes.

In the TCJA, the United States added the additional deferral benefit for properties developed in Qualified Opportunity Zones

(QOZs). This benefit allows a taxpayer to defer the capital gain from any asset, including stocks, if they reinvest the gain into QOZ projects.

PERMANENT GAIN ELIMINATION

In the United States, gain from the sale of real estate can first be deferred, then eventually eliminated. In my first book, *Tax-Free Wealth*, I refer to this as "buy, borrow, die." First, you buy real estate, then you borrow against the real estate (debt is not taxable as it must be repaid eventually), and then you die. In the interim, you may have sold and reinvested the proceeds from multiple properties over an entire lifetime. When you die, the United States allows the heirs a "step-up" in the "basis" of the property. Basis means the amount you paid for the property (including debt) less any depreciation taken over the lifetime of the project. When a property is sold and the proceeds are reinvested in a new property, the basis is reduced by any gain that was deferred. By the time someone dies, they may have taken millions of dollars in deductions for depreciation, and when they die, as if by magic, all that potential gain disappears.

For example, suppose you purchased a building for $1 million and over the years you took $800,000 of depreciation (everything but the land). Assume the property is worth $3 million when you die. If you had sold it immediately prior to your death, you would have paid tax on $2 million of appreciation plus the $800,000 of depreciation you took. Instead, if you wait until you die and your heirs sell the property, there is no tax at all. And since the United States has an estate tax exclusion of more than $12 million, there is no estate tax either. This amounts to an aggressive incentive for taxpayers to own investment real estate and to hold real estate throughout their life.

Tax Elimination Strategy	
1.	Buy
2.	Borrow
3.	Die

Home ownership

Some countries, notably the United States, provide significant tax incentives for owning a home. Not only are mortgage interest and taxes deductible, but some or all the gain is also not taxable when the home is sold.[16]

Sale of Personal Residence Exemption			
	Yes	No	Notes
Argentina	✓		
Australia	✓		
Canada	✓		
France	✓		
Germany	✓		
India	✓		
Italy	✓		
Japan	✓		Gain restrictions apply
Mexico	✓		Must meet specific qualifications
Singapore	✓		
South Korea	✓		
Spain	✓		
Taiwan	✓		Gain restrictions apply
United Kingdom	✓		Size restrictions apply
United States	✓		Gain restrictions apply

Compare this to the total lack of tax benefits for renting an apartment or home. The rent is not deductible to the tenant, nor are any of the other costs of maintaining the rental unit.

The policy that spurs real estate investment

Housing and construction have long been a priority for governments. While only some governments provide tax incentives for home ownership, nearly all developed countries provide tax incentives for developing and owning rental properties — both residential and commercial.[17,18]

Incentives for Developing & Owning Rental Properties			
	Yes	No	Notes
Argentina	✓		Investments in real estate projects until 31 December 2022 are exempt from the personal assets tax for two tax years after the investment is effective. One percent of the value of investments in real estate projects may be credited against the individual's personal assets tax. Owners that transfer real estate from 12 March 2021 to 31 December 2022 to corporations that develop projects covered by this regime will be able to defer the federal tax payment on the transfer.
Australia	✓		National Rental Affordability Scheme contribution incentive.
Canada	✓		Low-Income Housing Tax Credit (LIHTC) housing credit.
France	✓		Up to 21% tax credit for affordable rent. Reduced VAT tax rate for newly built dwellings for residential purposes.
Germany	✓		Special depreciation allowance for new rented houses.
India	✓		Reduction of goods & services tax to 1%–5%.
Italy	✓		10% flat rate for incomes coming from residential rental properties.
Japan	✓		Special depreciation on qualified buildings.
Mexico	✓		Tax deductions for acquisitions in real estate for taxpayers engaged in the construction and sale of real estate.
Singapore	✓		Allowances on qualifying capital expenditure to promote the intensification of industrial land use.
South Korea	✓		The Integrated Investment Tax Incentive System applies to real estate rentals.
Spain	✓		Tax relief to property developers to finance the construction of affordable housing.
Taiwan	✓		Accelerated depreciation and tax reductions through lower tax rates.
United Kingdom	✓		Debt guarantee incentives.
United States	✓		HOME Investment Partnerships Program; LIHTC program. Gain restrictions apply

Tax incentives are particularly important for ensuring the creation and availability of housing for the most vulnerable in society. The United States Department of Housing and Urban Development (HUD) believes the low-income housing tax credit "is the most important resource for creating affordable housing in the United States today."[19]

Historically, some governments have taken on direct responsibility for building residential housing. This was most prevalent in Russia and Poland during the Soviet years, but the United States and other countries around the world have done so as well.[20] In recent years, it is more common for governments to incentivize private development. The result is better housing at a lower cost to the government.[21]

Governments are motivated to make sure there is adequate housing. Shelter is one of the most basic human needs and homelessness is a major issue in many parts of the world, including Paris and San Francisco, where finding entire families camping out on street corners is common.[22] In South America, barrios made from cheap sheets of metal and plywood are common.[23] More and better access to quality, low-income housing could help solve these challenges.

Governments also have good reason to encourage commercial and industrial construction, which is critical for the development of the economy. While demand for commercial and industrial property may diminish due to technological advances like virtual meetings, it's unlikely to go away entirely due to manufacturing needs. Plus, many people enjoy and find themselves more productive working in an office with other people. Tax incentives to the developers and owners of commercial and industrial projects encourage continued development even when the need is projected and not urgent. Given that it typically takes anywhere from one to three years to acquire land, design, and construct a building, incentives for building commercial and industrial structures make sense.

Any country that has a net income tax allows for deductions of expenses used to generate income. While these deductions vary widely, deductions for the cost of equipment, buildings, and rent are common.[24]

Deductions for Business Expenses that Generate Income, Equipment, Buildings, and Rent		
	Yes	No
Argentina	✓	
Australia	✓	
Canada	✓	
France	✓	

Deductions for Business Expenses that Generate Income, Equipment, Buildings, and Rent (Continued)		
	Yes	No
Germany	✓	
India	✓	
Italy	✓	
Japan	✓	
Mexico	✓	
Singapore	✓	
South Korea	✓	
Spain	✓	
Taiwan	✓	
United Kingdom	✓	
United States	✓	

How the government strategy pays off

It's in a government's best interest to have housing available for those who cannot purchase or build their own home. To encourage the development of affordable housing, the government allows depreciation that more than offsets rental income, which in turn lowers the landlord's tax exposure. As a result, the government makes an early investment designed to stimulate the multi-family and affordable housing market. In return, it gets quality housing that it does not have to build or manage. Here is an example of how the numbers play out.

Suppose taxpayers decides to build a new fourplex for $1,000,000, with $200,000 attributable to the land and $800,000 to the improvements. The taxpayer invests $200,000 of their own money and the bank lends them $800,000. The government, in the case of the United States and some other countries, provides an immediate benefit in a depreciation deduction equal to about 30 percent of the cost of the project. This deduction is equal to $300,000. If the taxpayer is in a 33 percent tax bracket, the cost to the government the first year is $99,000. The government is not responsible for the debt and the construction or the management of the property.

Year 1 Government Costs for Building Purchase		
Building purchase		$ 1,000,000
Loan amount		$ 800,000
Amount invested		$ 200,000
Land value	20%	$ 200,000
Building and building components value	80%	$ 800,000
Depreciation and bonus depreciation value		
Land value	0%	$ –
Building and building components approximate bonus depreciation	30%	$ 300,000
Total Allowable Depreciation		**$ 300,000**
Tax Bracket	33%	
Year 1 government cost from reduction of taxable income due to depreciation		**$ 99,000**

Suppose the building produces a net operating income in year two of $100,000. After deducting the interest of $32,000 (assuming a 4 percent interest-only loan) and depreciation on the building of $18,000, there is taxable income of $50,000. At a 33 percent tax rate, the government then is paid $16,500, or an ROI of 16.67 percent. In addition, the interest is taxable to the bank at about 25 percent, so the government receives another $8,000. Now the return to the government is around 25 percent, and that doesn't include the taxes on wages paid to the property manager. A 25 percent return on an investment with fairly low risk and no responsibility other than the collection of the tax is a pretty nice return.

Government Rate of Return for Year 1 Investment Costs of Building Depreciation Deduction	
Year 2 Net Operating Income	$ 100,000
Interest Expense (4%)	$ 32,000
Year 2 Depreciation	$ 18,000
Taxable income	**$ 50,000**
Tax Bracket	33%
Taxes received by the Government for Operating Income	**$ 16,500**

Government Rate of Return for Year 1 Investment Costs of Building Depreciation Deduction (Continued)	
Taxes received	$ 16,500
Year 1 government costs	$ 99,000
Return on investment as a percentage	**16.67%**
Additional Taxable Interest Income from bank's loan	$ 32,000
Tax Bracket for Interest received by the bank	25%
Taxes Received	**$ 8,000**
Total Taxes Received from operating income and Bank interest	$ 24,500
Year 1 government costs	$ 99,000
Return on investment as a percentage	**25%**

Now let's say the building appreciates and is later sold for $1,500,000. In addition to recovering most of its initial investment of $99,000 through depreciation recapture, the government also gets an additional 20 percent of the $500,000 of appreciation through capital gains taxes. All of this in addition to the benefits of getting more housing built. A similar result would occur if the building were for a business instead of housing as illustrated in the taxpayer strategy below.

Sale of Building		
Gain on the sale		$ 500,000
Capital Gains Tax	20%	$ 100,000
Depreciation Recapture		$ 99,000
Total Tax received		$ 199,000

How the taxpayer strategy pays off

Of all investments, real estate provides the greatest opportunity for strategic use of tax incentives to increase the real rate of return, which is the percentage of annual profit from an investment adjusted for inflation. As I've covered in Chapter 7 of my first book, *Tax-Free Wealth*, the combination of tax incentives for real estate provides a powerful tool for building wealth.

Consider an entrepreneur whose business produces a net income of $500,000 per year. In isolation and without any other strategies, this income could be taxed as high as 40 percent or more. Now, suppose that business owners purchased a building for $1 million to use in their business, putting down 20 percent and borrowing the remaining 80 percent. In the United States, the first-year depreciation on this building would be approximately $300,000, offsetting a similar amount of business income and reducing overall taxable income to $200,000. That represents a tax savings of up to $120,000 in the first year alone. Later, when the business grows and needs a larger building, the owners might sell the building for $2,500,000 and use the proceeds to pay off the old debt of $800,000, leaving them with a $1,700,000 down payment on a new building costing $6,000,000. Assuming they use the like-kind exchange rules to avoid paying tax on the sale, the difference between the new purchase price of $6,000,000 and the deferred gain of $2,000,000 ($1,500,000 of gain plus $300,000 of first year depreciation and an assumed $200,000 of subsequent depreciation) is again subject to depreciation.

Year 1 Tax Savings from Purchase of Business Use Building	
Net income from Business	$ 500,000
Building Purchase	$ 1,000,000
Amount Invested = 20%	**$ 200,000**
Amount financed = 80%	$ 800,000
Approximate depreciation expense = 30%	$ 300,000
Total Net income from business after depreciation offset	$ 200,000
Total reduction of income from depreciation	$ 300,000
Total tax savings from reduction of income = 40%	**$ 120,000**

Building Sale with Additional Building Purchase	
Original Building purchase price	$ 1,000,000
Loan Amount	$ 800,000
Amount Invested	$ 200,000
Sale of building	$ 2,500,000
Pay off building loan	$ 800,000
Amount used as down payment for new building	**$ 1,700,000**
New building purchase	$ 6,000,000
Gain from Original building sale	($ 1,500,000)
Depreciation in year 1	($ 300,000)
Subsequent Depreciation	($ 200,000)
Total New Building Basis subject to depreciation	**$ 4,000,000**

Effectively, the owner only put in $200,000 of their own money (the down payment on the original building), received tax benefits over the years of $200,000 through depreciation ($300,000 bonus plus $200,000 subsequent depreciation at a 40 percent tax rate), paid no tax on the sale of the building, and will receive an additional first-year deduction of up to $1,200,000 ($4,000,000 new basis x 30 percent bonus depreciation). Assuming their income from the business has grown proportionately, the value of that $1,200,000 deduction could be as high as $480,000. In total, they have received $680,000 of tax benefits on an investment for which they paid $200,000.

Total Tax Benefits	
Year 1 depreciation	$ 300,000
Subsequent Depreciation	$ 200,000
New building basis depreciation = 30%	$ 1,200,000
Total	$ 1,700,000
Total tax benefit with a Tax Rate of 40%	**$ 680,000**

This is only one of the examples of how the government will effectively pay you for investing in areas in which it wants you to invest. Imagine if the project was low-income housing and, in addition to the depreciation, the investor also received tax credits of 70 percent of the cost of the real estate. The tax benefits get very big, very fast and can easily outweigh the original cost of the investment.

Chapter 4: Key Points

1. There are incentives for homeownership versus renting.
2. Real estate deductions must meet the four tests – of business purpose, ordinary, necessary, and documentation.
3. Real estate gets a deduction called depreciation on appreciating assets.
4. Cost segregation allows up to 30% or more of the depreciation to be taken in year one of ownership.
5. Certain government high-priority projects are incentivized through tax credits.
6. Tax benefits for selling property are low-taxed transactions and non-taxed transactions.
7. Buy, borrow, die strategy eliminates tax completely.

Chapter 5

Investment #4: Energy

> *"Global energy security is a vital part of America's national security."*
>
> —Joe Biden

Government purpose – environment, productive competitiveness, national security

In the spring of 1988, my wife and I discussed our next move. My term at the Ernst & Young National Tax Department was at an end, and we needed to decide which Ernst & Young office I would join. The firm wanted us to move to San Francisco. There were also partners in Utah, Long Beach, San Diego, and Phoenix who all wanted my services — a heady time when managing partners are vying for you.

Each location had pros and cons, but San Francisco and Long Beach were expensive, and the firm wasn't going to give me a cost-of-living increase. That left San Diego and Phoenix.

My wife had lived in Phoenix, so I took a trip out to Phoenix to meet everyone at the office. The desert is an interesting place. It has its own kind of beauty. I was immediately struck by the way the air seemed to move through my body and warm my bones. Growing up in Salt Lake City, where the winters nearly killed me, I knew this was the change I wanted in life.

We moved to Phoenix in the summer of 1988 and never left. I even enjoy the summers. In the summer of 2019, I decided to add solar paneling to the studio I built next to my house. When I considered solar power, I didn't initially think it would be a great investment. It was the terrific tax benefits that pushed me over the edge. As it turned out, our energy bills are so much lower in the summer now that it turned out to be a worthwhile investment after all. Funny to think, I would never have done it if it weren't for the tax incentives.

The tax incentives for energy investment

Many countries reserve the development and ownership of energy for the government. All the oil in the Middle East and most of the energy in Europe, Asia, and South America are owned and developed by the central governments. However, a few countries, including the United States, allow independent ownership of oil, gas, and other natural energy resources.[1]

Energy Natural Resources Private Ownership			
	Yes	No	Notes
Argentina		✓	Hydrocarbons are owned by the state & providence.
Australia		✓	Hydrocarbons are owned by the state.
Canada	✓		Offers private ownership in oil & gas.
France		✓	Hydrocarbons are owned by the state.
Germany	✓		Offers private ownership in oil & gas.
India		✓	Natural Resources are owned by the state.
Italy		✓	Natural Resources are owned by the state.
Japan	✓		Offers private ownership in oil & gas.
Mexico		✓	Natural Resources are owned by the state.
Singapore		✓	Imports oil & gas, other natural resources.
South Korea		✓	Natural Resources are owned by the state.
Spain	✓		Offers private ownership in oil & gas.
Taiwan	✓		Offers private ownership in oil & gas.
United Kingdom		✓	Natural Resources are owned by the state.
United States	✓		Offers private ownership in oil & gas.

Tax incentives are significant in countries that allow independent energy investment and ownership. And even for those who don't allow independent ownership of natural resources, many do allow independent ownership of renewable energy, such as solar, wind, and hydrogen — or they incentivize home, vehicle, and factory improvements that allow for clean energy or energy conservation. These incentives generally take the form of tax deductions and tax credits.

Deductions

Deductions are typically allowed on the production and sale of the energy. Oil, gas, and coal investments generally are allowed deductions for production costs and for depletion of the natural resources. Renewable energy, by nature, doesn't deplete, so deductions are limited to the cost of production. In the United States, production costs are broken down among costs of equipment, development, and operations.

Equipment costs are treated much the same as in any business, i.e., depreciation is allowed and, in some cases, a full write-off in the first year. Oil and gas development costs are also referred to as "intangible drilling costs" or IDC. IDC represents all the development costs for wells, less the cost of the land and the cost of equipment. In the United States, 100 percent of the IDCs are allowed as a deduction in the year of investment for any investor who takes on the risk of development and doesn't own their interest through a company with limited liability. Operating costs are also allowed as incurred, including the cost of operating the well, transporting the oil and gas, and taxes on the oil and gas.

Production Costs in the United States Include:	
1.	*Cost of Equipment*
2.	*Cost of Development*
3.	*Cost of Operations*

Conceptually, depletion is similar to depreciation. It is a deduction for the loss of oil and gas in the ground. As an additional incentive to oil and gas developers and investors, the United States allows a depletion deduction of 15 percent of the sales price of oil, regardless of the number of reserves remaining in the ground. This "percentage depletion" is not tied to the actual cost of the development or the amount of the reserves. Effectively, only 85 percent of income from oil and gas is taxable, and that amount is further reduced by operating costs.

Renewable energy deductions are almost always limited to equipment and operating costs. There is no depletion as the resource is, by definition, renewable, and presumably will not run out. So long as the sun keeps shining, the wind keeps blowing, and the rain keeps falling, there will always be solar, wind, and hydroelectric (and hydrogen) energy. And if they do deplete. . .well, a tax incentive isn't going to do you much good!

In the United States and many other countries, renewable energy equipment and development costs are deductible against ordinary taxable income.[2]

Renewable Energy Deductions			
	Yes	No	Notes
Argentina	✓		Accelerated depreciation, tax credits, R&D credits.
Australia	✓		Accelerated depreciation, R&D credits.
Canada	✓		Accelerated Capital Allowance, tax credits, R&D credits.
France	✓		R&D credits, regular business expense allowance.
Germany	✓		R&D credits, regular business expense allowance.
India	✓		Accelerated depreciation, R&D credits.
Italy	✓		R&D credits, regular business expense allowance.
Japan	✓		Accelerated depreciation, R&D credits.
Mexico	✓		Accelerated depreciation, R&D credits.
Singapore	✓		R&D credits, regular business expense allowance.
South Korea	✓		R&D credits, regular business expense allowance.
Spain	✓		Reduction of income derived from intangible assets, tax credits, R&D credits.
Taiwan	✓		Accelerated depreciation, R&D credits.
United Kingdom	✓		Accelerated depreciation, R&D credits, land remediation relief.
United States	✓		Accelerated depreciation, tax credits, R&D credits.

This means that in a 40 percent tax bracket, the government is sharing 40 percent of those costs. Later, when the energy is sold, the government will get 40 percent of the net income.

Credits

Tax credits for renewable energy can be significant — and the government doesn't always share in the income produced by them. In the United States, there is a credit equal to 26 percent of the cost of installing solar panels for homeowners and businesses. The credit to homeowners is a permanent benefit — a 26 percent reduction in the cost of installing the solar panels. Since homeowners don't normally receive a deduction for energy costs, the government doesn't share in the savings. Businesses installing solar panels, however, reduce the cost of their energy which, in turn, reduces their deduction for energy expenses. So, the government does, in effect, share the benefit of solar panels installed by a business.

The U.S. has a credit equal to 26% of the cost of installing solar panels for homeowners and businesses.

Businesses also enjoy a depreciation deduction for solar panels, less credits. For example, if the business pays $100,000 for panels and receives a $26,000 credit, it can deduct the equipment cost less 50 percent of the credit against income ($100,000 less $26,000 × 50% = $87,000). In a 40 percent tax bracket, this would result in a savings of almost $35,000 to go with the $26,000 credit, for a net cost to the business of only $39,000.

Purchase of Energy Equipment with Solar Credit Benefit		
Equipment cost		$ 100,000
Solar tax credit %	26%	
Solar tax credit		**$ 26,000**
Equipment cost		$ 100,000
Solar credit reduction percentage	50%	($ 13,000)
Total cost after reduction for solar credit		**$ 87,000**
Total cost net of solar credit		$ 87,000
Tax bracket	40%	
Tax savings from equipment costs reduction		**$ 34,800**
Original equipment cost		$ 100,000
Solar tax credit		($ 26,000)
Tax savings from equipment costs reduction		($ 34,800)
Net Cost of Equipment to Business		**$ 39,200**

The tax credit for installing solar panels is only one of many tax credits for renewable energy. In the United States, there are also tax credits for installing electric vehicle charging stations, purchasing electric vehicles, renewable energy production (IRC Section 45), installing energy efficient windows and roofs (IRC Section 25C), and building new energy efficient homes. Other countries offer similar credits.[3]

Renewable Energy Credits			
	Yes	No	Notes
Argentina		✓	No specified credit.
Australia	✓		Small-scale Technology Certificates.
Canada		✓	No federal tax credits but rebates for renewable energy regarding homes & vehicles. Additional territories offer incentives.
France	✓		Tax credit on expenses for energy transition.
Germany		✓	No specified credit.
India		✓	No specified credit.
Italy		✓	No specified credit.

Renewable Energy Credits			
	Yes	No	Notes
Japan	✓		Eco-car tax reduction; 2.2% – 2.7% tax reduction.
Mexico		✓	No specified credit.
Singapore		✓	No specified credit.
South Korea		✓	No specified credit.
Spain		✓	No specified credit.
Taiwan		✓	No specified credit.
United Kingdom		✓	No specified credit.
United States	✓		26% tax credit.

The policies that spur energy investment

Energy powers everything we do: from cars to factories to transportation of goods to travel, computers, refrigerators, and offices. Our entire society depends on energy. For years, people have tried to harness the energy of the sun. Thomas Edison said, "I'd put my money on the sun and solar energy, what a source of power. I hope we don't have to wait until oil and coal run out, before we tackle that."[4] Abraham Lincoln reportedly said, "As yet, the wind is an untamed, and unharnessed force; and quite possibly one of the greatest discoveries hereafter to be made, will be the taming, and harnessing of it."[5] And more recently, Elon Musk said of his companies, "Our goal is to fundamentally change the way the world uses energy. . .we want to change the entire energy infrastructure of the world to zero carbon."[6]

Since the industrial revolution, the world has built its entire economy, infrastructure, and defense on oil and gas.[7] Roads are routinely built using oil-based products with machines powered by oil. . .for use by vehicles running on oil. Europe uses natural gas for much of its winter heating. Japan invaded the United States in World War II primarily because the United States cut off its oil supplies.[8] Many other wars, including Vietnam, wars in the Middle East, and even World War I are thought by many to have been fought — and won or lost — on oil.[9]

Entire nations, including Saudi Arabia, Iran, United Arab Emirates, Kuwait, Russia, and Venezuela built their economies on oil and gas revenues. It would be difficult to underestimate the impact, advances, and advantages to society of massive quantities of easily transported and relatively inexpensive energy.

Climate change has brought clean energy into an entirely new focus for governments. As of this writing, President Joe Biden is promising a $400 billion investment in clean energy over 10 years. That is more than twice the investment it took to put somebody on the moon.[10] You can be assured that much of this expenditure will come in the form of tax incentives for investors, inventors, and developers to devise, develop, and install clean energy equipment. There is a lot of money to be had and other countries are following suit.

French President Emmanuel Macron famously added a tax on gasoline to fund the development of clean energy.[11] He promised that France would ban the sale of vehicles powered by fossil fuels by 2040, and be completely carbon neutral by 2050.[12] In addition, he promised to invest billions in pursuit of making France the number one manufacturer of electric vehicles in Europe.[13] Great Britain's Prime Minister Boris Johnson wants to make the United Kingdom the world leader in clean wind energy.[14] And Japan's economy minister Hiroshi Kajiyama said he wants to make renewable energy "a major power source" and plans to meet 22 to 24 percent of Japan's energy needs with clean energy by 2030.[15]

It's clear that the world is on a mission to reduce emissions with clean energy. Energy has always been a focus for governments and now the shift to conservation gives governments another reason to incentivize clean energy. Investors and entrepreneurs will see massive tax deductions and credits over the next decade for implementing their government's energy policy.

How the government strategy pays off

The government's primary purpose for incentivizing energy production is not necessarily economic. There are defense, environmental, and other considerations as well. Still, the economic impacts of energy investment should not be ignored. Consider the following example.

As previously mentioned, the U.S. government provides a tax credit of 26% on a $100,000 investment in solar panels for a business

($26,000). In addition, it allows a depreciation deduction in the first year of $87,000 ($100,000 less 50% × $26,000 credit amount). In a 40% tax bracket, it has contributed $61,000 of the cost.

Suppose the $100,000 solar panel array reduces the energy costs of a business by $7,400 per year. Like the homeowner, the government does not recoup the cost of the credit. However, the government does make a nice return on the contribution for depreciation. A reduced deduction to the business of $7,400 per year at 40% translates to income to the government of $2,960 per year. This is an 8.5% return on their investment of $35,000.

Government Benefit of Purchase of Energy Equipment with Solar Credit Benefit		
Equipment cost		$ 100,000
Solar tax credit %	26%	
Solar tax credit		**$ 26,000**
Solar credit	$26,000	
Solar credit reduction percentage for depreciation	50%	($ 13,000)
Total Year 1 depreciation deduction		**$ 87,000**
Total equipment costs		$ 100,000
Solar credit		$ 26,000
Solar depreciation tax benefit ($87,000 x 40%)		$ 35,000
Total Government Contribution		**$ 61,000**
Reduction of business energy expense		$ 7,400
Tax Bracket	40%	
Tax on reduction of energy expense		**$ 2,960**
Government's Depreciation Investment		$ 35,000
Tax on reduction of energy expense		$ 2,960
Rate of return on investment		8.5%

In addition, the government addresses its initiative to reduce carbon emissions. An investment of $100,000 should purchase a 100 kw system. A 100 kw solar system produces about 144,000 kwh/year of electricity. Each kwh of solar production saves 50 grams of CO_2 emissions. That means that a 100 kw solar array could save as much as 153 tons of CO_2 each year. Seems like a fair return on investment for the government.[16,17]

How the taxpayer strategy pays off

It's rare for a new opportunity to be as obvious and available as investment in energy. While natural resources have long enjoyed special tax treatments, the advantage of renewable energy is that it is not a depletable resource. Clean energy will be more like real estate investment. It will have a longer life span and will be less risky, as most renewable energy is found above ground (with the exception of thermal energy). Given that real estate is also a necessary component of clean energy, there is a natural alignment and combination of real estate and energy tax strategies. A government-paid strategy for owning clean energy might look something like this.

Allow me to share my own personal example. A few years ago, I purchased a building for my companies, Wheelwright Manahan and WealthAbility®, to occupy. At the time, I received all the real estate tax benefits discussed in Chapter 4. In 2021, I decided to add solar to the roof of the building. Here are my actual numbers for the solar investment.

That's effectively a 20.74% on my investment that is practically risk free. The only risk I take is that utility prices go down (unlikely) or that I don't use the power (equally unlikely).

Solar Panel Return on Investment		
Cost of purchase from the solar panel company		$ 104,242
Federal Tax Credit (26%)		$ 27,103
Bonus Depreciation ($104,242 – ($27,103/2))		$ 90,691
Tax Rate (37% Federal plus 3.8% NIIT plus 4.95% Arizona)	45.75%	
Tax Benefit of Depreciation		$ 41,491
Total Tax Benefits		$ 68,594
Net Cost to Taxpayer (me) ($104,242 – $68,594)		$ 35,648
Average annual savings on utility costs per solar company	$ 7,392	
Return on investment ($7,392/$35,648) over first five years		20.74%

Suppose you purchase a service station with a convenience store and a large amount of land for parking for $1 million. The convenience store and the structure that covers the gas pumps both have flat roofs. Suppose 20 percent of the value of the $1 million is allocated to the land and the remaining to the building and equipment. You put down 25 percent of the purchase price, $250,000, and borrow $750,000 from the bank.

In the United States, you would receive a depreciation deduction for the entire amount allocated to the building and equipment and, under the bonus depreciation rules, apply it entirely in the purchase year. The result is an $800,000 depreciation deduction with a cash value of $320,000 in the 40 percent bracket on an initial outlay of $250,000. The government has already paid for your investment — and then some.

But wait, there's more!

Working with the bank, you again get 75 percent financing to improve the property. You put in $50,000 toward the $200,000 cost of solar panels for both roofs and $25,000 of the $100,000 cost of electric charging stations in the parking lot. You get credits plus depreciation for all this equipment.

The solar panels result in a tax credit of $52,000 and a depreciation deduction of $174,000. At a 40% tax rate, the $174,000 deduction is worth an additional $69,600 for a total tax benefit of $121,600 for the solar installation.

Plus, there is a 30 percent tax credit for commercial installation of charging stations. The charging stations result in another $30,000 of tax credit plus $70,000 of additional depreciation for a total tax benefit of $58,000.[18]

Altogether, you have invested $325,000, the bank has invested $975,000, and the government has given you (not the bank) tax benefits totaling $499,000 ($320,000 from the real estate, $121,000 from the solar panels, and $58,000 from the charging stations). You receive all your investment plus a return of $174,000 (equaling 54 percent ROI) in the first year. You have no money in the deal — only the bank and the government have money in the deal — but you share in the profits at a rate of 60 percent of net profits after paying the bank.

Service Station with Solar Panels & Electric Charging Station Example		
Building Purchase		$ 1,000,000
Loan Amount		$ 750,000
Down Payment		$ 250,000
Land value	20%	$ 200,000
Building and building Components Value	80%	$ 800,000
Total Allowable Depreciation		**$ 800,000**
Tax Bracket	40%	
Year 1 government cost from reduction of taxable income due to depreciation		**$ 320,000**
Solar Panel Purchase		$ 200,000
Loan Amount		$ 150,000
Down Payment		$ 50,000
Depreciation & Bonus Depreciation Value		
Solar Panel Credit	26%	$ 52,000
Solar Credit Reduction Percentage for Depreciation	50%	$ 26,000
Solar Panel Depreciation Deduction (200,000 – 26,000)		$ 174,000
Tax Bracket	40%	
Tax Savings		**$ 69,600**
Solar Panel Credit		$ 52,000
Tax Savings		$ 69,600
Total Tax Benefit		**$ 121,600**
Electric Charging Station Purchase		$ 100,000
Loan Amount		$ 75,000
Down Payment		$ 25,000
Charging Station Credit	30%	$ 30,000
Charging Station Depreciation Deduction		$ 70,000
Tax Bracket	40%	
Tax Savings from Depreciation		**$ 28,000**
Charging Station Credit		$ 30,000
Tax Savings from Depreciation		$ 28,000
Total Tax Benefit		**$ 58,000**

Service Station with Solar Panels & Electric Charging Station Example	
Total Loans	
Building	$ 750,000
Solar Panels	$ 150,000
Charging Stations	$ 75,000
Total Loan Amount	**$ 975,000**
Total Amounts Invested	
Building	$ 250,000
Solar Panels	$ 50,000
Charging Stations	$ 25,000
Total Investment Amount	**$ 325,000**
Total Tax Savings Amounts	
Building	$ 320,000
Solar Panels	$ 121,600
Charging Stations	$ 58,000
Total Tax Savings Amounts	**$ 499,600**
Total Tax Savings Amounts	$ 499,600
Total Investment Amount	$ 325,000
Total Return on Investment	**$ 174,600**
Total Return on Investment as a percentage in Year 1	**54%**

At this point, some of you might be saying, ". . .but I don't have $325,000" or "I'm not in a 40% tax bracket." Please remember that this doesn't have to be your money. Real estate syndicators know that raising capital is a pivotal part of the investment process. While you personally may not have the funds or be in the highest tax bracket, there's someone else who has both the money and the tax bracket. They just may not have the time, knowledge, or energy to find the investment. There is always a place in the deal for those putting it together, a plan for those who have money and high tax brackets, and those who will manage the business. This is why Robert Kiyosaki is frequently quoted as saying, "Business and investing are team sports."[19]

Chapter 5: Key Points

1. Incentives for renewable energy generally take the form of tax deductions or tax credits.
2. In the United States, production costs are broken down across three areas: cost of equipment, development, and operations.
3. Government shares in the benefit of solar panels installed by a business.
4. In the United States, there are tax credits for installing electric vehicle charging stations, purchasing electric vehicles, producing renewable energy, installing energy efficient windows and roofs, and building new energy-efficient homes.

Chapter 6

Investment #5: Agriculture

> *"Agriculture is the most healthful, most useful, and most noble employment of man."*
>
> —George Washington

Government purpose – food, shelter, exports

Unlike me, who has a brown thumb when it comes to growing things (I can literally kill any plant in a matter of weeks), my wife, Louanne, has a green thumb. Plants love Louanne. She can get anything to grow, and nothing ever dies. She can even get orchids to stay alive on our kitchen table. At the beginning of the coronavirus pandemic, she started a vegetable garden. Everything in it flourished, especially the eggplant, which we planted because it was one of the few vegetable plants available at the beginning of the pandemic. (Everyone had apparently decided that if they couldn't go out, they should start gardening. Ironically, there were always plenty of harvested vegetables available at the store.)

Louanne has multiple gardens. She plants lettuce along with pansies in the winter (lettuce grows well in the winter in Arizona). She has roses, hibiscus, and bougainvillea in our front courtyard and basil, mint, and rosemary in our back courtyard. Once we get chickens to lay eggs, we may never have to go to the store again.

I love that we can be self-sufficient because of Louanne's green thumb. It means that we truly will never go hungry, regardless of the economy. And we know the food from our garden is organic and will taste better than anything purchased at the grocery store. No special labels required.

The incentives for agricultural investment

The pandemic made it clear just how important our food production, packaging, and delivery is to the people's well-being and government stability. At the beginning of the pandemic, social media was overwhelmingly focused on empty grocery-store shelves. People quickly started hoarding basic necessities, worrying that they may never again be able to buy toilet paper or frozen pizza. Apps that calculated how much toilet paper you would need during the year quickly turned up for your phone. Food delivery services, both for groceries and takeout, were overwhelmed with demand. I distinctly remember going into Costco (a big warehouse retailer in the United States) at the beginning of the pandemic and noticing that almost every cart had a case of bottled water. People were freaking out.

It's no wonder that governments have long reserved some of the best tax incentives for agriculture. From deductions for every possible expense to special write-offs for specific crops and entire sections of the law devoted to agricultural co-ops, agricultural incentives are plentiful.

Deductions

Most countries allow same-year deductions for almost all agricultural production expenses rather than capitalizing them and expensing them over a longer period of time.[1]

Agriculture Deductions			
	Yes	No	Notes
Argentina	✓		Expenses are deductible to the extent incurred in producing taxable income, subject to certain restrictions and limitations.
Australia	✓		Farming businesses can generally claim a deduction for most of the costs when they are incurred.
Canada	✓		Can use cash-based accounting and report expenses at the time they are actually paid.
France	✓		Can use cash-based accounting and report expenses at the time they are actually paid.
Germany	✓		Can use cash-based accounting and report expenses at the time they are actually paid.
India		✓	N/A Agricultural income earned by the taxpayer in India is exempt from tax.

Agriculture Deductions			
	Yes	No	Notes
Italy		✓	N/A Italy uses assigned yields rather than actual yields or income generated.
Japan	✓		The amount of selling, general, and administrative expense (SG&A), and other business expenses that were incurred during the year.
Mexico	✓		Expenses deemed as absolutely necessary for the generation of taxable income are deductible. Additionally, under the Agricultural, Forestry, and Fisheries Regime, small-scale producers' income is tax exempt.
Singapore		✓	As long as the expense is incurred wholly and exclusively in the production of income, the expense can be deductible. However, capital allowances are required for plant and machinery assets.
South Korea	✓		Income from grains and other food crops are exempt from taxation. Other agriculture farming incomes are considered as business income and the basic framework under which they are subject to income tax or corporate tax is the same as for other industries.
Spain	✓		Small entrepreneurs can use the simplified cash-based accounting method for expenses. However, the fixed index method can also be used, which may produce more favorable results.
Taiwan	✓		Income from self-undertaking in farming, fishing, animal husbandry, forestry and mining-amount of income shall be the whole year's income after deduction of necessary expenses.
United Kingdom	✓		Can use cash-based accounting and report expenses at the time they are actually paid.
United States	✓		In addition to current expenses being deductible, many farm and ranch assets are deductible in the year purchased, including some farm and ranch buildings.

Feed for cattle, seeds, fertilizer for crops, and agricultural equipment are all deductible immediately upon purchase in most countries.

These deductions are *in addition* to the normal business deductions that are already afforded to agriculture. After all, agriculture is a business. And it's a business more people are interested in as they become concerned about food quality and supply chain interruptions.

It wasn't that long ago that the thought of an agriculture-related side business was unthinkable — unless you were rich and wanted a vineyard and your own wine label. Now, a family farm or a co-operative vegetable garden is relatively commonplace, even in the inner cities.[2] Those who invest in these farms, ranches, and even vineyards should understand that most of the expenses are deductible against ordinary income taxes if they follow the rules properly.

One caution: Farms don't always make money, and many countries prohibit deductions for hobbies.[3]

	Hobby Loss Rules Apply		
	Yes	No	Notes
Argentina		✓	No specific hobby loss rules.
Australia	✓		Business has produced a profit in three of the past five years (including the current year).
Canada	✓		Direct expenses are claimed against any income from the farm activities up to but not exceeding the income declared.
France	✓		Hobby designation is presumed when losses arise and other sources of income meet certain thresholds.
Germany	✓		Activities with continuous losses (evaluated over a period of 10 years) are considered as a hobby.
India		✓	N/A Agricultural income earned by the taxpayer in India is exempt from tax.
Italy		✓	N/A Italy uses assigned yields and not on the basis of actual yields or income generated.
Japan		✓	No specific hobby loss rules.
Mexico		✓	No specific hobby loss rules.
Singapore		✓	Uses Traditional carry forward rules. Must meet same business & same shareholder tests.
South Korea		✓	No specific hobby loss rules.
Spain		✓	No specific hobby loss rules.
Taiwan		✓	No specific hobby loss rules.
United Kingdom	✓		Hobby farmers can offset losses in agriculture against income from elsewhere, with restrictions on losses over five years.
United States	✓		IRC § 183(d) is a safe harbor for the taxpayer. It allows a presumption that the taxpayer is engaged in for profit if in 3 of 5 consecutive years (2 of 7 in the case of breeding, training, showing, or racing of horses), the activity is profitable.

So, you can't deduct your veggie garden. You need a legitimate business.

The IRS has a bright-line test for whether something is a business or a hobby. If the activity makes money three out of five years, it is considered a business. Where horses are involved (raising, training, and racing), the rule is two out of seven years. This is a problem because given the number of deductions available, it can be difficult to show a profit on a farm for every three out of five years.

There are proper rules to follow to operate a farm or ranch. Every country has a tax law that prohibits deductions for hobbies.

The good news is that the three-out-of-five-year rule is not the only test. If the intent is to produce a profit, even a farm or ranch that shows frequent losses can qualify as a business.

The key to qualifying as a business lies in showing positive cash flow from the business, and even though a farm or ranch may have big deductions and show a tax loss, it may still produce positive cash flow.

How is this possible? Depreciation. Agriculture, like any business in the United States, receives an immediate deduction for equipment. Agriculture can also get an immediate deduction for the construction of many types of buildings, such as greenhouses and other single-purpose structures. These deductions are also available in Australia and the United Kingdom.[4]

Typically, the equipment and buildings are partially funded through bank loans. This can create a phantom deduction that far outweighs the taxable income or loss. Let's look at an example.

Suppose you borrow $500,000 for equipment and for construction of farm buildings. The loan may be for a 20-year term with a 4 percent interest rate. That makes your annual payment about $36,000. And suppose in your country, the building you purchase is depreciated over five years. That means that each year, you receive a depreciation deduction of $100,000. So, even if you have $60,000 of positive cash flow each year after making your loan payment, you will still show a taxable loss of over $20,000 in each of the first five years. This would be an example of how you could easily show you have a profit motive while still having a loss for tax purposes.

Purchase of Farm Building - Using Bonus Depreciation		
Building & Equipment Purchase		$ 500,000
Loan Amount		$ 500,000
Interest Rate	4%	
Interest Expense		$ 20,000
Principle		$ 16,891
Total Payment per Year		**$ 36,891**
Depreciation		
Building & Equipment Year 1 Depreciation	20%	$ 100,000
Total Depreciation Year 1		**$ 100,000**
Year 1		
Operating Income		$ 97,000
Loan Payment		$ 36,891
Cash Flow		$ 60,109
Less: Depreciation Expense		$ 100,000
Plus: Principle Paid		$ 16,891
Tax Loss		**$ (23,000)**

Credits and Non-Taxed Income

In addition to the deductions, there are multiple tax credits available for agriculture, from credits for alcohol fuels and biodiesel fuel to credits for distilled spirits and agricultural chemicals (Section 45O). In the United States, agricultural cooperatives have their own favorable tax rules distinguished from other taxable entities. There is an entire subchapter of the Internal Revenue Code (Subchapter T) devoted to the tax rules for cooperatives.[5]

Cooperative Rules and Regimes			
	Yes	No	Notes
Argentina	✓		National law N° 20.337 called Law of Cooperatives (LC).
Australia	✓		Australia's cooperative's rules are broken down by territory.
Canada	✓		Cooperative's regulations SOR/99-256.
France	✓		France has individual statutes; however, the 10 September 1947 cooperative act is the main source for rulings.
Germany	✓		The 1889 (Reich) Cooperatives Act is the foundation for tax rulings.
India	✓		Individual states maintain their own rules for cooperatives. For multi-state cooperatives, the rules are held in the Multi-State Co-operative Societies Act, 2002.
Italy	✓		Exceptions from tax liability for production cooperatives under certain conditions.
Japan	✓		Reduced corporate tax rates for agricultural cooperatives that provide banking, insurance, farm input supply, marketing, and technical advice services to their members.
Mexico	✓		Cooperatives can be included in AGAPE regime for special tax treatment.
Singapore	✓		Co-operative Societies Rule 2009.
South Korea	✓		Framework Act on Cooperatives (Act No. 11211).
Spain	✓		Agricultural Cooperatives, fall under Protected Cooperatives regime and receive specific tax incentives.
Taiwan	✓		There is not a specific designation, rules are largely located in the Income Tax Act.
United Kingdom	✓		Co-operative and Community Benefit Societies Act 2014.
United States	✓		Subchapter T.

In addition, there are tax benefits for captive insurance companies that were enacted so farmers and ranchers could set aside funds on a tax-deferred basis for unexpected and otherwise uninsurable losses. These incentives are all in addition to the substantial direct subsidies received by farmers and ranchers.[6]

There are also special rules in the United States to allow farmers and ranchers to hedge (insure) their bets on prices for their crops and livestock, including beneficial tax rules for purchasing and trading commodity futures and other hedging transactions called straddles. All these rules and incentives help farmers and ranchers to successfully conduct business and protect themselves from inevitable price and production fluctuations.

The policies that spur agricultural investment

The pandemic turned delivery services into major corporations practically overnight. Farmers, ranchers, and packagers became "front-line" and "essential" workers even though they never dealt with those stricken with COVID-19. And people no longer took for granted that the shelves in their grocery store would always be fully stocked.

Every country has policies to encourage local production of food and necessities. Not only is this important for basic survival, but it's also an important economic policy and a critical national defense strategy. During the Middle Ages, a common strategy for taking over a city was to lay siege and starve the residents out. A city or country starved for food is ripe for invasion or destruction.

This is why the United States Department of Agriculture lists food security as its number one priority.[7] The European Union states that the goal of its Common Agricultural Policy (CAP) is first and foremost to ensure a stable supply of affordable food.[8] Australia's Ag2030 initiative aims to grow agricultural output to $100 billion by 2030 and provides government support to do so.[9] England's focus on less restrictive policies than the European Union reflects its aim to promote fair and sustainable farming practices that are good for the country and profitable for farmers. (Interestingly, the EU's restrictive agricultural policy is why English farmers largely voted in favor of Brexit, believing that the EU's regulations put too many restrictions on British agriculture, including fishing.[10,11,12] And due to its topography, Japan uses technology to get the most out of every acre of productive land. It ranks as one of the most technologically advanced countries for agriculture and food packaging.[13]

Why the government strategies pay off

Suppose a taxpayer decides to start a business of sustainable fir tree production with an eye on the annual market for Christmas trees. They purchase a hundred acres of land for $100,000 and spend $200 per acre planting timber. The cost of planting is tax deductible. The government does not share in the cost of the land, but at a 40 percent tax rate, the government does share $80 per acre of the cost of planting, for a total cost to the government of $8,000 ($200 × 100 × 40%). The average cost of maintaining the trees each year is $2,000 per acre.

After seven years, the cost to the government of sharing production expenses is $5,600 per acre ($2,000 × 7 years × 40%) or $560,000 for the hundred acres. Beginning in year eight, the taxpayer sells 200 trees per acre (about 1/8th of the trees) for $25 each for a total of $500,000. After deducting the $200,000 of maintenance expenses each year, this results in a taxable profit of $300,000 per year going forward, of which the government receives 40 percent or $120,000.

The government received almost all its investment back in year seven and then receives another $120,000 per year after that for no additional investment cost ($300,000 × 40%). On a total investment of $568,000, the government receives an annual return of $120,000 for a return on investment of over 21 percent. In addition to the profit, the government reduces greenhouse gases by 871 tons per year. Not a bad return on investment for the government.

Purchase of Land & Timber	
Government Shared Expense for Planting (100 acres)	$ 8,000
Tax benefit per Acre For Maintenance ($2,000 x 40%)	$ 800
Total tax benefit Per Year (100 acres)	$ 80,000
Tax Benefits for total Years	7
Total Amount of Tax Benefits	$ 560,000
Total Government Investment	$ 568,000
Annual Tax on Income	$ 120,000
Return on Investment as a percentage	**21.13%**

How the taxpayer strategy pays off

Farming, ranching, and other agricultural production can be a risky investment. In recognition of this and of the importance of successful agriculture to a nation's well-being, most countries allow specific tax benefits to offload some of this risk to the government. In fact, agricultural tax benefits are so great, they essentially offset the entire initial investment costs.

STOP
&
THINK
Agricultural tax benefits are so great, they can essentially offset the entire initial investment costs.

Suppose, for example, that you decide to develop a winery, growing your own grapes. As in the fir tree business noted above, while the land is not deductible, virtually every other expense related to the development of the vineyard is immediately deductible. Since land doesn't wear out and only grows more valuable when it becomes a vineyard, the investment in the land is a simple, secure, long-term investment unlikely to decrease in value and may be readily financed through traditional bank loans.

You and your investors contribute $300,000 to the venture and obtain a loan for $700,000 for the equipment, buildings, and working capital. The equipment, vines, fertilizer, and labor required to develop the vineyard are all immediately deductible. In addition, the construction of greenhouses and other single-purpose structures are also deductible. This contrasts with other real estate improvements that typically are deducted over a period of several years. It's very possible that you can deduct 100 percent of the entire $1 million investment in the first year. If you and your investors are in a 40 percent tax bracket due to income from other sources, the value of the deductions is $400,000 more than your original investment. If you lease the land, you can deduct the cost of the lease payments as well.

Purchase of Vineyard Building & Equipment – Using Bonus Depreciation		
Building & Equipment Purchase		$ 1,000,000
Loan Amount		$ 700,000
Initial Investment		$ 300,000
Percentage of Building & Equipment subject to Bonus Depreciation	100%	
Total Depreciation Expense in year 1		$ 1,000,000
Tax Bracket	40%	
Total Tax Deduction		$ 400,000

Eventually, you may want to add a building for a store and restaurant. A cost segregation (see Chapter 4) can be done to allow much of the building costs to be immediately deductible. Banks are eager to lend money for buildings that produce income. While you and your investors may invest $200,000 for the building, the bank may be willing to lend as much as $600,000 for the remainder of the cost of the building and equipment. Even a 25 percent tax bracket results in the government contributing the full cost of the down payment ($800,000 × 25% = $200,000).

Operating costs, including labor, will be similarly deductible. When combined with the depreciation deduction for the building, the winery, store, and restaurant may produce significant cash flow for many years without much, if any, taxable income.

Adding Additional Store & Restaurant Building: Using Cost Segregation & Bonus Depreciation	
Building Purchase	$ 800,000
Loan	$ 600,000
Amount Invested	$ 200,000
Percentage of buildings subject to Bonus Depreciation after Cost Segregation	x 100%
Total Depreciation Expense in year 1	$ 800,000
Tax Bracket	x 25%
Total Tax Savings	$ 200,000

A note about debt

Through the first five investments, you have probably noticed the importance of debt as part of the tax strategy. This illustrates how important debt is to an economy and how much the government wants to encourage the use of debt. Debt should not be taken lightly. If the business, real estate, technology, energy, or agriculture investment does not produce enough income to pay the debt, the lender will not be happy and will likely make life difficult, if not impossible, for the investor. This is why understanding financial statements and accurately projecting and managing cash flow is critical to the success of a debt-financed business.

Debt should not be taken lightly.

Understanding financial statements and accurately projecting and managing cash flow is CRITICAL.

An investor may choose to avoid debt. This would be the "safe" way to go, according to much traditional wisdom. But is it? In each of the five investments discussed, it's clear that, with the use of debt, the government essentially pays for the entire initial investment in the project. At that point, the investors have no money on the table.

All the money on the table is either the government's money or the bank's money. While the government and the bank expect to be repaid, the government is willing to risk its money in return for potential future profits. Only the bank will foreclose if you don't pay back the loan.

In my experience, those who are afraid of debt simply don't trust the asset that is being purchased to produce enough income to pay the debt service costs. Remember that the purpose of an asset is to create income. The purpose of debt is to acquire assets. If you trust the asset, because of your education, research, and team, you should have no problem undertaking the debt.

The scenarios I have illustrated put all the risk in the operations, not the acquisition. The acquisition becomes fully funded by the government and the bank. The government is more than willing to fund the initial investment; however, since you and your investors control the operations, it's up to you to make the venture a success and repay the bank. That's where the real risk remains. Becoming well educated about the investment, operations, and future cash flow is the key to success.

Chapter 6: Key Points

1. Agriculture receives some of the best tax incentives both in deductions and credits.
2. Tax laws prohibit deductions for hobbies (e.g., veggie garden) – it must be a legitimate business.
3. United States Department of Agriculture lists food security as it's #1 priority.
4. Debt as part of a tax strategy should not be taken lightly. It's critical to understand financial statements and accurately project and manage cash flow.

Chapter 7

Investment #6: Insurance

Government purpose – peace, economy, retirement, security, welfare

> *"My mother had taught shorthand and typing to support us since my father died, and secretly she hated it and hated him for dying and leaving no money because he didn't trust life insurance salesmen."*
>
> —Esther Greenwood in Sylvia Plath's *The Bell Jar*[1]

I first started investing in real estate in 2003, shortly after I met Robert and Kim Kiyosaki. My business partner, Ann, and I played Robert and Kim's *CASHFLOW*® board game and were immediately hooked on real estate. Over the next few years, we acquired 30 rental properties, most of which were in Arizona and Utah, with a few in other places, such as Idaho and Florida. Our first encounter with a potential lawsuit came only a few years into investing.

One of our Utah tenants, who had been a great tenant, lost his job. Soon thereafter, my property manager called to tell me that the tenant said they had fallen on the steps leading up to the house and wanted compensation for hurting their knee. My immediate reaction was to tell our property manager to call our insurance agent and let them know about the claim.

I mentioned earlier that my mother always told me that the two most important professionals on your team are a good CPA and a good insurance agent. Well, I had been a CPA for many years at that point and was now learning why a good insurance agent was so important. Of course, I also learned that one definition of tenant. . .can be "plaintiff."

Our insurance agent promptly called the insurance company's home office and soon an insurance adjuster was on the phone to our property manager to find out what had happened. The adjuster then called me with a few follow-up questions and told me not to worry. They would take care of things and let me know. I heard from the adjustor only one more time — when they called to let me know that the matter was resolved and the tenant didn't get a payout.

That wasn't my only experience with the value of insurance. I've used insurance multiple times in my business and am grateful for agents who have looked out for my best interests and the interests of my businesses. I am also now at an age where life insurance is an important consideration.

When I was young, I made sure I had a good term insurance policy on my life. My wife was a teacher and, even working full-time, never made much money. I didn't want to risk leaving my family with little or no financial means if something were to happen to me.

Now, my children are grown, and I don't have the same concerns. Instead, I am at the age where my income is strong, and I want my heirs to have enough to take care of their needs and to pay off any debts in case I die prematurely. So now I have a whole life policy. My wife is happy because she won't have to worry about any debts when I die. My older son is relieved because he has some special and expensive medical needs, and while he currently is employed and living on his own, there is always a chance that could change and he will need financial assistance.

A whole life policy provides security for both my wife and my family. In addition, the cash value built up in the policy provides me with some security so that if businesses or investments fail, I will always have that to fall back on. I have come to see permanent insurance (whole life is permanent instead of just for a short term) as a way to relieve pressure for me, my wife, and my family. As I look at my investments, life insurance is included in the amount I have set aside as "safe" assets.

The incentives that spur insurance investments

Tax incentives for insurance include both typical incentives, such as deductions, as well as unique incentives, such as the nontaxable nature of life insurance proceeds and the nontaxable nature of investment earnings. Let's start with the usual business tax incentive — deductions

Tax Incentives for Insurance Include:	
1.	Deductions
2.	Nontaxable nature of life insurance proceeds
3.	Nontaxable nature of investment earning

Deductions

Deductions for insurance premiums must be separated between premiums for property and casualty insurance and premiums for life insurance. So long as the need for property and casualty insurance is an ordinary and necessary expense and the amount of the premium is reasonable for the business, business-paid property and casualty premiums are fully deductible. This is regardless of business type. The premiums are deductible, and any claims are taxable.

The same does not hold true for personal insurance, including life insurance. Whether on a home, an automobile, art or jewelry, personal expenses, including expenses for insurance, are not deductible and claims are not taxable.

The primary exception is for health insurance. In the United States and many other countries, healthcare insurance premiums are deductible or, if paid by an employer, not taxable as compensation.[2]

Health Insurance Deductibility			
	Yes	No	Notes
Argentina	✓		Medical insurance payments for employees and their families are deductible.
Australia	✓		Sickness, life, and accident insurance premiums are deductible if individual is below annual income ceiling.

(Continued)

Health Insurance Deductibility (Continued)			
	Yes	No	Notes
Canada	✓		Employment Insurance premiums are deductible.
France	✓		A corporate income tax and a business license tax - ('taxes professionnelle' and minimum 'taxe professionnelle' assessed on the added value) exemption will be applicable to health insurance following specific criteria. This exemption is limited to health insurance.
Germany	✓		Contributions to a health insurance plan are completely tax deductible as far as these contributions are paid for primary basic healthcare.
India	✓		Medical insurance deductions are available, however there is a ceiling on the amount of deduction available.
Italy	✓		Contributions for medical assistance made to Italian National Medical Service Funds (Fondi Integrative al Servizio Sanitario Nazionale) both by the employer and the employee are not taxable, however, there is a payment ceiling.
Japan	✓		Japanese governmental health, nursing, welfare pension, and employment insurance premiums are deductible in calculating taxable income.
Mexico	✓		Health insurance premiums for individuals, if the beneficiary is the taxpayer, and/or their family.
Singapore	✓		Group medical insurance which is provided in lieu of medical cost that would have been reimbursed by employers and where the benefit is available to all staff.
South Korea	✓		Insurance premiums for which the beneficiary is the employee are also deductible; however, they are treated as salaries for the employees and are subject to WHT on earned income.
Spain	✓		The global cost of the insurance is tax deductible for the company (no limits on the amount).
Taiwan	✓		Taiwan National Health Insurance is deductible on the individual's itemized return.
United Kingdom		✓	Private health insurance is not tax deductible.
United States	✓		Generally speaking, any expenses an employer incurs related to health insurance (for employees or for dependents) are 100% tax-deductible as ordinary business expenses, on both state and federal income taxes.

The Tax Foundation estimates that health insurance premiums are the single biggest tax benefit provided by government to U.S. individuals[3]. The tax benefit of deducting or not taxing health insurance premiums is larger than all the corporate tax benefits combined, coming in at $215 billion in the United States alone.[4] Additionally, compensation for physical injuries and other health issues is not taxable.[5]

Compensation for Injury			
	Yes	**No**	**Notes**
Argentina		✓	All compensation/benefit is considered taxable.
Australia	✓		Personal injury structured settlement payments are tax exempt.
Canada	✓		All amounts received by a taxpayer or the taxpayer's dependent, as the case may be, that qualify as special or general damages for personal injury or death will be excluded from income regardless of the fact that the amount of such damages may have been determined with reference to the loss of earnings of the taxpayer in respect of whom the damages were awarded. However, an amount which can reasonably be considered to be income from employment rather than an award of damages will not be excluded from income.
France	✓		Lump sum awards for injury are not taxable, however interest that is earned on damages are. Additionally there are specific rules on periodic payments.
Germany	✓		Compensation for bodily injury or heath issues are typically not taxable.
India	✓		No specific exclusion. But the reimbursement does not fall within the definition of Income.
Italy	✓		Revenues paid by the National Institute for the Insurance against on-the-job injuries are tax exempt.
Japan	✓		Proceeds of injury insurance, compensation, or consolation money for mental or physical injuries are not taxable.
Mexico	✓		Benefits exceeding 10 times the minimum salary are liable for tax.
Singapore	✓		Death gratuities injuries or disability payments/ Workmen compensation is not taxable.

(Continued)

Compensation for Injury (Continued)			
	Yes	No	Notes
South Korea	✓		No public charges of the state or local governments shall be imposed on any money or valuables offered as insurance benefits. Additionally, national pension, medical insurance, unemployment insurance and work injury insurance that are borne by employer.
Spain	✓		Compensation as a consequence of civil liability for personal injury, in the amount legally or judicially recognized is exempt income.
Taiwan	✓		Compensation for death or injury and that are obtained in pursuance of the National Compensation Act.
United Kingdom	✓		Per ITTOIA05/S731 of the U.K. law, injury settlements are generally not taxable with specific court requirements.
United States	✓		Amounts paid to reimburse the taxpayer, whether directly or indirectly, are not taxable.

This is an enormous incentive to purchase health insurance when you consider the combination of deductions for health insurance and non-taxability of compensation for health-related injuries

INCOME

Premiums paid for life insurance are deductible in some countries if paid by the business.[6] In other countries, they are not deductible because life insurance proceeds are not taxable income in those countries.[7]

Life Insurance Premiums – Deductible to the Business			
	Yes	No	Notes
Argentina	✓		Life insurance premiums are deductible as they are considered expenses incurred in producing income.
Australia		✓	Generally, life insurance premiums are not tax deductible, with rare exceptions when life insurance is funded through a superannuation.
Canada	✓		If the life insurance policy is used as collateral for a loan.

Life Insurance Premiums – Deductible to the Business			
	Yes	No	Notes
France	✓		Key-man life insurance premiums are deductible but are subject to conditions and limitations.
Germany		✓	Life insurance premiums are not deductible.
India		✓	Only individuals and Hindu Undivided Family (HUF) qualify for deductions.
Italy		✓	Life insurance premiums are not deductible.
Japan	✓		Life insurance premiums (excluding the portion of so-called policyholder dividends) relating to new (former) life insurance, medical care insurance and new (former) private pension insurance, such premiums paid can be deducted.
Mexico		✓	Life insurance premiums are not deductible.
Singapore	✓		Premiums paid on group term life or personal accident insurance policies are tax deductible to the employer.
South Korea	✓		Insurance premiums paid to an insurance company are deductible if the business enterprise is the listed beneficiary.
Spain		✓	Life insurance premiums are not deductible.
Taiwan		✓	Life insurance premiums are not deductible.
United Kingdom	✓		Key-man life insurance is deductible if certain conditions are met.
United States		✓	Life insurance premiums generally are not deductible.

Are Life Insurance Proceeds Taxable?			
	Yes	No	Notes
Argentina		✓	Only proceeds during lifetime are taxable.
Australia		✓	Typically, not taxable to a financial dependent beneficiary.
Canada		✓	If your estate is named as the beneficiary, proceeds of the death benefit will be subject to estate taxes.
France		✓	No, except for large policies.
Germany		✓	Tax on a portion of death proceeds are payable under certain high cash value policies.
India		✓	
Italy		✓	Only proceeds during lifetime are taxable.

(Continued)

Are Life Insurance Proceeds Taxable? (Continued)			
	Yes	No	Notes
Japan		✓	
Mexico		✓	Life insurance payments are tax free if the insurance company is a Mexican insurer.
Singapore		✓	Generally tax-exempt if derived directly by an individual.
South Korea	✓		Inheritance tax generally imposed on the total proceeds received.
Spain		✓	
Taiwan		✓	Not taxable if the proceeds are below TWD 30 million.
United Kingdom		✓	
United States		✓	

Insurance proceeds are, however, subject to inheritance taxes — if the policy is owned by the person who died. If heirs own the policy, the proceeds escape both income taxation and estate taxation. I'll get into that strategy a little later in this chapter. In addition, the increase in the investment value of a whole life or universal life policy (commonly referred to as the cash surrender value (CSV)) is not taxable as long as the policy remains in effect. Only if the policyholder cancels the policy does the investment value become taxable. The result is that while the policy grows in value, it effectively is never taxed if the policy is held until the death of the policyholder (n.). The policyholder can use the investment value for collateral for a non-taxable loan and still not have to pay tax on the increase in the value.

Life insurance proceeds are not taxable income. However, they are subject to inheritance taxes if the policy is owned by the person who died.

Some insurance policies that effectively allow for both deductions on the front end and nontaxable income on the back end. Captive insurance, as previously discussed in the chapter on agriculture, which is effectively self-insurance for a farm or small business, is one example. In this case, the business receives a deduction for premiums and the insurance company, which is also owned by the business owner, is not subject to income tax. While the tax law clearly provides for captive insurance as a benefit to small business and agriculture, in recent years the Internal Revenue Service (IRS) has challenged captive insurance policies as it has found many cases where this insurance product has been abused by taxpayers. Unfortunately, this is one case where the IRS is throwing the baby out with the bath water — attacking even good, conservative captive insurance companies.

Of course, the government has a right to attack abusive behavior by taxpayers and should do so. They can always challenge whether premiums are appropriate and whether an insurance company properly spreads the risk among enough people to make it true insurance. It will be up to the courts to decide whether captive insurance will survive IRS attacks or whether this benefit will simply disappear without an act of Congress.

Common whole life insurance policies also provide the opportunity for deductions and nontaxable income. And these policies are not under attack by the IRS. All whole life policies allow the owner to use the CSV as collateral for a loan back to the policy owner, while the CSV continues to increase tax free. The policyholder (now the borrower) can use the borrowed funds for investing in business, technology, energy, real estate, or agriculture. Because the money is used for investment, the interest paid back to the insurance company is deductible. This is different than borrowing from a 401(k) or pension plan because the money is not coming directly out of the policy. Instead, the policy is used as collateral for the loan. In the United States and many other countries, the nature of the interest expense is determined by how the funds are used, not the source of the funds. This regime is commonly referred to as the "interest tracing rule."[8]

Interest Expense			
	Yes	No	Notes
Argentina	✓		Follows Interest Tracing rules.
Australia	✓		Rules are related to economic substance.
Canada	✓		Follows Interest Tracing rules.
France	✓		Follows Interest Tracing rules, however, there is a yearly limit on interest expense.
Germany	✓		Follows Interest Tracing rules, however, there is a yearly limit on interest expense.
India	✓		Follows Interest Tracing rules, however, there is a yearly limit on interest expense on non-resident associated enterprises.
Italy	✓		Follows Interest Tracing rules.
Japan	✓		Follows Interest Tracing rules, however there may be restrictions for related party under related party rules.
Mexico	✓		Follows Interest Tracing rules.
Singapore	✓		Follows Interest Tracing rules.
South Korea	✓		Follows Interest Tracing rules.
Spain	✓		Follows Interest Tracing rules.
Taiwan	✓		Follows Interest Tracing rules, additional rules on non-financial institution interest ceilings and inter-company loans.
United Kingdom	✓		Follows Interest Tracing rules.
United States	✓		Follows Interest Tracing rules.

The policies that spur insurance incentives

The most important policy for any government is peace and stability. This is one of the reasons for an agriculture policy and is also a primary driver of insurance policy. Insurance, by definition, evenly distributes risk among a large group of people. Where one person is unable to handle a crisis, a group of people might be able to handle that same crisis with very little disruption. Life insurance does this by spreading the risk of premature death over a large population. Property and casualty, as well as health insurance, also spread risk over a large population. The result is that many people contribute to reduce the risk of a catastrophic event. Since the risk of the event is low, the relative cost shared among many people, is also low.

Outside of defense, the other critical policy of every government is economic development. Due to the long-term horizon of life insurance companies, they tend to hold many of their reserves in long-term, stable investments, such as real estate and corporate bonds. Insurance companies often put up the money for medium and large businesses to finance their investments at relatively attractive terms. In addition, life insurance can be one way for individuals to safely channel their savings into productive investments.[9]

The payment of life insurance benefits also serves to reduce dependence on the government. According to Cummins,[10] from 2010 to 2017, the life insurance industry in the United States distributed over $1 trillion in contract payments, including life insurance benefits, annuity payouts, and disability income payments. This is equivalent to 20 percent of the Social Security benefits paid over the same period.

How the government's strategy pays off

The most interesting part of the government's insurance incentive strategy is that it has no initial outlay. That means that anything the government gets back is 100 percent profit. Because the revenue is nontaxable, the premiums are nondeductible. If the life insurance is ever discontinued and the CSV is distributed, the earnings on the insurance are taxed, providing the government with additional revenue at no additional cost.[11]

Let's take a simple example. Suppose an individual pays an annual premium of $40,000 for a policy with a $1 million face value. The $40,000 premium comes from money that presumably was taxed. No cost to the government there. The premiums paid are taxable income to the insurance company. And let's assume that the insurance company makes a typical profit of about $4,000 on the initial premium and $8,500 on the subsequent annual premiums and the agent receives a commission of roughly 80 percent of the first-year premium and five percent of each succeeding-year premium. Suppose the insurance agent has a net profit margin of about 40 percent. In all, at a 40 percent federal and state combined tax rate, the government receives $800 per year from the insurance company (taxed at roughly 20%) and another $5,000 for the first year from the agent ($32,000 x 40% margin x 40% tax rate) and roughly $320 per succeeding year for a net of about $2,000 per year ($320 from the agent and $1,700 from the insurance company).

Government Life Insurance Tax Benefits		
Insurance policy		$ 1,000,000
Premium - post tax		$ 40,000
Insurance company profit for premium	10%	
Profit		$ 4,000
Tax bracket	20%	
Tax on insurance premium		$ 800
Agent Initial commission percentage	80%	
Commission		$ 32,000
Profit margin	40%	
Profit Year 1		$ 12,800
Tax bracket	40%	
Tax on commission		$ 5,120
Tax Year 1		
Tax on insurance premium		$ 800
Tax on commission		$ 5,120
Total Tax Year 1		**$ 5,920**
Year 2 and Subsequent Years		
Insurance company profit for premium	21%	
Profit		$ 8,400
Tax bracket	20%	
Tax on insurance premium		$ 1,660
Agent ongoing Initial commission percentage	5%	
Commission		$ 2,000
Profit margin	40%	
Profit Year 2		$ 800
Tax bracket	40%	
Tax on commission		$ 320

Government Life Insurance Tax Benefits (Continued)		
Tax Year 2		
Tax on insurance premium	$	1,660
Tax on commission	$	320
Total Tax Year 2	**$**	**1,980**

When the insurance is paid out, even assuming no estate tax on the insurance and no income tax, the government continues to benefit. Not only do they receive the benefit of the recipient not relying on the government for social services payments, but should the profits be invested, they also receive a share of any investment income.

The net result of all these factors is significant returns to the government, along with good policy reasons for the insurance and, in effect, a negative initial cost to the government because there is no deduction and because the government gets to tax the recipients of the premiums.

How the taxpayer strategy pays off

While the government may not pay the entire investment in a life insurance policy, it can still make a hefty contribution that results in an investment that is never subsequently taxed by the government. . . meaning it's a permanent tax benefit. Suppose, for example, that you took out a life insurance policy with a $1 million face value. A 40-year-old man in good health should have an annual premium on that policy of about $40,000, so we'll use those numbers for this example. After three years, the cash surrender value (CSV) will approximate $100,000 and, by the end of the seventh year, the CSV will approximate the total premiums paid ($280,000). At that point, every dollar contributed results in a dollar or more of CSV.

Assume that in year four, you begin borrowing against the policy. Your wealth strategy is based on purchasing duplexes for $250,000 per door. You borrow $100,000 from the insurance company at 4 percent interest and use it as a down payment. You hire an expert to do a cost segregation on the real estate. This results in an immediate depreciation deduction (with bonus depreciation) of $125,000 or 25 percent of the $500,000 cost. The deduction nets a tax benefit in your 40 percent tax bracket of $50,000, roughly half the amount of the loan.

Remember, you still have $100,000 invested in the life insurance policy and the policy will continue to grow at about the same 4 percent as the interest you pay. The $4,000 of annual interest is deductible (as a rental property expense) and nets a tax benefit of $1,600 (in your 40 percent tax bracket). The $4,000 that is earned inside the policy is not taxed.

In year seven, you can borrow another $100,000 and do another $500,000 real estate deal, resulting in another $50,000 tax benefit. At this point, your CSV equals your premiums paid. You now have $1,000,000 of real estate or solar, business, agriculture, or technology — remember you can get similar leveraged tax benefits in any of these investments. The real estate income pays back your loans, and in addition to any net profits, you have received $100,000 of tax benefits and your CSV in your insurance policy continues to grow tax free.

Loan & Loan Expense		
Year 4		
Borrowed amount		$ 100,000
Interest	4%	
Interest expense per year		$ 4,000
Yearly Interest expense related to rental(s)		$ 4,000
Tax bracket	40%	
Yearly Tax Benefit		$ 1,600
Year 7		
Borrowed amount		$ 100,000
Interest	4%	
Interest expense per year		$ 4,000
Yearly interest expense related to rental(s)		$ 4,000
Tax bracket	40%	
Yearly Tax Benefit		$ 1,600

Duplex Purchase & Cost Segregation		
Year 4		
Duplex purchases - 2		$ 500,000
Down payment from life insurance loan		$ 100,000
Cost segregation	25%	$ 125,000
Tax bracket	40%	
Tax benefit from depreciation		$ 50,000
Year 7		
Duplex purchases - 2		$ 500,000
Down payment		$ 100,000
Cost Segregation	25%	$ 125,000
Tax Bracket	40%	
Tax Benefit from Depreciation		$ 50,000

Tax Benefits	
Total tax benefits from depreciation	$ 100,000
Total tax benefits from Interest expense: Years 4–7	$ 6,400
Total Tax Benefits	$ 106,400

On top of it all, the face value of your policy is growing. Due to certain life insurance regulations, after year seven, your premium probably drops to $8,000 per year, which increases your CSV by at least $8,000 per year and the face value of the policy by more than $20,000 per year. At age 65, you have a paid-up policy (no more premiums), and you have $784,000 of CSV (which continues to grow even without additional premiums). With a good wealth strategy, you have invested at least $500,000 of the CSV and added $2,000,000 of bank debt for a total investment of $2,500,000. This has resulted in bonus depreciation of roughly $625,000. In your 40 percent tax bracket, you have received cumulative tax benefits of over $250,000.

And the face value of your policy is $1,600,000. Even if you die without repaying your loans, your net insurance proceeds would be $1,100,000 which is more than your original face amount of $1,000,000 (see Figure 7.1).[12]

At Age 65 Total Assets & Tax Benefit		
Total Assets Purchased		$ 2,500,000
Amount of Bank Loan		$ 2,000,000
Down Payment from Life Insurance loan		$ 500,000
Total Cost Segregations on Assets	25%	$ 625,000
Tax Bracket	40%	
Total Tax Benefits from Depreciation		$ 250,000
Face Value of Life Insurance Policy		$ 1,600,000
Life Insurance Loan Amount		$ 500,000
Net Insurance Proceeds		$ 1,100,000

FIGURE 7.1

This effectively frees up $1,100,000 of other assets that you can spend and still leave a nice inheritance nest egg. Your total investment over the 25 years of paying premiums is $424,000. Your net CSV is $284,000 ($784,000 less $500,000 of loans outstanding) along with tax savings of $250,000 and an increase in the face value of $600,000 (net of $100,000 after outstanding loans). Your actual return on investment in the life insurance, not counting any returns from the investments you made from life insurance loans is 6.070 percent.

ROI on Investment	
Tax savings	$ 250,000
Face Value	$ 1,600,000
Total gains	$ 1,850,000
Investment over 25 years	$ 424,000
Annual Internal Rate of Return	6.070%

At this point, the policy has been paid up and no more premiums are required.[13]

One last thing. If handled properly, the insurance can also be paid to your heirs without estate or gift tax. Yet another tax advantage of life insurance.

Chapter 7: Key Points

1. The two most important professionals on your team are a good CPA and a good insurance agent.
2. Consider whole life insurance as a type of safe asset.
3. Tax incentives for insurance include typical deductions and unique nontaxable incentives.
4. Deductions are separated between premiums for property and casualty and premiums for life insurance.
5. If heirs own the life insurance policy, the proceeds escape income and estate taxation.
6. Captive insurance allows deductions on the front end and nontaxable income on the back end.
7. Whole life policies allow the owner to use the cash surrender value (CSV) as collateral which can be used to invest in business, technology, energy, real estate, or agriculture.

Chapter 8

Investment #7: Retirement Savings

> *"The question isn't at what age I want to retire, it's at what income."*
> —George Foreman

Government purpose – keep the peace, take care of the elderly

My dad loved to work. Even when we went to our cabin at Bear Lake, Idaho, he spent the time working on the cabin or the property. While most people look forward to retirement, my dad thought it meant "being taken out of service," and he wanted nothing of it. At 88 years old, he still ran a small business and worked on writing his own and my mother's memoirs. A year after he stopped working, he died. He had simply accomplished all he wanted to do in life and peacefully expired in bed.

I can't say that I share my dad's love of work — at least not to the extent he did. While I enjoy working, I also love to play and travel. I'm fine sitting on a beach reading a book or relaxing on a cruise ship. But what I don't want is to do those things on the cheap. Don't give me a cruise ship with a tiny, windowless room or force me to travel coach just to stay in a cheap hotel room and eat beef jerky. So, while I don't crave work the way my dad did, I don't want to retire poor either.

As I've travelled the world speaking, I have asked many people if they have a goal to retire poor. Not surprisingly, no one has told me yes. In fact, everyone I ask wants to retire rich! And yet, most financial planners and CPAs take the view that it's okay to have less money when you retire because you will have fewer expenses. That view only holds true if your idea of retirement is sitting at home reading a book or watching television.

The fact is that most retirement plans are based on this idea of "needing" less money when you retire. I expect most people, given a choice, would rather have more money when they retire so they can golf on the best courses, eat at the best restaurants, travel first class (or private), and stay in the nicest hotels.

Retirement investing is strongly encouraged by governments around the world. Every government has some type of retirement program embedded in their tax law.[1]

Retirement Programs by Country

	Yes	No	Notes
Argentina	✓		Argentina's Retirement and Pension Fund.
Australia	✓		Superannuation guarantee (SG).
Canada	✓		RRSP, TFSA, RPP, & DPSP Programs.
France	✓		CNAV National Pension System, ARRCO, and AGIRC.
Germany	✓		Government Pension System, with occupational pension schemes (Riester Rente & Rurup Rente, and private savings plans).
India	✓		Employees Provident Fund Organization & New Pension System.
Italy	✓		Government Pension System.
Japan	✓		Old-age pension.
Mexico	✓		Government Pension System.
Singapore	✓		Central Provident Fund.
South Korea	✓		Korean public pension.
Spain	✓		Spanish public pension; occupational tax- qualified pension plans.
Taiwan	✓		The Public Service Pension Fund, Labor Insurance, Old Labor Pension Fund and its successor, the New Labor Pension System.
United Kingdom	✓		National Employment Savings Trust & Private Pensions.
United States	✓		401K, IRA, Pension & Profit-Sharing Plans.

These programs can be broken into two distinct groups. The first is the qualified retirement plan. This is the program most widely publicized by the government and corporations. Wall Street loves qualified plans because most qualified plan investments end up in the hands of Wall Street via bonds, ETFs, mutual funds, or stock portfolios.

Qualified plans include pension plans, profit sharing plans, individual retirement plans, such as IRAs, RRSPs and Supers, and other defined contribution plans such as 401(k) plans. All these plans have a tax benefit upon contribution and a tax liability upon distribution, with the sole exception of the Roth IRA and Roth 401(k) and portions of the Superannuation.

Governments also have a significant amount of control over qualified plans, such as how much and when you or your company can contribute, who can or must benefit, how you can interact with the plan and the plan's assets, which assets can be held by the plans, when you can take money out of the plans, and, last but certainly not least, the taxation of the plan and the plan benefits.

Conversely, non-qualified plans include everything that can be used for retirement planning that is not subject to the explicit control by the government. This can range from simple savings accounts to business ownership, limited partnerships, and other investments. Trusts are also frequently used for non-qualified plans.

Non-qualified plans are distinguished by the lack of direct government control. While the government controls all taxation to some extent, non-qualified plans have none of the explicit control that defines qualified plans. There are no limits, for example, on the amount of money added to a non-qualified plan, the investments of a non-qualified plan, the beneficiaries of a non-qualified plan, when money is distributed by a non-qualified plan, the owner's interactions with the plan — including borrowing and lending activities — and passing on the benefits of the plan or the plan's assets to children, grandchildren, or charities. Non-qualified plans, unlike qualified plans, can last for generations and can accomplish much more than simple retirement planning. In total, non-qualified plans have nearly none of the restrictions of qualified plans and, as will be explained below, can have all the benefits of qualified plans. In addition, non-qualified plans do not merely defer income taxes; they can be devised in such a way as to legally avoid income taxes indefinitely.

Two Types of Retirement Programs:	
1.	Qualified Retirement Plan
2.	Non-qualified Retirement Plan

Qualified plans are highly regulated by the government.

Non-qualified plans are not specifically incentivized by the government for retirement purposes.

The incentives that spur retirement investing

Tax incentives that spur retirement investing include deductions for putting the money into the retirement account, deferring or postponing tax on the investment income to a later year, and in some cases, lower tax rates when the money is eventually used — or even complete exemption from taxation when the money is used in some cases.

The incentives are different depending on whether the plan is "qualified" or "non-qualified." Qualified plans, as mentioned above, are highly regulated by the government and allow specific tax benefits depending on whether the government's rules are followed. In contrast, non-qualified retirement plans are simply any plan an individual makes for retirement — savings, stocks, real estate, or other investments — that are not part of a qualified plan. Non-qualified plans are not specifically incentivized by the government for retirement purposes. Rather, they come under the general rules for investment discussed previously, such as business, technology, real estate, agriculture, and energy.

Deductions

The primary incentive of most qualified plans is the deduction from income on the front end of the investment, which is equal to the amount of the contribution. Except for Roth (and similar) plans, taxpayers are allowed to deduct the investment made into the plan from their income in the year the contribution is made, thus lowering their tax in the year of contribution. The income is then taxed later when the taxpayer retires and draws funds out of the plan. Most countries limit the amount of contribution to the qualified plan each year.[2]

	Are there Contributions Limits?		
	Yes	No	Notes
Argentina	✓		Defined Pension, 11% required contribution by employee into the Integrated Pension System. Additionally employer contributions are 22.88% of which 10.17% is for the benefits granted by SIPA and the remaining 12.71% is divided between the Family Allowances Subsystem (4.44%), National Employment Fund (0.89%), the National Institute for Retirees and Pensioners (INSSJP) (1.5%), and social work (6%).
Australia	✓		Under the Superannuation program Employer's minimum contribution is 10% of payroll with ceiling of 2.5 times average indexed earnings annual cap of $27,500 for employees that are full time and make more than AUD 450 a month.
Canada	✓		Depending on the program, limits are as follows: $15,390–$30,780.

(Continued)

Are there Contributions Limits? (Continued)			
	Yes	No	Notes
France	✓		ARRCO - earned on 6% of earnings below social security ceiling and on 16% of earnings up to three times social security ceiling. AGIRC - earned on 6% of earnings below the ceiling of the general public pension scheme and on 16.24% of earnings up to eight times the social security ceiling.
Germany	✓		Private Pensions - Contribution levels up to 4% of the social security contribution threshold. Riester Pensions - To receive full state subsidies, pension participants must invest at least 4% of their previous year's income in a Riester plan.
India	✓		Under EPF Schemes employees with basic wages less than or equal to INR 15 000 per month; the employee contributes 12% of the monthly salary and the employer contributes 3.67 percent. This combined 15.67% accumulates as a lump-sum. Must contribute 12% of monthly salary.
Italy		✓	Employee contributions are tax-deductible up to an upper limit on total employee and employer contributions of EUR 5 164 a year, however TFR is excluded from this limit.
Japan	✓		The ceiling to contributions of JPY 620,000 a month.
Mexico	✓		6.5% of individual's earnings - Ceiling on contributions is 25 times minimum wage.
Singapore	✓		Employees contribute 20% of monthly wages and their employers contribute 15.5% - Maximum monthly wage for contribution purposes is currently set at $4,500 per month.
South Korea	✓		The maximum monthly pension contribution to be paid by an employee is KRW 235,800.
Spain	✓		30% of total net income received by the individual in the year, €2,000 per year. For tax-qualified pension plans, contributions are tax deductible up to €10,000 per year, if the additional €8,000 is contributed to the plan by the company.
Taiwan	✓		Under the Labor Pension Scheme up to 6% of salary can be contributed by employees. Employers must contribute 6% of employees' salaries (up to EUR 3,491/NTD 150,000) to employee accounts and can contribute more if they wish.
United Kingdom		✓	There are no legal maximum contributions, however, for every pound paid in, the tax authorities will pay an extra 28 pence into the account up to the level of a person's salary: subject to an annual limit. The lump sum is tax free, while annuities are taxed.

Are there Contributions Limits? (Continued)			
	Yes	No	Notes
United States	✓		401K Contributions ceiling is $20,500; SIMPLE Plans ceiling is $14,000, total contributions for traditional IRA and Roth IRA ceiling is $6,000 ($7,000 if you're age 50 or older), and Profit Sharing ceiling is $61,000.

Qualified plans can be divided into two primary types: defined benefit and defined contribution. A defined benefit plan, typically referred to as a pension plan, is favored by government institutions like firefighters, police officers, Congress, and other public servants. Prior to the advent of the 401(k) and other popular defined contribution plans, many large corporations also had defined benefit plans.

Two Primary Types of Qualified Plans	
1.	Defined benefit.
2.	Defined contribution.

A defined benefit plan defines the amount of the benefit to be paid out to participants rather than defining the amount of the contribution that is made on behalf of the participants. Defined benefits are usually tied to length of service and pay rates of the individuals and funded entirely by the employer. The government entity or company is required to fund the plan to ensure that the benefits are available to the participants.

Since the benefit, not the contribution, is defined, defined benefit plans for those about to retire can be loaded up with deductible contributions to the plan to provide for benefits over the life of the participant. This can be beneficial to a small business owner with few employees. For example, supposed the business owner is 60 years old and their employees are in their 20s and 30s, and the owner is due to retire in five years. Since the benefits will be paid out over the owner's remaining lifetime, they will have to put in a great deal of money those last five years to fund their lifetime of benefits.

Frequently, a business owner's income is highest in their later years as the business has been developed and does not have the start-up costs of the early years. This means that the business owner's income is going to be in a higher bracket these last few years before they retire. Setting up a defined benefit plan allows them to deduct large contributions to the plan when their tax brackets are at their highest rates. While they are also required to contribute to their employees' plan, those contributions will be much lower as they are so much further away from their retirement age.

A defined contribution plan focuses on the amount of contribution to the plan. Defined contributions may be made by the employer, the employee, or a combination of the two. The 401(k) plan in the United States is a defined contribution plan that almost always has an employer and an employee contribution aspect. Many 401(k) plans include an employer match of contributions by the employee. (This is the "bait" my friend Andy Tanner cites in his book *401(k)aos* as the primary reason employees are willing to contribute to 401(k) plans. Andy's book is a good primer on why 401(k) plans can be a bad deal for employees.)

The benefit provided by a defined contribution plan is largely dependent on the success of the earnings in the plan. If the value of the plan assets goes to zero, there are zero benefits. The company's only liability is to fulfill its fiduciary duty to manage the assets logically and conservatively. The primary goal of the company is to not lose money. I suspect this is the reason most defined contribution plans invest in conservative asset portfolios.

Several years ago, I was looking for potential buyers for my CPA firm. I considered one large national firm, with a strong regional presence. The regional managing partner told me that they had a robust personal financial planning arm with over $4 billion under management. When I asked about the earnings goals for the assets, they told me simply that their goal was to not lose money. There was no goal at all to increase the value of the invested funds, some, or all of which was surely tied to defined contribution retirement plans.

Deferral

In addition to the deduction for contributions to qualified plans, the income from such plans is also deferred to a later year when the plan benefits are distributed to the beneficiaries (you and your fellow employees). Many people wrongly assume this means income earned within a qualified plan is nontaxable. Rather, you simply defer the tax to the time when the money is withdrawn. This does not, contrary to widely held belief, result in higher rates of returns within qualified plans versus non-qualified plans. Let's look at an example.

Suppose you contributed $100,000 to a qualified plan, of which you are the sole beneficiary. Assume the plan earns 5 percent annually on your investment. The amount earned in one year is $5,000, and there is a resulting deferred tax liability equal to your tax rate when the amount is withdrawn. Unless your plan is to retire poor, you can logically assume the same marginal tax rate when you retire as when you were working.

If your tax rate at the time you made the plan contribution was 40 percent, or $40,000, you can reasonably expect the tax on the distribution will also be 40 percent or $40,000 when you withdraw and use the money. The earnings will also be taxed at the same 40 percent rate. This is best illustrated in a simple financial statement diagram.

Qualified Retirement Plan (QRP) Tax vs. Pay Tax

Year 1	QRP Tax		Year 1	Pay	
Initial Amount		$ 100,000	Initial Amount		$ 100,000
Initial Tax	0%	$ –	Initial Tax	40%	**$ 40,000**
Tax when distributed	40%	**$ 40,000**	Tax when distributed	0%	$ –
Total Remaining after tax		$ 60,000	Total Remaining after tax		$ 60,000

The primary benefit of a qualified plan is the compounding of the earnings during the period when they are not subject to tax. For example, suppose that instead of contributing the $100,000 to a retirement plan, you paid the $40,000 of tax now and invested the $60,000 in different investments at the same 5 percent rate of return.

The $60,000 at 5 percent would result in $3,000 of earnings. However, that $3,000 would also be taxed at 40 percent, so the after-tax earnings would be only $1,800 instead of the $3,000 of after-tax earnings had you invested through a qualified plan.

Over 30 years, here is the difference between investing through a qualified plan instead of outside of a retirement plan, assuming the same 40 percent tax rate during retirement.

Investment through Qualified Plan vs. Outside of Plan (Compounding Gains over 30 Years)

Qualified Retirement Plan option			Outside of Plan option		
Year 1			Year 1		
Initial Amount		$ 100,000	Initial Amount		$ 100,000
Initial Tax	0%	$ 0	Initial Tax	40%	($ 40,000)
Interest Rate	5%		Amount to be invested after taxes		$ 60,000
Years	30		Interest Rate	5%	
Growth Over 30 years pre-taxed		$ 332,194	Years	30	
			Growth Over 30 years after Tax		$ 142,726
Retirement plan value after 30 years		$ 432,194	Tax on Growth	40%	($ 57,090)
			Total Net Growth		$ 85,635
Tax Rate on Distribution	40%		Initial Taxed Amount of investment		$ 60,000
Tax		($ 172,878)	Total Net Growth (After Taxes)		$ 85,636
Total value after tax		$ 259,317	Total value after tax		$ 145,636

Note: Assumes Compounding is 1 period per year

Of course, this assumes that the income is taxable every year, such as interest income. If the income earned is taxed at a preferential rate outside of the plan, such as dividends or capital gains, then the difference will not be as pronounced.

Taxed Now		Deferred		Permanent	
Capital Gains		Regular IRA		Roth IRA	
Initial Investment	$ 10,000	Initial Investment	$ 10,000	Initial Investment	$ 10,000
Gain Per Year	10%	Tax Benefit Added to Investment	$ 4,000	Gain Per Year	10%
Years	30	Gain Per Year	10%	Years	30
Taxed Per Year	20%	Years	30		
		Total After 30 Years	$244,000		$174,000
		Tax upon Withdrawal 40%	$ 97,717	Tax upon Withdrawal 0%	
Total After Tax	$100,627	Total After Tax	$146,575	Total After Tax	$174,494

If you could invest tax-deferred outside of a qualified plan, you would always be better off, as you would have much more control over the amount of the investment, availability of investments, leverage of investments, and distributions from the investments. In addition, as I will explain later in this chapter, non-qualified plans can be set up to escape taxation indefinitely and, with proper planning, permanently. This can never be done with qualified plans as the government will always require restrictions in exchange for the tax benefits.

In summary, the primary benefit of a standard qualified plan, assuming similar retirement tax rates to working tax rates, is the avoidance of the double tax that most countries assess on earnings, i.e., once on the earnings of the individual and then again on the earnings from the investment of those earnings.

STOP
&
THINK
The benefit of a qualified plan is the avoidance of the double tax on earnings.

The policies that spur retirement incentives

The key to every successful government throughout history is maintaining peace and order among the citizens. Making sure it provides basic necessities, such as food, shelter, and water is the first and most crucial step in doing this. It's no wonder that governments around the world do everything in their power to make sure people have enough resources to avoid an uprising. This is the basis for government pension schemes.

From the government's perspective, the best government pension scheme, of course, is one it doesn't directly fund. Rather, it's much more advantageous to convince the citizens to fund their own pension. Big corporations latched onto this idea years ago when they drifted away from defined benefit plans funded entirely by the company to defined contribution programs, like 401(k)s, where the company merely matched all or a portion of the amount funded by the employee — while knowing many employees wouldn't fund it at all.

Governments do the same by giving tax benefits to encourage contributions to retirement plans. Curiously, this is one area of tax benefits where countries are not completely aligned with each other. In the United States, for example, there are stiff penalties for withdrawing retirement plan assets earlier than a predetermined retirement age (currently 59 and a half years). Canada does not have any penalty for early withdrawal of RRSP funds,[v] and Australia has very liberal laws regarding how Super funds are invested, used, and withdrawn.[4] But regardless, these plans all come down to a government-incentivized savings plan.

It's interesting to see just how small an incentive is necessary to create a large investment in these plans. Conceptually, a deferral of income is not a huge incentive. The incentive ends up costing the government more than it should simply because the returns on investment to the government can be so much lower than they would be outside of the plan, given the restrictions on types of investments and use of debt inside a qualified plan.

Another benefit of qualified plans to the government is a boost to the stock market. As most governments require the assets to be invested in stocks or bonds, the stock market gets a natural boost from the investment in these plans. About 30 percent of investments in the U.S. stock market are from qualified plan investors. Since the stock market is basically a legal Ponzi scheme,[5] it depends on new investment to increase in price.

Most pension investments are made up of established stocks. New investment has the effect of pushing up the price of these stocks, and the price is determined by supply and demand. Each year, as funds from qualified plans go into the stock market, they are typically buying existing stocks, which means there is more money chasing the same amount of stock. The end result, as Jean Chatzky famously said on CNN is pensions are constantly required to invest new money as the population grows, which in turn fuels the stock market. Governments see the stock market as a sign of a healthy economy and stability in the marketplace, so growth in the stock market is routinely viewed favorably by most governments.[6]

Governments that Require Pensions to be Invested in Paper Assets, such as Stocks and Bonds and Limitations of Purchases

	Yes	No	Notes
Argentina		✓	Argentine Sovereign Pension Reserve Fund Is required to purchase private corporate bonds, along with investing into companies domiciled in Argentina.
Australia		✓	No quantitative portfolio restrictions.
Canada	✓		Canada requires pensions be invested in qualified investments, many of which are stocks, bonds, and debt obligations.
France	✓		Minimum of 50% in EU government bonds.
Germany		✓	30% in quoted stocks (10% on unquoted). 50% in bonds.
India		✓	50% of the augmented fund can be invested into future markets or commodity markets, and it's mandatory for PFRDA (Pension Fund Regulatory and Development Authority) to administer the function of the fund managers.
Italy		✓	Liquidity: 20%, Shares of closed-end investment funds: 20%.
Japan		✓	N/A

(Continued)

Governments that Require Pensions to be Invested in Paper Assets, such as Stocks and Bonds and Limitations of Purchases (Continued)			
	Yes	No	Notes
Mexico	✓		At least 51% of the funds' assets must be invested in inflation-linked or inflation-protected securities.
Singapore		✓	By default, gains in the pension scheme are from interest payments from Special Singapore Government Securities (SSGS).
South Korea	✓		Up to 40% in quoted shares.
Spain	✓		90% of assets must be invested in organized, officially recognized markets; Deposits and other money market assets must be 1–15%.
Taiwan	✓		Requires asset investments for growth, including Stock & Bonds.
United Kingdom		✓	No quantitative portfolio restrictions.
United States	✓		Although there is no list of approved investments for retirement plans, there are special rules contained in the Employee Retirement Income Security Act of 1974 (ERISA) that apply to retirement plan investments. For example, participant-directed accounts and IRAs cannot invest in collectibles, such as art, antiques, gems, certain coins, or alcoholic beverages. They can invest in certain precious metals only if they meet specific requirements.

How the government strategy pays off

There is a definite cost to the government for providing retirement benefits. The question is whether the cost is worth the eventual benefits. Let's look at an example.

Suppose a taxpayer invests $25,000 per year into a qualified retirement plan and is allowed to deduct the investment. Assuming a 32 percent marginal tax rate at a total income level of $200,000, the government pays $8,000 per year for this investment plus deferred taxes on the interest.[7] At the end of 30 years, the plan now has about $2,095,042,[8] assuming a 6 percent rate of return. Let's assume that upon retirement this money is paid out over 20 years and continues earning 6 percent per year. The amount paid out will be about $172,000 per year and will produce $32,000 per year in taxes for 20 years.[9] This produces a rate of return to the government of about 1.1 percent.

Qualified Retirement Plan Example		
Yearly Investment		$ 25,000
Rate of Return	6%	
Tax Bracket	32%	
Yearly Deferred Taxes		$ 8,000
Total Plan Balance after 30 years		$ 2,095,042
Rate of Return	6%	
Yearly Withdrawal		$ 172,000
Taxes Paid Per year		$ 32,008
Taxes Paid over 20 years		$ 640,160
Deferred Taxes over 30 years		$ 481,853
Taxes paid in excess of Deferral ($640,160–$481,853)		$ 158,307
Total Percentage of Gain		33%
Rate of Return over 30 years		1.1%

While this is only a modest rate of return to the government, given the large amount of risk in the marketplace for investments, the biggest benefit is the government not making other social payments to make up for the taxpayer not having retirement funds.

If the government instead invested directly in the market at the same 6 percent, it would only have to invest about $4,400 (roughly 55% of the actual $8,000) per year to receive the same $32,000 per year it receives under the qualified retirement plan scenario.

How the taxpayer strategy pays off

When it comes to qualified and non-qualified retirement plans, the government definitely favors one over the other. Let's take a look at the differences between the plans, and we'll see which type of investing is in fact most favored by the government and which provides the most tax benefits to the investor.

Let's first look at the tax benefits of investing through a qualified plan, and then we'll contrast it with a non-qualified scenario. Essentially, the first six investments covered in this book (Partnering with the Government, Business, Technology | Research and Development, Real Estate, Energy, and Agriculture) could be considered non-qualified retirement plans when done strategically.

Suppose you invest $25,000 per year into a defined contribution retirement plan for 30 years with a 6 percent compounded annual rate of return.[10]

As explained above, after 30 years, you will have roughly $2,095,000 in your retirement account. If you plan to live for 20 years after retirement, and assuming you can continue to receive 6 percent on your investment annually, you should be able to withdraw about $172,000 per year.

Now, also assume you were earning $200,000 per year while you were working. In retirement, you will be living on about $172,000 per year or just under what you were earning while you were working ($200,000 less $25,000 retirement contribution = $175,000 working net income). At $175,000 per year, your average tax rate of 18.91 percent produced total income taxes (in the United States) of about $33,000 per year.

At an income of $172,000, your marginal tax rate will be 32% but your average (effective) tax rate will only be 19 percent. This means you are only paying a total of $32,000 each year in taxes and over 20 years, you will pay a total of $640,000. You took a deduction at 32% (your top marginal rate) for the entire time you were contributing, resulting in total taxes saved of $240,000 versus the $142,500 on the $25,000/year investment at 19%, you end up permanently saving $97,500 on the $750,000 contributed. In addition, consider that you would only have $1,024,263 if you had to pay tax on the 6 percent earnings each year, so you really have saved $497,500 ($400,366 ($2,095,042 × (1 – 0.32) – $1,024,263) of additional investment plus $97,500 savings from the tax rate differential). While you put in $750,000 over 30 years, the government effectively contributed an amount equal to 66 percent of your original contribution through the combination of a lower effective tax rate at retirement plus allowing you to defer the tax to a later year.[11]

Notice that the benefit comes primarily from the fact that by using a qualified retirement plan, you are only taxed once on your earnings instead of twice (once when you earn the original wages and when you earn the investment).[12]

Now let's compare the qualified retirement plan results with the non-qualified plan results and use real estate for our example. Suppose we take the same $25,000 of annual contribution and instead of investing it in a qualified retirement plan, we instead invest it in real estate. Following the pattern in Chapter Three, we borrow $100,000 and buy a $125,000 investment property. Let's use the same 6 percent return on investment as in the retirement plan, and let's assume a 3 percent interest rate on the bank mortgage. To simplify, we will make the loan interest only (no principal paid down). Here is what this looks like on your financial statement (see Figure 8.1).

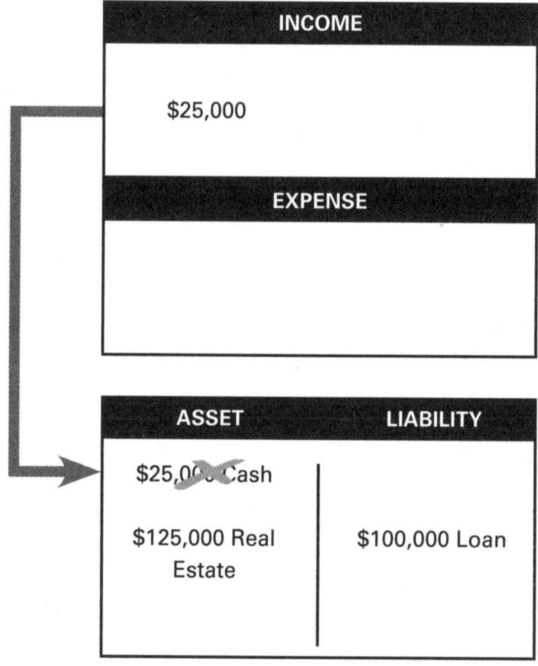

FIGURE 8.1

Now let's look at what happens in year one. Depreciation on the property should approximately equal the contribution, resulting in a $25,000 loss that more than offsets the $25,000 of income. The property generates 6 percent cash flow on the $125,000 purchase price, for income of $7,500. The bank gets $3,000 of interest ($100,000 x 3%), for a net cash flow of $4,500.

Investment Property Example		
Building Purchase		$ 125,000
Loan		$ 100,000
Yearly Investment		$ 25,000
Building Depreciation - 60% of Building over 27.5 years	60%	$ 2,727
Bonus Depreciation	20%	$ 25,000
Depreciation Expense		$ 27,727
Reduction of investment/Taxable Income		
Depreciation Expense		$ 27,727
Yearly Investment		$ 25,000
Remaining Depreciation Expense		$ 2,727
Rate of Return	6%	
Income		$ 7,500
Loan Interest Rate	3%	
Interest Expense		$ 3,000
Reduction of Rate of Return by Interest Expense		
Income		$ 7,500
Interest Expense		$ 3,000
Net Cash Flow		**$ 4,500**

The net tax situation is interesting. The depreciation is enough to offset both the income earned to make the down payment and the net income from the property.

Net Cash Flow	$ 4,500
Remaining Depreciation Expense	$ 2,727
Net Taxable Income after Depreciation Expense	**$ 1,773**

Each year, for 30 years, this is repeated. For simplicity, let's assume the net cash flow is invested at 6 percent and the earnings are taxable at the 32 percent rate. Every five years, the combination of income from the property and tax benefits will be enough to purchase another property of about $100,000, with $20,000 down and an $80,000 loan.

		Cash Flow from Investment	
Year	Cash flow	$1,773 Tax at 32%	Income After Tax
1	$ 4,500	$ (567)	$ 3,933
2	$ 9,000	$ (567)	$ 7,865
3	$ 13,500	$ (567)	$ 11,798
4	$ 18,000	$ (567)	$ 15,731
5	$ 22,500	$ (567)	$ 19,664
6	$ 27,000	$ (567)	$ 23,596
7	$ 31,500	$ (567)	$ 27,529
8	$ 36,000	$ (567)	$ 31,462
9	$ 40,500	$ (567)	$ 35,395
10	$ 45,000	$ (567)	$ 39,327
11	$ 49,500	$ (567)	$ 43,260
12	$ 54,000	$ (567)	$ 47,193
13	$ 58,500	$ (567)	$ 51,125
14	$ 63,000	$ (567)	$ 55,058
15	$ 67,500	$ (567)	$ 58,991
16	$ 72,000	$ (567)	$ 62,924
17	$ 76,500	$ (567)	$ 66,856
18	$ 81,000	$ (567)	$ 70,789
19	$ 85,500	$ (567)	$ 74,722
20	$ 90,000	$ (567)	$ 78,655
21	$ 94,500	$ (567)	$ 82,587
22	$ 99,000	$ (567)	$ 86,520
23	$ 103,500	$ (567)	$ 90,453
24	$ 108,000	$ (567)	$ 94,385
25	$ 112,500	$ (567)	$ 98,318
26	$ 117,000	$ (567)	$ 102,251
27	$ 121,500	$ (567)	$ 106,184
28	$ 126,000	$ (567)	$ 110,116
29	$ 130,500	$ (567)	$ 114,049
30	$ 135,000	$ (567)	$ 117,982

Even if the property does not otherwise appreciate, after 30 years, the value of the investments will be $4,350,000 with loans totaling $3,480,000. The properties at that time can either be converted to a larger, single property if tax-free exchanges are available (See Chapter 4), or simply held for the investment income. The result is an annual income at retirement of $135,000.

The retirement income of $135,000 seems like it's less than the amount of income withdrawing from the qualified retirement plan by $37,000/year. However, unlike the qualified plan, there should be no tax because of annual depreciation deductions.[13] ($172,000 from the qualified plan nets $140,000 after tax so the real difference is only $5,000/year.) In addition, there is no reduction in principle, so you will not be able to outlive your retirement. Now, suppose the real estate, in addition to the 6 percent cash flow, appreciates at 3 percent per year. The results are even more striking.

Buildings with Appreciation			
Year	Building Purchase	Appreciation at 3%	Fair Market Value
1	$ 125,000	$ –	$ 125,000
2	$ 125,000	$ 3,750	$ 253,750
3	$ 125,000	$ 7,613	$ 386,363
4	$ 125,000	$ 11,591	$ 522,953
5	$ 225,000	$ 15,689	$ 763,642
6	$ 125,000	$ 22,909	$ 911,551
7	$ 125,000	$ 27,347	$ 1,063,898
8	$ 125,000	$ 31,917	$ 1,220,815
9	$ 125,000	$ 36,624	$ 1,382,439
10	$ 225,000	$ 41,473	$ 1,648,912
11	$ 125,000	$ 49,467	$ 1,823,380
12	$ 125,000	$ 54,701	$ 2,003,081
13	$ 125,000	$ 60,092	$ 2,188,174
14	$ 125,000	$ 65,645	$ 2,378,819
15	$ 225,000	$ 71,365	$ 2,675,183
16	$ 125,000	$ 80,255	$ 2,880,439

Buildings with Appreciation (Continued)			
Year	Building Purchase	Appreciation at 3%	Fair Market Value
17	$ 125,000	$ 86,413	$ 3,091,852
18	$ 125,000	$ 92,756	$ 3,309,608
19	$ 125,000	$ 99,288	$ 3,533,896
20	$ 225,000	$ 106,017	$ 3,864,913
21	$ 125,000	$ 115,947	$ 4,105,860
22	$ 125,000	$ 123,176	$ 4,354,036
23	$ 125,000	$ 130,621	$ 4,609,657
24	$ 125,000	$ 138,290	$ 4,872,947
25	$ 225,000	$ 146,188	$ 5,244,135
26	$ 125,000	$ 157,324	$ 5,526,459
27	$ 125,000	$ 165,794	$ 5,817,253
28	$ 125,000	$ 174,518	$ 6,116,770
29	$ 125,000	$ 183,503	$ 6,425,273
30	$ 225,000	$ 192,758	$ 6,843,032

At $6,843,032, the net equity in the properties would be $3,363,032 (the debt doesn't increase). Compare this to the total of $2,095,042 by investing through a qualified retirement plan in the stock market. And you don't have to eat into your principal each year in order to take out your $135,000 in cash flow. This leaves you with a lifelong income that never runs out as well as a tidy nest egg to leave to your family or favorite charity.

As you can see, a strategic investment plan in non-qualified retirement assets is by far a smarter financial choice. But it also requires a high financial IQ, which many people don't have. The easier choice, which requires little financial IQ, is the qualified retirement plan. This is why most people choose the qualified plan. While not nearly as successful, it requires less work and less financial education.

Chapter 8: Key Points

1. There are two types of government retirement programs 1) qualified retirement plan and 2) nonqualified retirement plan.
2. Qualified plans are highly regulated by the government.
3. Nonqualified plans are not specifically incentivized by the government for retirement purposes.
4. There are two primary types of qualified plans 1) defined benefit and 2) defined contribution.
5. With proper planning, nonqualified plans can be set up to escape taxation indefinitely.
6. All qualified plans rely on the compounding effect of deferred taxation.

Chapter 9

Conclusion

"Congress can raise taxes because it can persuade a sizable fraction of the populace that somebody else will pay."

—Milton Friedman

I was frequently asked during the 2020 election whether I preferred Donald Trump or Joe Biden as President. My answer from a tax standpoint was, "It doesn't matter." Confused, thinking that Donald Trump had lowered taxes and Joe Biden promised to raise taxes, the questioner always asked the follow-up question, "Why doesn't it matter who is President when it comes to taxes?"

My answer, quite simply, was that all politicians prefer to use taxes to manipulate the economy. As such, there will always be tax incentives. The better question would be, "If Joe Biden wins the Presidency, where should I invest my money to produce the least amount of taxes?" In that, Joe Biden has always been clear — invest in renewable energy.

Certain tax benefits are unlikely to ever change, from deductions for business expenses to tax credits for technology and deductions for agriculture and retirement. Others, such as tax benefits for real estate and energy, can change drastically depending on who is in charge.

While the world is focused on changes in climate, politics, and health, one thing has not changed: All countries' tax laws continue to be used as incentives for political priorities. U.S. President Joe Biden focuses on renewable energy, childcare, and education — all done in large part through tax incentives. While priorities can shift, the true priorities of all governments are manifested in their tax laws.

Certain strategic initiatives, such as energy, jobs, technology, housing, insurance, agriculture, and retirement seem to always be in vogue. As I've shown you in this book, when combined with debt, which is also a favorite governmental tool, these incentives can be so great that they effectively fund most, if not all, of the investment through tax incentives.

The common fallacy is that the rich don't pay taxes because they cheat. Over my 40-year career as a tax advisor, I have rarely seen a rich taxpayer cheat. What I do see, and what should be obvious from the previous chapters, is that the rich understand that if they invest their money in government-incentivized activities, they can get a lot richer and pay a lot less tax.

STOP & THINK
The rich understand if they invest their money in government incentivized activities, they can get a lot RICHER and pay a lot LESS tax.

Conversely, I have frequently found that those who cheat on taxes are in the middle class and lower middle class. Sometimes, this is by offering a business customer a discount for paying cash. (In my experience, these cash discounts are not to avoid credit card fees. More often, they are to avoid taxes.) Sometimes, it's as simple as poor bookkeeping records and paying for personal expenses with business funds. And sometimes it's even more nefarious, where a company maintains two sets of bookkeeping records, one for their own information and one for the tax auditor This cannot happen with large businesses because they must present the same financial statements to the government tax auditors as they do to the bank and their investors.

The good news is that tax laws are eminently fair. That is, they apply equally to everyone who desires to use them in the way the government intended. Rather than cheat, wouldn't it be better to help the government do their job by actively partnering with the government to provide jobs, housing, energy, technology, and food? Rather than accuse the rich of cheating, wouldn't it be better to understand that in many cases, the tax law is simply working as intended? While it's true that many rich people do not pay much tax, it's equally true that those same people contribute significantly to government priorities. This is not to say there are not rich people who cheat or take advantage. As my friend, Ken McElroy would say, "People are people." But instead of vilifying success, I've long believed that it's better to understand what makes people successful, even when it comes to taxes.

Every taxpayer is a partner with the government

Most people are silent partners. They get a paycheck with taxes withheld and file their annual tax return. A few people are active partners. They (along with their advisors) examine what the government wants done and determine whether it would make sense to invest their capital in government-favored investments. While the specific investments and specific incentives may change from year to year or from country to country, the goals of the government are the same — to protect its citizens; improve technology; generate energy; create a sense of security; and provide food, jobs, and housing.

So, what is the next step for you? Start with reviewing your own personal investment strategy. Determine which of the government-sponsored investments fits well within your strategy. Then sit down with a tax advisor who truly understands how the tax law works in your country to determine the next steps to massively reduce your taxes by doing what your government wants done. Does it take effort? Absolutely. Can you do it on your own? Absolutely not. As my friend, Robert Kiyosaki always says, "Investing is a team sport."

Your Next Steps

1. Review your personal investment strategy.
2. Determine which of the government-sponsored investments fits within your strategy.
3. Meet with your tax advisor to identify next actions to take.

Rather than look for loopholes, underreport income, or make up phony deductions, take the time to ask what your government wants done and then take full advantage of the tax benefits offered. The government is more than willing to pay you to make the investments it wants. Why make investments with your own money when the government wants to partner with you and is more than happy to pay you to make an investment?!!

Chapter 9: Key Points

1. Ask yourself – "where should I invest my money in order to produce the least amount of taxes?"
2. The true priorities of all governments are manifested in their tax laws.
3. The rich understand that investing their money in government-incentivized activities makes them much richer and they pay a lot less taxes.
4. Tax laws are eminently fair in that they apply equally to everyone who desires to use them the way the government intended.
5. Every taxpayer is a partner with the government.

Bonus Chapter

How to Get the Government to Pay for Your Ferrari

> *"The Ferrari is a dream — people dream of owning this special vehicle and for most people it will remain a dream apart from those lucky few."*
>
> —Enzo Ferrari

Government purpose – reward for being a good partner

Several years ago, I was in Chile with Robert Kiyosaki and a few other Rich Dad Advisors. We were invited to speak to a room of about 600 investors and business owners. My job, of course, was to talk about tax benefits from investing and real estate.

This was a two-day event, and the sponsor of the event was the local Bentley and Lamborghini dealer. On one side of the stage was a lime-green Lamborghini and on the other was a stately Bentley. On the first morning, as I was on stage with Robert, he asked me to explain how to deduct a Bentley. I explained what I knew to be true in the United States and most countries. So long as the vehicle is used for business, it was typical in your business to drive a Bentley, and, of course, you maintained good documentation, the costs associated with the Bentley should be deductible, including a share of the cost of purchasing the Bentley (depreciation).

At lunch, one of the participants, a tax attorney in Santiago, approached me and told me he was enjoying the event. He explained that automobiles were considered luxuries in Chile and none of the cost could be deducted under Chilean tax law.

Later that night, as the speakers were having dinner together and talking about the day, I shared my experience with the Chilean tax attorney. Robert paid close attention to my story but made no comment at the time. The next morning, as we got ready for the event, he came to me and said, "Tom, today I would like you to explain how to deduct a Bentley legally in Chile."

After the panic subsided a bit, I simply said "OK" and decided to trust in the process to see what would happen. That afternoon, Robert asked me to show how to deduct a Bentley in Chile. I briefly went through the example below, with Robert interjecting about how he had done the same thing when buying his Porsche.

At the end of the event, the Chilean tax attorney came to shake my hand. He told me that the way I had explained how to deduct a Bentley in Chile would absolutely work. He also indicated he would never have thought of doing it that way.

Originally, nor had I. No longer did I tell people that while most business expenses are deductible, there are certain expenses that are never deductible. Instead of asking the question, "Is this expense deductible?", I began asking the question, "How do I make this expense deductible?" As I went about doing this and showing this example to other people, I soon discovered that not only could the Bentley, Porsche, Ferrari, or BMW (my favorite car) be deductible, but also, with proper planning, it is relatively simple to have the government pay for the entire cost of the car.

As they say, "The proof is in the pudding." My good friend and client, Brad Sumrok, a professional real estate investor and fellow financial educator, agreed to share his own personal example with us.

Brad came to me several years ago and told me that he had four financial goals in life. First, he wanted to earn $1,000,000. Second, he wanted to have $1,000,000 in his bank account. Third, he wanted to pay $1,000,000 in taxes. And fourth, actually I never got to the fourth because I stopped him immediately when he got to number three.

I clearly remember telling him, "Brad, are you crazy? Why would you want to pay $1,000,000 in taxes?" His response was that he always had figured that if he made a lot of money, he would have to pay a lot of tax. I immediately explained about government incentives and that he never needed to pay that much in taxes. As it was, by the time he got to me at the end of 2017, he had made enough money that his tax bill was going to be right around $935,000. We went through some strategies that were appropriate to him as a real estate investor and the following year he quite literally reduced his taxes to zero, completely legally and doing what the government wanted him to do, i.e., invest in housing for people to rent.

In 2021, Brad decided he wanted to purchase a Ferrari. He searched diligently and found the exact Ferrari he wanted. The cost of the Ferrari was $285,000. He put down $95,000 and financed the remaining $190,000. The loan payment is $3,500/month for five years. The transaction for the car looks like this (see Figure 10.1).

TYPICAL FERRARI ACQUISITION

INCOME
$95,000

EXPENSE
$3,500 x 12 = $42,000 payment

ASSET	LIABILITY
$ 95,000 Cash	
$ 285,000 Ferrari	$ 190,000 Car Loan

FIGURE 10.1

Most people would stop right there. They save up to pay for the down payment and then pay the loan each month out of new earnings. Brad took a different approach. He took the money he would have used had he purchased the car for cash ($285,000) and invested in an apartment building with some other investors (called a "syndication"). The property is called Rosemont. Due to the U.S. rules for bonus depreciation, his share of the first-year depreciation on the building was $260,700. Brad lives in Florida, so he doesn't pay any state taxes, only federal taxes. His federal tax rate for 2021 was 37%, resulting in a net tax savings the first year of $96,459. Because he uses his car solely for his business, he also receives an $18,000 first year deduction for the car, resulting in net tax savings of $6,660. This is a total of first-year tax benefits of $103,119. He used $95,000 of that tax reduction for the down payment on the car and pocketed the additional $8,119 (see Figure 10.2).

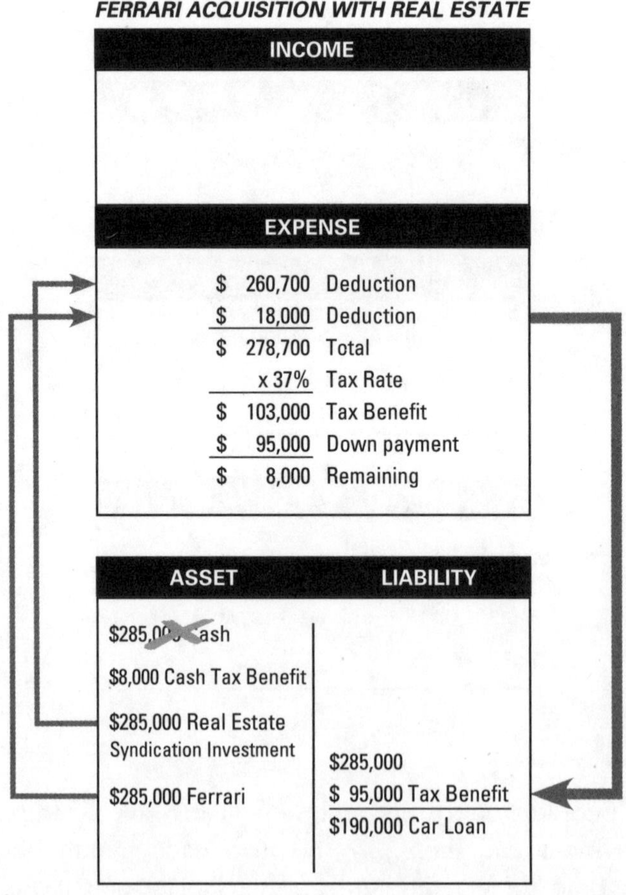

FERRARI ACQUISITION WITH REAL ESTATE
INCOME
EXPENSE
$ 260,700 Deduction
$ 18,000 Deduction
$ 278,700 Total
x 37% Tax Rate
$ 103,000 Tax Benefit
$ 95,000 Down payment
$ 8,000 Remaining
ASSET
LIABILITY
$285,000 Cash
$8,000 Cash Tax Benefit
$285,000 Real Estate Syndication Investment
$285,000 Ferrari
$285,000
$ 95,000 Tax Benefit
$190,000 Car Loan

FIGURE 10.2

Brad still has the $3,500/month of car loan to pay, or $42,000/year. The annual cash flow to Brad from his $285,000 investment is $53,580 (18.8%). After paying for the Ferrari loan, he still has $11,580 left over. His depreciation deduction from the real estate in the second year and beyond is about $22,000 and depreciation deduction from the Ferrari of about $9,000 each year. Taxable income from the deal is $22,580 ($53,580 – 22,000 – 9,000). Tax on the net income is $8,300 which is less than the net cash flow of $11,580 (see Figure 10.3).

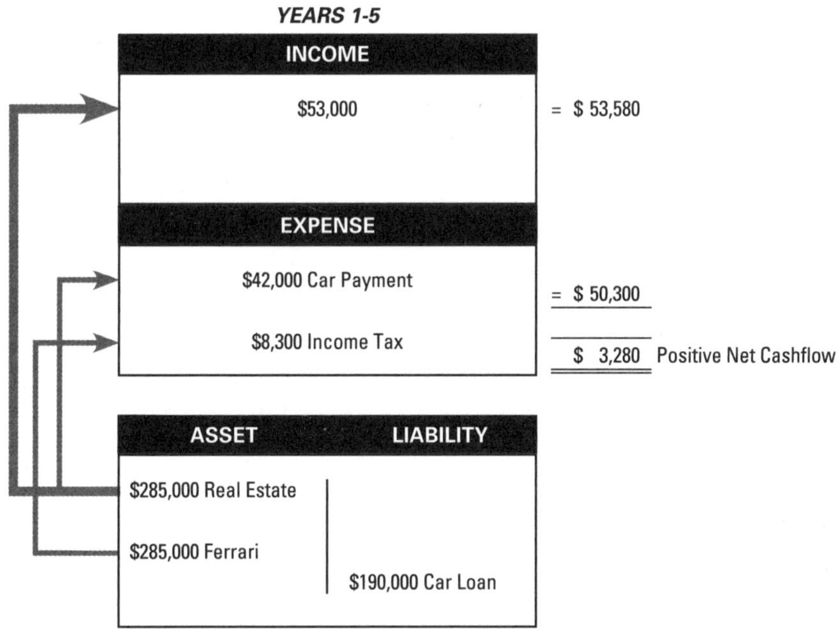

FIGURE 10.3

After five years, Brad owns the Ferrari outright (loan is paid off), and he still has $53,580 each year of cash flow from the real estate. In this case, the government made the down payment on the car, and the real estate paid off the car loan (see Figure 10.4).

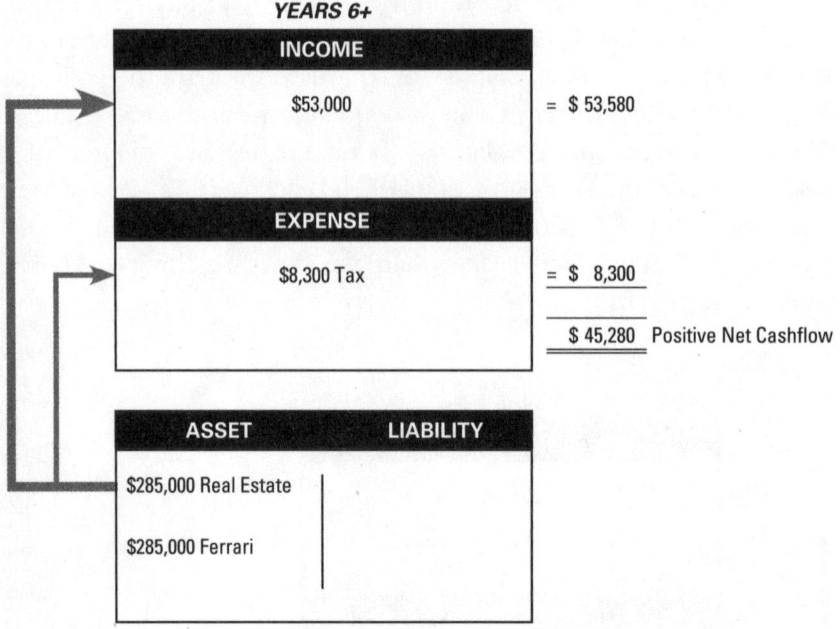

FIGURE 10.4

Note that the government gets what it wants while Brad is getting what he wants. The government wants safe, affordable housing, which Brad is providing. It also gets a good return on its investment. The tax benefits to Brad the first year are $113,119. This is the government's sole investment. The government receives $8,300 of tax from Brad. This is a return of 7.34 percent. While not as much as several returns noted in previous chapters, it's still better than the government's return on qualified retirement plans.

Remember that the government isn't actually funding cars, houses, or other luxuries. Rather, it's funding sound investments for which it reaps substantial rewards in the form of direct economic benefit and in benefits to society. Because something is profitable to you, the taxpayer, doesn't make it wrong, unethical, or illegal. If you want to reduce your taxes enough to afford a Ferrari, it's really a simple matter of investing in government priorities. Brad's example proves that doing what the government wants done creates way more income and far less taxes.

Endnotes

Preface

1. *The Wall Street Journal*, Markets, Amazon.com annual income
2. Tom Huddleston, Jr., "Amazon had to pay federal income taxes for the first time since 2016 – here's how much," CNBC.com, Feb 4, 2020
3. United States Securities and Exchange Commission, Tesla, Inc. 2020 Annual report, Form 10-K, p. 96, https://www.sec.gov/Archives/edgar/data/1318605/000156459021004599/tsla-10k_20201231.htm
4. Jim Tankersley and Emily Cochrane, "SALT Increase That Burned Blue States Is Targeted By Democrats," *The New York Times*, Dec 19, 2019

Introduction

1. Office of Economic Cooperation and Development (OECD), "Tax Incentives for Research and Development: Trends and Issues", 2002

Chapter 1, Partnering With the Government

1. Friends, The One With George Stephanopoulos, Episode 4, October 13, 1994, FICA Explained: The FICA or Federal Insurance Contributions Act is a US federal law that requires employers to withhold three different types of employment taxes from their employees' paychecks – Social Security tax, Medicare tax, Medicare surtax
2. James C. Davies, "Toward a Theory of Revolution," American Psychological Review, Vol 27, No. 1 Feb 1962, pp 5-19
3. Kristin Tax, "The sheer size of our government workforce is an alarming problem," The Hill April 14, 2019
4. Ilostat Explorer, Public Employment by Sectors
5. Ilostat Explorer, Public Employment by Sectors. https://www.ilo.org/shinyapps/bulkexplorer38/?lang=en&segment=indicator&id=PSE_TPSE_GOV_NB_A https://tradingeconomics.com/united-states/employed-persons
6. David S. Painter, *Journal of American History*, Volume 99, Issue 1, June 2012, pp. 24–39
7. Gregory Brew, "How Oil Defeated The Nazis," OilPrice.com, June 5, 2019

8. Jason Murdock, "Who Has Been Affected by the Huge SolarWinds Cyberattack so Far?," Newsweek December 18, 2020
9. Raphael Satter, "Up to 1,500 businesses affected by ransomware attack, U.S. firm's CEO says," Reuters July 6, 2021
10. Frantisek Markovic, "China's Huawei Faces New Allegations Over Cyber Security," *Forbes*, Jul 24, 2019
11. Natalie Obiko Pearson, "Huawei Rejected by Three in Four Canadians on Eve of 5G Decision," Bloomberg, Oct 11, 2021
12. Justine Brown, "5 federal agencies with a role in ensuring enterprise cybersecurity," Coidive Aug 17, 2016
13. Ianchovichina, Burger, and Arampatzi, "Developing but growing less happy: what explains this paradox in the Arab world?," World Bank Dec 18, 2015
14. The Editors of Encyclopedia Britannica *Arab Springs*, Britannica Jan 27, 2021
15. All Things Considered, "Andrew Yang Talks Universal Basic Income During the Coronavirus Crisis," NPR Mar 22, 2020
16. Matt Weidinger, "What's in Kamala Harris's pandemic UBI Plan?," American Enterprise Institute (AEI) Aug 26, 2020
17. Eric Morath, "Biden's Minimum-Wage Proposal: When Would It Reach $15 an Hour?," *The Wall Street Journal* Feb 9, 2021
18. U.S. Department of The Treasury, "Treasury and IRS announce Families of Nearly 60 Million Children Receive $15 Billion in Frist Payments of Expanded and Newly Advanceable Child Tax Credit," July 15, 2021
19. United Nations University, "Housing Privatization in Central and Eastern Europe: From Policy to Practice"
20. Rebecca Winthrop and Eileen McGivney, "Why wait 100 years? Bridging the gap on global education," Brookings, June 10, 2015
21. Rakesh Kochhar, "The middle class is large in many Western European countries, but it is losing ground in places," Pew Research Center Apr 17, 2017
22. David Madland and Nick Bunker, "Middle-class societies invest more in Public Education," Center for American Progress Action Fund, Nov 2011
23. PewTrusts, "How States are Improving Tax Incentives for Jobs & Growth," The Pew May 3, 2017
24. United Nations, "Design & Assessment of Tax Incentives in Developing Countries," p. 4, United Nations 2018
25. Gallup, "Taxes," 2021

Chapter 2, Investment #1: Business

1. Argentina - https://taxsummaries.pwc.com/argentina/corporate/deductions
   Australia - https://taxsummaries.pwc.com/australia/corporate/deductions
   Canada - https://taxsummaries.pwc.com/canada/corporate/deductions
   France - https://taxsummaries.pwc.com/france/corporate/deductions
   Germany - https://taxsummaries.pwc.com/germany/corporate/deductions
   India - https://taxsummaries.pwc.com/india/corporate/deductions
   Italy - https://taxsummaries.pwc.com/italy/corporate/deductions
   Japan - https://taxsummaries.pwc.com/japan/corporate/deductions
   Mexico - https://taxsummaries.pwc.com/mexico/corporate/deductions
   Singapore - https://taxsummaries.pwc.com/singapore/corporate/deductions
   South Korea - https://taxsummaries.pwc.com/republic-of-korea/corporate/deductions
   Spain - https://taxsummaries.pwc.com/spain/corporate/deductions
   Taiwan - https://taxsummaries.pwc.com/taiwan/corporate/deductions
   United Kingdom - https://taxsummaries.pwc.com/united-kingdom/corporate/deductions
   United States - https://taxsummaries.pwc.com/united-states/corporate/deductions
2. Argentina - https://santandertrade.com/en/portal/establish-overseas/argentina/tax-system
   Australia - https://business.gov.au/finance/taxation/tax-deductions
   Canada - https://www.canada.ca/en/revenue-agency/services/tax/businesses/small-businesses-self-employed-income/business-income-tax-reporting/business-expenses.html
   France - https://www.frenchbusinessadvice.com/Deductible-Expenses-Of-Benefits-Of-Companies-In-France
   Germany - Spanien_form_210_erlaeuterungen.pdf
   India - https://taxsummaries.pwc.com/japan/corporate/deductions
   Italy - https://www.agenziaentrate.gov.it/portale/documents/180690/1186737/Regolemento+282_2011.en_Regolemento+282_2011.en.pdf/cd1ede25-1e81-445c-9575-f9beabe1094e?version=1.0
   Japan - https://taxsummaries.pwc.com/japan/corporate/deductions
   Mexico - https://www.foley.com/-/media/files/insights/publications/2017/08/general-comments-on-deduction-of-expenses-by-mexic/files/general-comments-on-deduction-of-expenses-by-mexic/fileattachment/002802general-comments-on-deduction-of-expenses-by.pdf
   Singapore - https://www.iras.gov.sg/irashome/Businesses/Self-Employed/Learning-the-basics/Keeping-Proper-Records-and-Accounts/

South Korea - https://taxsummaries.pwc.com/republic-of-korea/corporate/deductions

Spain - https://www.limitconsulting.com/2014/11/what-expenses-can-you-offset-against-tax-in-spain/

Taiwan - Regulations Governing Application of Agreements for the Avoidance of Double Taxation with Respect to Taxes on Income Ministry of Finance 2010.01.07

United Kingdom - https://www.gov.uk/expenses-if-youre-self-employed/how-to-claim

United States - https://www.irs.gov/businesses/small-businesses-self-employed/what-kind-of-records-should-i-keep

3. Argentina - https://taxsummaries.pwc.com/argentina/corporate/deductions

Australia - https://taxsummaries.pwc.com/australia/corporate/deductions

Canada - https://www.canada.ca/en/revenue-agency/services/tax/technical-information/income-tax/income-tax-folios-index/series-3-property-investments-savings-plans/series-3-property-investments-savings-plan-folio-6-interest/income-tax-folio-s3-f6-c1-interest-deductibility.html#toc6

France - https://www.jonesday.com/en/insights/2012/02/new-limitation-of-interest-deductibility-by-french-corporate-taxpayers#:~:text=209%20IX%20of%20the%20French,capitalization%20rules%20introduced%20in%202007

Germany - https://www.dlapiper.com/en/us/insights/publications/2014/04/german-interest-deduction-limitation-rules/#:~:text=The%20deductibility%20of%20interest%20expenses,amortization)%20under%20German%20tax%20laws.&text=That%20principle%20must%20be%20implemented%20consistently%20in%20German%20tax%20law

India - https://taxsummaries.pwc.com/india/corporate/deductions#:~:text=Interest%20expenses,tax%2Ddeductible%20without%20any%20limit

Italy - https://taxsummaries.pwc.com/italy/corporate/deductions#:~:text=Generally%2C%20interest%20expense%20is%20fully,reported%20in%20the%20financial%20statements)

Japan - https://taxsummaries.pwc.com/japan/corporate/deductions#:~:text=Interest%20expenses%20on%20borrowing%20are,some%20extent%20in%20certain%20cases

Mexico - https://www.foley.com/-/media/files/insights/publications/2017/08/general-comments-on-deduction-of-expenses-by-mexic/files/general-comments-on-deduction-of-expenses-by-mexic/

fileattachment/002802general-comments-on-deduction-of-expenses-by.pdf

Singapore - https://home.kpmg/content/dam/kpmg/sg/pdf/2017/02/taxalert-201714.pdf

South Korea - https://taxsummaries.pwc.com/republic-of-korea/corporate/deductions

Spain - https://www.accountinginspain.com/deduction-of-financial-expenses-in-spain-in-2015/

Taiwan - https://taxsummaries.pwc.com/taiwan/corporate/deductions#:~:text=Interest%20expenses,not%20exceed%2015.6%25%20per%20annum

United Kingdom - https://www.gov.uk/government/publications/corporation-tax-tax-deductibility-of-corporate-interest-expense/corporation-tax-tax-deductibility-of-corporate-interest-expense#:~:text=From%201%20April%202017%2C%20the,replaced%20with%20the%20new%20rules

United States - https://taxsummaries.pwc.com/united-states/corporate/deductions

4. Argentina - https://www2.deloitte.com/content/dam/Deloitte/ar/Documents/tax/dttl-tax-argentinahighlights-2019.pdf

Australia - https://www2.deloitte.com/content/dam/Deloitte/us/Documents/Tax/us-tax-ice-country-highlights-australia.pdf

Canada - https://www.canada.ca/en/revenue-agency/services/tax/technical-information/income-tax/income-tax-folios-index/series-3-property-investments-savings-plans/series-3-property-investments-savings-plan-folio-6-interest/income-tax-folio-s3-f6-c1-interest-deductibility.html

France - https://www2.deloitte.com/content/dam/Deloitte/us/Documents/Tax/us-tax-ice-country-highlights-france.pdf

Germany - https://www2.deloitte.com/content/dam/Deloitte/us/Documents/Tax/us-tax-ice-country-highlights-germany.pdf

India - https://www.incometaxindia.gov.in/tutorials/tax%20treatment%20of%20dividend%20received.pdf

Italy - https://www2.deloitte.com/content/dam/Deloitte/us/Documents/Tax/us-tax-ice-country-highlights-italy.pdf

Japan - https://www2.deloitte.com/content/dam/Deloitte/global/Documents/Tax/dttl-tax-japanhighlights-2020.pdf?nc=1#:~:text=Taxation%20of%20dividends%20%E2%80%93%20Dividends%20received,corporation%20for%20a%20certain%20period

Mexico - https://www2.deloitte.com/content/dam/Deloitte/us/Documents/Tax/us-tax-ice-country-highlights-mexico.pdf

Singapore - https://www.iras.gov.sg/irashome/Individuals/Locals/Working-Out-Your-Taxes/What-is-Taxable-What-is-Not/Dividends/

South Korea - https://assets.kpmg/content/dam/kpmg/xx/pdf/2018/08/south-korea-2018.pdf

Spain - https://taxsummaries.pwc.com/spain/corporate/income-determination#:~:text=The%20Spanish%20company%20has%20at,for%20at%20least%20one%20year.&text=The%20tax%20exemption%20does%20not,expense%20in%20the%20paying%20company

Taiwan - https://www.grantthornton.tw/globalassets/1.-member-firms/taiwan/media/tw_images/publication-pdf/taiwan-tax/2019/corporate-tax-guide-taiwan-2019.pdf

United Kingdom - https://www2.deloitte.com/content/dam/Deloitte/us/Documents/Tax/us-tax-ice-country-highlights-united-kingdom.pdf

United States - https://home.treasury.gov/news/press-releases/kd3761

5. Argentina - https://www.dlapiperintelligence.com/goingglobal/corporate/?t=&c=AR&mc=PR

   Australia - https://efprgroup.com/wp-content/uploads/2019/04/EFPR-eBook_Business-Tax-Guide-AUS_18EFP005_3.19.pdf

   Canada - https://www.mondaq.com/canada/tax-authorities/753682/limited-liability-corporation#:~:text=A%20Limited%20Liability%20Corporation%20(LLC)%20is%20a%20hybrid%20structure%20with,through%20treatment%20for%20tax%20purposes

   France - https://www.bloomberglaw.com/product/tax/document/XPV1U618?bc=W1siU2VhcmNoIFJlc3VsdHMiLCIvcHJvZHVjdC90YXgvc2VhcmNoL3Jlc3VsdHMvMjdlYTUzMzkwZTAxMjBmZDhkMmMxODBiMjFmZjViOTEiXV0--4d92a1cfe4347a66064493844f371d91b348f876&guid=15126eb2-e124-47c5-ae3b-56060c2f50a0&search32=V2Su-1D2TSdAHOPd_MJsWw%3D%3DFWPK7aId_1Nv_aoH7LxilgYyoGai3ccuxq3Or1jlIZgES8vFnL92tuEL8M7NPPTi-ao9MwgM6R7zWsGJVOPOePZEXT1rKMT1StEhSdxCxYDgwIughMcTmI3QRbg26w6h4E-sp3mdRPERrl3vgDdc49pyZK9Owpa432GAcdjSlcWkJ2lRE-8KnD02wcFtKDRj2P658D9BFRGwLqIW4NJNSSYNnJOOV_a1HCqMymXYQuNx099MmFSC4BpEa9z5tdMedo6Zz6yfk9UqFM9KrhMNbER87pYzukPYFF9AVCfJgrpTy0b-eppF6c43fz4r8SfE0LQA2mj2wAlX-rnn1UGR9LY510nif4xgHIPNaSCZC4pQFyX2JBPrVe60A8Lr3-fF0hqEUtLGkBHtAxRn1Q5Q1WWoiJ_Z2pdNNFiy6X3uJuwOPJJJBGSMZAmyAGQV0L4J

Germany - https://www.bloomberglaw.com/product/tax/document/XPV21M18?bc=W1siU2VhcmNoIFJlc3VsdHMiLCIvcHJvZHVjdC90YXgvc2VhcmNoL3Jlc3VsdHMvMmM2MmE0NmJjMjNiMTg1M2VlZTdmZWY4ZjljZGRlOTUiXV0--376da2a6d0669c910fc2f06475ffb50f208ff092&guid=0026de25-58e8-4366-b930-6f3834721a40&search32=4UDAU_1vwV9kSc9V4r17Lw%3D%3DITn6SMi9DoYZI72tcxG70WD8tDTQVRjJM_pmL34knxGqYMVbsIrKmajkVL2TGzi0j-afMRwaGswd3vVcriSr74koDu4f6OpEe-83WEpAnMxxmq_TULag8dDZFTvDh5wp7uvXEACCuAss3HihR7u9l0_L4lfg8RtgOKCtHwNio3SyEeS6vNK52MWMMGU2NrV7Z8BcpkKfdt3ZjwizvNsMd9o_lHqh2n9YcQJTYa3czPZzX5NTtj-feOejnrqID9MyHyv_NKFGBKdlocjfI8xwjxBlQnmi2Xj2qPjwtDfaTVH5SvkmRjwUT9Ld3itJvirauNZVOqVnoYOJMG4z6l2LqZUZoIPjPyRvFaAO0cB7tY27hy79Q-3O758WseP6GARJ7_QiZt8K_slXAdvkGE216xLLS7C3xozsHelHHmwPmLFO62yia2DxhAp-64YIhTsq

India - https://ssrana.in/corporate-laws/company-laws-india/company-law-india/#:~:text=Types%20of%20legal%20entities%20in,Limited%20Liability%20Partnership%20(LLP)

Italy - https://www.bloomberglaw.com/product/tax/document/XPV1IN18?bc=W1siU2VhcmNoIFJlc3VsdHMiLCIvcHJvZHVjdC90YXgvc2VhcmNoL3Jlc3VsdHMvZDlhOWIyNDJmYTNlMjQxYzAxOWI2ZDY1NTMxNjBiYTAiXV0--cc97b512063785a60bf1826705f113a5ca9c3dae&guid=ee7427ea-230b-4280-a462-7c982c6d1055&search32=JXLMHaEpaQoLeZ26s9LuEQ%3D%3D0GYr2sVYsPCI58cAOWSc9zZjPJwG_Pe_YwH3ci2lC2i7HClaoaqTubBCOhCWOosc8R9MCCA_MoOkngUPGmiKYxDaXgkv2i3DEHJwsGZcZgIrsP5PDNfBgZ7pZFuJABJmPNqlGjzog2Z_PB-USXeJLRrISsUaUftx9EqinmZnQwyDabLE_z596K18H_kd--9FazP4rgckYx67TxDwFy1dxkFjQZWOjrnxtRZodio-YgwpXoAdAJgiSPCBqTPUflesM9y1yNmQ9AHUU_35gRDnM3heRTSgyDX-9z-xirvEQmvSbbGlS8_5wWJPtzuUS6_64DHPM1VJsl2x3V4vhJ9tP410gAinC523mIHgIVDd6Du7OC2bS2uEc7WXQHfq69c-wxgBk2kR7z77MXcaTE2VI7e1hWfUUV-iuyZHigoGUz8ygqShYbAgZMWl3JgCaQea

Japan - https://uk.practicallaw.thomsonreuters.com/Cosi/SignOn?redirectTo=%2f8-549-4101%3ftransitionType%3dDefault%26contextData%3d(sc.Default)%26firstPage%3dtrue

Mexico - https://www.procopio.com/uploads/model/Block/4520/pdf/78/forms-of-doing-business-in-mexico-compared-to-the-u-s--836.pdf

Singapore - https://www.rikvin.com/incorporation/types-of-business-entities-in-singapore/
South Korea - https://thelawreviews.co.uk/title/the-inward-investment-and-international-taxation-review/south-korea
Spain - https://www.angloinfo.com/how-to/spain/working/starting-a-business/business-structures
Taiwan - https://medium.com/@yuwanju/taiwans-limited-partnership-act-still-has-room-for-improvement-53b0bc1a63e7
United Kingdom - https://www.offshore-protection.com/uk-llp-company-formation
United States - https://www.taxpolicycenter.org/briefing-book/what-are-pass-through-businesses

6. Argentina - https://tradingeconomics.com/argentina/corporate-tax-rate
Australia - https://tradingeconomics.com/australia/corporate-tax-rate
Canada - https://tradingeconomics.com/canada/corporate-tax-rate
France - https://tradingeconomics.com/france/corporate-tax-rate
Germany - https://tradingeconomics.com/germany/corporate-tax-rate
India - https://tradingeconomics.com/india/corporate-tax-rate
Italy - https://tradingeconomics.com/italy/corporate-tax-rate
Japan - https://tradingeconomics.com/japan/corporate-tax-rate
Mexico - https://tradingeconomics.com/mexico/corporate-tax-rate
Singapore - https://tradingeconomics.com/singapore/corporate-tax-rate
South Korea - https://tradingeconomics.com/south-korea/corporate-tax-rate
Spain - https://tradingeconomics.com/spain/corporate-tax-rate
Taiwan - https://tradingeconomics.com/taiwan/corporate-tax-rate
United Kingdom - https://tradingeconomics.com/united-kingdom/corporate-tax-rate
United States - https://tradingeconomics.com/united-states/corporate-tax-rate

7. Argentina - https://tradingeconomics.com/argentina/personal-income-tax-rate
Australia - https://tradingeconomics.com/australia/personal-income-tax-rate
Canada - https://tradingeconomics.com/canada/personal-income-tax-rate
France - https://tradingeconomics.com/france/personal-income-tax-rate
Germany - https://tradingeconomics.com/germany/personal-income-tax-rate
India - https://tradingeconomics.com/india/personal-income-tax-rate

Italy - https://tradingeconomics.com/italy/personal-income-tax-rate
Japan - https://tradingeconomics.com/japan/personal-income-tax-rate
Mexico - https://tradingeconomics.com/mexico/personal-income-tax-rate
Singapore - https://tradingeconomics.com/singapore/personal-income-tax-rate
South Korea - https://tradingeconomics.com/south-korea/personal-income-tax-rate
Spain - https://tradingeconomics.com/spain/personal-income-tax-rate
Taiwan - https://tradingeconomics.com/taiwan/personal-income-tax-rate
United Kingdom - https://tradingeconomics.com/united-kingdom/personal-income-tax-rate
United States - https://tradingeconomics.com/united-states/personal-income-tax-rate

8. 26 U.S. Code § 1202 – Partial exclusion for gain from certain small business stock, Cornell Law School
9. Australia - https://www.ato.gov.au/business/income-and-deductions-for-business/in-detail/small-business-income-tax-offset/
   Canada - https://www.canada.ca/en/revenue-agency/programs/about-canada-revenue-agency-cra/federal-government-budgets/budget-2018-equality-growth-strong-middle-class/passive-investment-income/small-business-deduction-rules.html
   India - https://taxsummaries.pwc.com/india/corporate/deductions
   South Korea - https://taxsummaries.pwc.com/republic-of-korea/corporate/tax-credits-and-incentives
   Taiwan - https://taxsummaries.pwc.com/taiwan/corporate/taxes-on-corporate-income
   United States - https://www.irs.gov/newsroom/qualified-business-income-deduction
10. In addition to exclusions related to the gain from the sale of small business stocks, some countries allow for tax-free reorganizations.

Are Corporate Reorganizations Tax Free?

	Yes	No	Notes
Argentina	✓		Tax-free reorganizations may be structured under an Argentine law that allows tax attributes, such as loss carry forwards, to be conveyed from the predecessor to the surviving company. The results that may arise as a result of the reorganization, meeting all legal requirements, will not be subject to income tax.

Are Corporate Reorganizations Tax Free?			
	Yes	No	Notes
Australia	✓		No taxes are directly payable on a share acquisition, but a buyer may have an obligation to remit to the ATO 12.5% of the purchase price. Corporate tax can apply to a net capital gain on the sale of shares. Where the share disposal results in a company leaving an Australian income tax consolidated group, the cost base for the shares sold is effectively reconstructed with reference to the underlying tax cost base of the assets of the leaving company. Otherwise, the cost base is generally the historical cost of the shares adjusted for related acquisition and sale costs.
Canada	✓		Certain types of corporate acquisitions, divisions, and other restructurings which are generally not taxable at the corporate or stockholder level. The transaction must meet strict statutory and non-statutory requirements.
France	✓		If certain conditions are met and certain commitments are taken by the absorbing corporation, the absorbing corporation will not report any gain or loss upon the receipt of assets from the absorbed corporation and the absorbing corporation's basis in the assets acquired from the absorbed corporation will be the same basis as in the absorbed corporation's hands.
Germany	✓		If shareholders receive shares and not assets, not capital gains will be realized upon the transaction.
India	✓		Through amalgamations, corporate reorganizations can become tax neutral.
Italy		✓	The gain arising from the subsequent sale of the shares received in exchange by the contributing company may benefit of the 95% exemption provided for by the participation exemption regime.
Japan	✓		Qualified reorganizations under the law can create tax-free reorganizations for both the corporate and the shareholders.
Mexico	✓		To the extent certain requirements are met, Mexican tax provisions state it will be deemed that no disposal of assets or goods takes place where a legal merger occurs. Therefore, no corporate ISR, VAT, or tax on acquisition will be triggered.
Singapore		✓	Stamp duty is required, however if certain conditions are met, there is stamp duty relief for share transfers.

Are Corporate Reorganizations Tax Free?			
	Yes	No	Notes
South Korea	✓		If a South Korean company becomes a wholly owned subsidiary of another company through a comprehensive share exchange or transfer satisfying certain statutory requirements, payment of corporation tax on capital gains resulting from this exchange or transfer may be deferred until the disposal of such shares.
Spain	✓		Under the special tax neutrality regime, share transfer capital gains or losses are not included in taxable income.
Taiwan	✓		Provided that the requirements set out in the Business Mergers and Acquisitions Act are met, a transfer of securities will be exempt from securities transaction tax.
United Kingdom	✓		The reconstruction of a group or a merger may sometimes involve the transfer of a business or businesses from one or more companies to another company or companies in consideration of the issue of stock by the acquiring company to the shareholders of the company transferring the business. In these circumstances the company transferring the assets as part of the transfer of the business will not suffer a tax charge but rather the acquiring company takes over the tax position of the company transferring the business.
United States	✓		Section 368 Tax-free Reorganization.

Argentina - https://uk.practicallaw.thomsonreuters.com/9-519-0298?transitionType=Default&contextData=(sc.Default)

Australia - https://content.next.westlaw.com/5-519-5448?__lrTS=20210311093019485&transitionType=Default&contextData=(sc.Default)&firstPage=true#co_anchor_a800743

Canada - https://www.canada.ca/en/revenue-agency/services/forms-publications/publications/t4037/capital-gains.html#Whatisthe

France - https://uk.practicallaw.thomsonreuters.com/2-502-1280?transitionType=Default&contextData=(sc.Default)

Germany - https://www.lw.com/upload/pubcontent/_pdf/pub1204_1.pdf

India - https://uk.practicallaw.thomsonreuters.com/7-598-4529?transitionType=Default&contextData=(sc.Default)#co_anchor_a457344

Italy - https://uk.practicallaw.thomsonreuters.com/0-503-4014?transitionType=Default&contextData=(sc.Default)

Japan - https://uk.practicallaw.thomsonreuters.com/4-502-1868?transitionType=Default&contextData=(sc.Default)
Mexico - https://uk.practicallaw.thomsonreuters.com/7-381-3182?transitionType=Default&contextData=%28sc.Default%29#co_anchor_a995391
Singapore - https://uk.practicallaw.thomsonreuters.com/7-502-1598?transitionType=Default&contextData=(sc.Default)&firstPage=true#co_anchor_a738723
South Korea - https://uk.practicallaw.thomsonreuters.com/4-505-7541?transitionType=Default&contextData=(sc.Default)
Spain - https://home.kpmg/xx/en/home/insights/2021/04/spain-taxation-of-cross-border-mergers-and-acquisitions.html
Taiwan - https://uk.practicallaw.thomsonreuters.com/w-011-9291?transitionType=Default&contextData=(sc.Default)
United Kingdom - https://www.lw.com/upload/pubcontent/_pdf/pub1204_1.pdf
United States - https://www.law.cornell.edu/uscode/text/26/368

11. Argentina - https://uk.practicallaw.thomsonreuters.com/9-519-0298?transitionType=Default&contextData=(sc.Default)
Australia - https://content.next.westlaw.com/5-519-5448?__lrTS=20210311093019485&transitionType=Default&contextData=(sc.Default)&firstPage=true#co_anchor_a800743
Canada - https://www.canada.ca/en/revenue-agency/services/forms-publications/publications/t4037/capital-gains.html#Whatisthe
France - https://uk.practicallaw.thomsonreuters.com/2-502-1280?transitionType=Default&contextData=(sc.Default)
Germany - https://www.lw.com/upload/pubcontent/_pdf/pub1204_1.pdf
India - https://uk.practicallaw.thomsonreuters.com/7-598-4529?transitionType=Default&contextData=(sc.Default)#co_anchor_a457344
Italy - https://uk.practicallaw.thomsonreuters.com/0-503-4014?transitionType=Default&contextData=(sc.Default)
Japan - https://uk.practicallaw.thomsonreuters.com/4-502-1868?transitionType=Default&contextData=(sc.Default)
Mexico - https://uk.practicallaw.thomsonreuters.com/7-381-3182?transitionType=Default&contextData=%28sc.Default%29#co_anchor_a995391
Singapore - https://uk.practicallaw.thomsonreuters.com/7-502-1598?transitionType=Default&contextData=(sc.Default)&firstPage=true#co_anchor_a738723

South Korea - https://uk.practicallaw.thomsonreuters.com/4-505-7541?transitionType=Default&contextData=(sc.Default)

Spain - https://www.taxathand.com/article/16069/Spain/2020/2021-budget-law-includes-measures-affecting-companies-individuals-and-nonresidents

Taiwan - https://uk.practicallaw.thomsonreuters.com/w-011-9291?transitionType=Default&contextData=(sc.Default)

United Kingdom - https://www.lw.com/upload/pubcontent/_pdf/pub1204_1.pdf

United States - https://www.law.cornell.edu/uscode/text/26/1202

12. Argentina - https://www.bloomberglaw.com/product/tax/document/XPV1GKH8#A0Q9H2P4A5A0Q9H2P4A5

Australia - https://www.ato.gov.au/business/gst/accounting-for-gst-in-your-business/choosing-an-accounting-method/

Canada - https://www.canada.ca/en/revenue-agency/services/tax/businesses/small-businesses-self-employed-income/business-income-tax-reporting/accounting-your-earnings.html

France - https://www.bloomberglaw.com/product/tax/document/XPV1V518#section(2)(2)(c)_0

Germany - https://www.bloomberglaw.com/product/tax/document/XPV21MH8?bc=W1siU2VhcmNoIFJlc3VsdHMiLCIvcHJvZHVjdC90YXgvc2VhcmNoL3Jlc3VsdHMvOGViNGYyMjA3NmNiMTIwOTE3YThjNGEyZGQ4ZGUzYzAiXV0--7249df39792106eeb22515e7122c9075cdcbbde1&guid=982ac7ea-6e93-45aa-b2d0-dc51af0f96f9&search32=T1dam4wrc16PBQ-BaTecdw%3D%3DPwNzcQYiCvwPnznEnANqq8gQb8Uc8sv_l4IAfyHztVh6qCpCk_z3B1gonBN5OetD3nAJskRp3lUrixdP5StA9skOUcWFRq0gRXbnH9cI9vSD4NWCutByzQBvElZ0DdxqaQ48_kr9Kc2z_Y-0LR_ADge1miE78ZZbwpk0og-pUj1YB2XYOEBZaZqnNoncjUEoYqZ8vRmceRJlIKx5whdD2849VE__NIxcLSnQOEKI9CcxETewrTlRPrPVQHP1fj2BsQZldPbxfHi85dlc-JoMmqIcKAqfVTxj49eq-jyDuM2r3Ffhp06TgkRY3MWYUUPjLyeu97lU7e0o3cQ5h87oPkdrtj0vEFVc1MK2S-6YPZuv020j3uMq99ZrsOx2VG11fanvDShvxoW1nM9BP7m-DedyLqrPuFSy1uHcZEzl-y7nFVVoaq0YR36I1jpMqboo6QJA7Mt2gQ9f9Rp5JU7JzjEbHfxxbSkuSSbrodL7g8PmGvqT13jMWdjZsGeR3CWSZpf6xN97OvQrW1w92Xj5LwDHkx_hhBHHzHE2zR65XNoKMVKpMqlbLPe6eWkLFrEoPKk52LZ5D0Krt4kwRo_fkgjNLIrGqtawuU6KHqJ60b1xfCubmlhzy-FcV-Z2alGS

India - https://www.bloomberglaw.com/product/tax/document/XPV1TEH8#section(4)(4)(c)(4)(c)(8)

Italy - https://www.bloomberglaw.com/product/tax/document/XPV1IEH8?bc=W1siU2VhcmNoIFJlc3VsdHMiLCIvcHJvZHVjdC90YXgvc2VhcmNoL3Jlc3VsdHMvYmQ2OTBiNDE0MWZjMWFkOTU5YzgxM2U0ZmIzMjZiMTkiXV0--e6e5030c8a63dcd4b81facedc4d25c1f9778c542&guid=5186adaa-dd6f-4412-8e1b-7fa9eb377302&search32=zY1a44S6PY_SnQ498Sf_2A%3D%3DzNdjkQnr1MxBUhjJuV_OfeqZScWu0cgpT6xDw5RL5gyev4dytLcmt-0ovEeE9JdjWyvJGmdVQCCvmhPhFzZH7yQOwXed_x3eioqvkp5XkY4d3dO7bR7RDjL_zFfq8ICLJCMK7WzLGDEsW4DCLVtz668H1C5sceTEdIRYvZI52efZsn_FHjSqjBafyA_ljNbdzon0HAYtD50jNMhjwcJF5_4chS9SpyNnprmL8rUroUVDkXXE6JUZJ8laYwdV-yaHWe2EMamtLHO1FVtipEaFQRb5JxahMZMuRSS-azWwd5X7VC0TG5Wn36PfgqZB7uRKcx8L_j4ZrX8M3zxFeVvI8iLVSr0Cvdm7gDwgY_Tvxio5KrrL-0yVJcrY1_rnQgJlq1AocKaEjXvImkmUIWSckaBlGkBxUQzkrI1r4_AmUEDke98vR2tjb9qsWbBQ_BwJGCd16enwr2hvUHLFh8Y6nKt2yKF8vgwmrFz1mrLBpRwqLzp_aQKULU2EFHayU5TuZBkv-gak7-QQoEe7_yskY_Ab3VzjIj-KWyZaQ48pQ5z8xUIImSeIn37DydmA-QbKm9qqshx3MYn_Gog0QyWPVKnioir0G7QAH4e_VuO_HNn9VeS9xThQmc3CII-mHcXv

Japan - https://www.bloomberglaw.com/product/tax/document/XPV2DQ18#section(2)

Mexico - https://taxsummaries.pwc.com/mexico/corporate/income-determination#:~:text=Income%20is%20generally%20recognised%20on,reported%20on%20a%20cash%20basis.

Singapore - https://www.iras.gov.sg/irashome/Schemes/GST/Cash-Accounting-Scheme/

South Korea - https://santandertrade.com/en/portal/establish-overseas/south-korea/tax-system

Spain - https://www.bloomberglaw.com/product/tax/document/27886501416

Taiwan - https://gcis.nat.gov.tw/elaw/English/lawEnDtlAction.do?method=viewLaw&pk=168

United Kingdom - https://www.gov.uk/simpler-income-tax-cash-basis/who-can-use-cash-basis

United States - https://www.law.cornell.edu/uscode/text/26/448

13. Argentina - https://www.bloomberglaw.com/product/tax/document/XPV1GKH8#section(2)(2)(c)_0

Claiming Revenue When Received			
	Yes	No	Notes
Argentina		✓	Taxpayers engaged in building activities are able to use the cash method but must compute gross income from long-term construction projects. The percentage of total gross income expected to be earned on completion of the building (i.e., the expected gross profit percentage) may be applied to the amount received during the taxable year for purposes of computing the gross income for that taxable year. The percentage must be approved by the tax authorities.
Australia	✓		Using cash method.
Canada	✓		Using cash method.
France	✓		Long-term contracts can be recognized over time or at completion.
Germany	✓		Revenues may only be recognized if they are realized at the balance sheet date. Based on the realization principle.
India	✓		If an ongoing service is identified as part of the agreement, the period over which revenue shall be recognized for that service is generally determined by the terms of the agreement with the customer. If the agreement does not specify a period, the revenue shall be recognized over a period no longer than the useful life of the transferred asset used to provide the ongoing service.
Italy	✓		Using revenue recognition standard Financial Accounting Standards Board (FASB).
Japan	✓		Using revenue recognition standard from the Accounting Standards Board of Japan (ASBJ).
Mexico	✓		Follows International Financial Reporting Standards (IFRS) guidance for revenue recognition.
Singapore	✓		Using cash accounting scheme for small businesses.
South Korea	✓		Follows International Financial Reporting Standards (IFRS) guidance for revenue recognition.
Spain	✓		If payment term is longer than one year.
Taiwan	✓		Follows International Financial Reporting Standards (IFRS) guidance for revenue recognition.
United Kingdom	✓		Using cash accounting scheme for small businesses.
United States	✓		Can use cash accounting for small business.

Australia - https://www.ato.gov.au/business/gst/accounting-for-gst-in-your-business/choosing-an-accounting-method/

Canada - https://www.canada.ca/en/revenue-agency/services/tax/businesses/small-businesses-self-employed-income/business-income-tax-reporting/accounting-your-earnings.html#kp_sls_xpns

France - https://assets.kpmg/content/dam/kpmg/fr/pdf/2019/09/fr-global-assurance-ifrs-compared-french-gaap-overview_sept19.pdf

Germany - https://accounting-app.pwcplus.de/article/215204/?download=215480&file=similarities_and_differences_ifrs_german_gaap.pdf

India - https://www.mca.gov.in/Ministry/pdf/Ind_AS18.pdf

Italy - https://www.protiviti.com/IT-it/insights/bulletin-vol-5-issue-12

Japan - https://www.ark-outsourcing.com/news/detail_51.html

Mexico - https://www.ifrs.org/issued-standards/list-of-standards/ifrs-15-revenue-from-contracts-with-customers/

Singapore - https://www.iras.gov.sg/irashome/Schemes/GST/Cash-Accounting-Scheme/

South Korea - https://www.iasplus.com/en/jurisdictions/asia/korea

Spain - https://www.bloomberglaw.com/product/tax/document/27886501416

Taiwan - https://www.sfb.gov.tw/en/home.jsp?id=236&parentpath=0,4#:~:text=The%20R.O.C.%20(Taiwan)%20has%20fully%20adopted%20IFRSs%20since%202015.

United Kingdom - https://www.gov.uk/simpler-income-tax-cash-basis/who-can-use-cash-basis

United States - https://www.irs.gov/publications/p538

14. Revenue procedure 97-27 https://www.irs.gov/pub/irs-tege/rp97_27.pdf
15. Argentina - https://taxsummaries.pwc.com/argentina/corporate/deductions

    Australia - https://taxsummaries.pwc.com/australia/corporate/deductions

    Canada - https://taxsummaries.pwc.com/canada/corporate/deductions

    France - https://taxsummaries.pwc.com/france/corporate/deductions

    Germany - https://taxsummaries.pwc.com/germany/corporate/deductions

    India - https://taxsummaries.pwc.com/india/corporate/deductions

    Italy - https://taxsummaries.pwc.com/italy/corporate/deductions

    Japan - https://taxsummaries.pwc.com/japan/corporate/deductions

    Mexico - https://taxsummaries.pwc.com/mexico/corporate/deductions

    Singapore - https://taxsummaries.pwc.com/singapore/corporate/deductions

    South Korea - https://taxsummaries.pwc.com/republic-of-korea/corporate/deductions#:~:text=Generally%2C%20loss%20carrybacks%20are%20not,an%20NOL%20for%20one%20year.

Spain - https://taxsummaries.pwc.com/spain/corporate/deductions
Taiwan - https://taxsummaries.pwc.com/taiwan/corporate/deductions
United Kingdom - https://taxsummaries.pwc.com/united-kingdom/corporate/income-determination
United States - https://taxsummaries.pwc.com/united-states/corporate/deductions

16. Aaron Holmes, "From Amazon to GM, here are all the major tech and transportation companies who avoided federal income tax expenses last year," Business Insider, Nov 24, 2019
17. Francine McKenna, "Even with its losses, Tesla won't take a big hit from lower tax rate," MarketWatch, Dec 15, 2017
18. Argentina - https://taxsummaries.pwc.com.argentina/corporate/tax-credits-and-incentives

Australia - https://taxsummaries.pwc.com/australia/corporate/tax-credits-and-incentives
Canada - https://taxsummaries.pwc.com/canada/corporate/tax-credits-and-incentives
France - https://www.impots.gouv.fr/portail/internationalenbusiness/tax-incentives#NB
France - https://www.french-property.com/guides/france/working-in-france/starting-a-business/financial-assistance/bank-finance
Germany - https://taxsummaries.pwc.com/germany/corporate/tax-credits-and-incentives
Germany - https://www.gtai.de/gtai-en/invest/investment-guide/incentive-programs/grants-for-hiring-personnel-65422
India - https://taxsummaries.pwc.com/india/corporate/tax-credits-and-incentives
Italy - https://taxsummaries.pwc.com/italy/corporate/tax-credits-and-incentives
Japan - https://taxsummaries.pwc.com/japan/corporate/tax-credits-and-incentives
Mexico - https://taxsummaries.pwc.com/mexico/corporate/tax-credits-and-incentives
Singapore - https://taxsummaries.pwc.com/singapore/corporate/tax-credits-and-incentives
South Korea - https://taxsummaries.pwc.com/republic-of-korea/corporate/tax-credits-and-incentives
Spain - https://taxsummaries.pwc.com/spain/corporate/tax-credits-and-incentives
Taiwan - https://taxsummaries.pwc.com/taiwan/corporate/tax-credits-and-incentives

United Kingdom - https://taxsummaries.pwc.com/united-kingdom/corporate/tax-credits-and-incentives

United States - https://taxsummaries.pwc.com/united-states/corporate/tax-credits-and-incentives

19. Argentina - https://taxsummaries.pwc.com.argentina/corporate/tax-credits-and-incentives

Australia - https://taxsummaries.pwc.com/australia/corporate/tax-credits-and-incentives

Canada - https://www.rcgt.com/en/tax-planning-guide/sections/section-5-employees/incentives-workers/

France - https://taxsummaries.pwc.com/france/corporate/tax-credits-and-incentives

Germany - https://uk.practicallaw.thomsonreuters.com/3-503-3433?__lrTS=20200406104020799&transitionType=Default&contextData=%28sc.Default%29#co_anchor_a823596

India - https://www.taxscan.in/deduction-new-employee-u-s-80jjaa-extended-footwear-leather-industries/17228/

Italy - https://taxsummaries.pwc.com/italy/corporate/tax-credits-and-incentives

Japan - https://taxsummaries.pwc.com/japan/corporate/tax-credits-and-incentives

Mexico - https://taxsummaries.pwc.com/mexico/corporate/tax-credits-and-incentives

Singapore - https://www.corporateservicessingapore.com/guide-to-corporate-tax-credit-and-incentives-in-singapore-for-2020/

South Korea - https://taxsummaries.pwc.com/republic-of-korea/corporate/tax-credits-and-incentives

Spain - https://taxsummaries.pwc.com/spain/corporate/tax-credits-and-incentives

Taiwan - https://content.next.westlaw.com/9-633-4823?__lrTS=20201022201048957&transitionType=Default&contextData=(sc.Default)&firstPage=true

United Kingdom - https://uk.practicallaw.thomsonreuters.com/7-503-4973?transitionType=Default&contextData=(sc.Default)&firstPage=true#co_anchor_a969654

United States - https://taxsummaries.pwc.com/united-states/corporate/tax-credits-and-incentives

20. Argentina - https://taxsummaries.pwc.com.argentina/corporate/tax-credits-and-incentives

Australia - https://taxsummaries.pwc.com/australia/corporate/tax-credits-and-incentives

Canada - https://taxsummaries.pwc.com/canada/corporate/tax-credits-and-incentives

France - https://www.impots.gouv.fr/portail/internationalenbusiness/tax-incentives#NB

Germany - https://taxsummaries.pwc.com/germany/corporate/tax-credits-and-incentives

India - https://taxsummaries.pwc.com/india/corporate/tax-credits-and-incentives

Italy - https://taxsummaries.pwc.com/italy/corporate/tax-credits-and-incentives

Japan - https://taxsummaries.pwc.com/japan/corporate/tax-credits-and-incentives

Mexico - https://taxsummaries.pwc.com/mexico/corporate/tax-credits-and-incentives

Singapore - https://taxsummaries.pwc.com/singapore/corporate/tax-credits-and-incentives

South Korea - https://taxsummaries.pwc.com/republic-of-korea/corporate/tax-credits-and-incentives

Spain - https://taxsummaries.pwc.com/spain/corporate/income-determination

Taiwan - https://taxsummaries.pwc.com/taiwan/corporate/tax-credits-and-incentives

United Kingdom - https://taxsummaries.pwc.com/united-kingdom/corporate/tax-credits-and-incentives

United States - https://taxsummaries.pwc.com/united-states/corporate/tax-credits-and-incentives

21. Paulo Aguiar do Monte, "Public versus private sector: Do workers' behave differently?" Economy, pp. 229–243, Volume 18, issue 2, May–August, 2017
22. Argentina - https://taxsummaries.pwc.com.argentina/individual/deductions

Home Office Allowed		
	Yes	No
Argentina		✓
Australia	✓	
Canada	✓	
France		✓
Germany	✓	

Home Office Allowed		
	Yes	No
India		✓
Italy		✓
Japan	✓	
Mexico	✓	
Singapore	✓	
South Korea	✓	
Spain	✓	
Taiwan		✓
United Kingdom	✓	
United States	✓	

Australia - https://www.ato.gov.au/individuals/income-and-deductions/deductions-you-can-claim/home-office-expenses/
Canada - https://taxsummaries.pwc.com/canada/individual/deductions
Germany - https://taxsummaries.pwc.com/germany/individual/deductions
Japan - https://www.nta.go.jp/english/taxes/individual/12015.htm
Mexico - https://taxsummaries.pwc.com/mexico/individual/deductions
Singapore - https://www.iras.gov.sg/taxes/individual-income-tax/employees/deductions-for-individuals/employment-expenses
South Korea - https://taxsummaries.pwc.com/republic-of-korea/corporate/deductions
Spain - https://taxsummaries.pwc.com/spain/individual/deductions
United Kingdom - https://www.gov.uk/expenses-if-youre-self-employed
United States - https://www.irs.gov/businesses/small-businesses-self-employed/home-office-deduction

23. Home office Depreciable life is based on United States Commercial Building Asset Life
24. Argentina - https://taxsummaries.pwc.com.argentina/corporate/deductions

	Depreciation Limitations on Vehicles
	Notes
Argentina	Depreciation of automobiles whose original cost exceeds ARS 20,000 is not deductible, otherwise 20% deduction per year for 5 years.
Australia	Value capped at $60,733; Vehicles under $30,000 may qualify for 100% expense in the year, vehicles over $30,000 will receive 15% first-year depreciation.

	Depreciation Limitations on Vehicles
	Notes
Canada	Depreciation ceiling for vehicles is between $30,000 & $55,000 depending on the vehicle. Only 30% of the value can be depreciated per year.
France	Depending on the CO_2 emissions per kilometer, first-year deductibility ranges between 9,900€ to 30,000€.
Germany	Up to 25% first-year depreciation using declining-balance method.
India	40% first-year depreciation starting in 2018.
Italy	Up to 20% for light vehicles, and restrictions may apply.
Japan	Useful life is six years; can use straight-line depreciation at 16.7% or double declining method at 33.3% in year 1. Amounts will be subject to proration for the months in service.
Mexico	Depreciation ceiling is MXN 175,000 over four years; Up to MXN 250,000 for electric cars.
Singapore	20% first-year capital allowance, remainder over the useful life depending on the vehicle (5 - 16 years).
South Korea	Company cars limited to KRW eight million annually.
Spain	Maximum depreciation rate per year is 16%, maximum useful life period is 14 years.
Taiwan	Auto Useful live five years: There are several different methods for depreciation that can be used - straight-line, fixed percentage on diminishing book value, sum-of-years-digit, unit-of-production, and working-hour.
United Kingdom	6% of value for capital allowance on CO_2 cars over a certain CO threshold. Low CO_2 emissions may receive a higher deductibility for capital allowance.
United States	$18,200 first-year depreciation, bonus depreciation included.

Australia - https://www.ato.gov.au/Business/Depreciation-and-capital-expenses-and-allowances/Simpler-depreciation-for-small-business/Assets-and-exclusions/?anchor=Carcostlimit#Carcostlimit

Canada - https://www.canada.ca/en/department-finance/news/2019/12/government-announces-the-2020-automobile-deduction-limits-and-expense-benefit-rates-for-businesses.html

France - https://www.frenchbusinessadvice.com/Corporate-Vehicles-And-Taxation

Germany - https://taxfoundation.org/new-accelerated-depreciation-policies-to-spur-investment-australia-austria-germany-new-zealand/

India - https://search.incometaxindia.gov.in/Pages/results.aspx?k=vehicle%20depreciation

Italy - https://www.adrioninterreg.eu/wp-content/uploads/2017/06/Adrion_tabel_on_depreciation_updated_2017_09_29-002.pdf

Japan - https://www.nta.go.jp/english/taxes/individual/12013.htm

Mexico - https://taxsummaries.pwc.com/mexico/corporate/deductions

Singapore - https://www.iras.gov.sg/irashome/Businesses/Companies/Working-out-Corporate-Income-Taxes/Claiming-Allowances/Capital-Allowances/Calculating-Capital-Allowances/#title5

South Korea - https://taxsummaries.pwc.com/republic-of-korea/corporate/deductions

Spain - https://www.limitconsulting.com/2014/11/standard-depreciation-rates/

Taiwan - https://taxsummaries.pwc.com/taiwan/corporate/deductions

United Kingdom - https://www.gov.uk/work-out-capital-allowances/rates-and-pools

United States - https://www.journalofaccountancy.com/news/2021/aug/irs-updates-car

Chapter 3, Investment #2: Technology | Research and Development

1. SARS.gov, "Research and Development (R&D) Incentive," Oct 3, 2021
2. Inland Revenue Authority of Singapore, "Productivity & Innovation Credit (PIC) Scheme," Nov 8, 2021
3. Argentina - https://www2.deloitte.com/content/dam/Deloitte/us/Documents/Tax/us-tax-argentina-2020-survey-of-giii.pdf

   Australia - https://business.gov.au/grants-and-programs/research-and-development-tax-incentive

   Canada - https://www.canada.ca/en/revenue-agency/services/scientific-research-experimental-development-tax-incentive-program/overview.html

   France - https://www.oecd.org/sti/rd-tax-stats-france.pdf

   Germany - https://www.natlawreview.com/article/german-act-tax-incentives-research-and-development-fzulg-force

   India - https://www2.deloitte.com/content/dam/Deloitte/us/Documents/Tax/us-tax-countrypage-india.pdf

   Italy - https://taxsummaries.pwc.com/italy/corporate/tax-credits-and-incentives

   Japan - https://www.oecd.org/sti/rd-tax-stats-japan.pdf

   Mexico - https://taxsummaries.pwc.com/mexico/corporate/tax-credits-and-incentives

Singapore - https://www.pwc.com/sg/en/tax/assets/researchdevt_taxsavings.pdf

South Korea - https://taxsummaries.pwc.com/republic-of-korea/corporate/tax-credits-and-incentives

Spain - https://www.oecd.org/sti/rd-tax-stats-spain.pdf

Taiwan - https://taxsummaries.pwc.com/taiwan/corporate/tax-credits-and-incentives

United Kingdom - https://www.gov.uk/guidance/corporation-tax-research-and-development-rd-relief

United States - https://pro.bloombergtax.com/brief/rd-tax-credit-and-deducting-rd-expenditures/

4. Republique Francaise, *Tax Incentives,* March 2020
5. Argentina - https://www2.deloitte.com/content/dam/Deloitte/us/Documents/Tax/us-tax-argentina-2020-survey-of-giii.pdf

Australia - https://www.oecd.org/sti/rd-tax-stats-australia.pdf

Canada - https://taxsummaries.pwc.com/canada/corporate/tax-credits-and-incentives

France - https://www.oecd.org/sti/rd-tax-stats-france.pdf

Germany - https://www.natlawreview.com/article/german-act-tax-incentives-research-and-development-fzulg-force

India - https://taxsummaries.pwc.com/india/corporate/tax-credits-and-incentives

Italy - https://taxsummaries.pwc.com/italy/corporate/tax-credits-and-incentives

Japan - https://www.oecd.org/sti/rd-tax-stats-japan.pdf

Mexico - https://taxsummaries.pwc.com/mexico/corporate/tax-credits-and-incentives Singapore - https://taxsummaries.pwc.com/singapore/corporate/tax-credits-and-incentives

South Korea - https://taxsummaries.pwc.com/republic-of-korea/corporate/tax-credits-and-incentives

Spain - https://www.oecd.org/sti/rd-tax-stats-spain.pdf

Taiwan - https://taxsummaries.pwc.com/taiwan/corporate/tax-credits-and-incentives

United Kingdom - https://www.gov.uk/guidance/corporation-tax-research-and-development-rd-relief

United States - https://taxfoundation.org/research-and-development-tax/

6. R&D Tax Credit by State - https://www.kbkg.com/research-tax-credits/research-development-tax-credit-state-benefits

7. Isabella Jibilian and Katie Canales, "The US is readying sanctions against Russia over the SolarWinds cyber-attack. Here's a simple explanation of how the massive hack happened and why it's such a big deal," *Business Insider*, April 15, 2021
8. Paul Mozur, "New Rules in China Upset Western Tech Companies," *New York Times*, Jan 28, 2015
9. Michael Goodier, "The definitive list of where every country stands on Huawei," New Statesman, July 29, 2020
10. Sjaak Wolfert, Lan Ge, Cor Verdouw, and Marc-Jeroen Bogaardt, "Big Data in Smart Faming – A review," Science Direct, Jan 23, 2017
11. "World Development Indicators," The World Bank, Feb 19, 2022
12. "The rise of 3D-Printed Houses," *The Economist*, Aug 21, 2021
13. Insight Report, "Making Affordable Housing a Reality in Cities", World Economic Forum, June 2019
14. Institute for Energy Research (IER), "The United States was Energy Independent in 2019 for the First Time Since 1957," Institute for Energy Research, May 11, 2020
15. EIA, Energy Information Administration (US DOE), https://www.eia.gov/energyexplained/us-energy-facts/imports-and-exports.php
16. Union of Concerned Scientists (UCS), "Benefits of Renewable Energy Use," Union of Concerned Scientists, Dec 20, 2017
17. Jeffery A. McNeely, "Nature and COVID-19: The pandemic, the environment, and the way ahead," The Royal Swedish Academy of Sciences, Sep 9, 2020
18. Sebastian Anthony, "SpaceX says it will put humans on Mars by 2026, almost 10 years ahead of NASA," Extreme Tech, June 18, 2014
19. Tom Sanger, Star Fischer, and Travis Riley, "5 Common Misconceptions about the R&D Tax Credit – and Whether You Qualify," MossAdams, Mar 12, 2021

Chapter 4, Investment #3: Real Estate

1. OECD Affordable Housing Database, 2019
2. Argentina – https://taxsummaries.pwc.com/argentina/individual/deductions
   Australia - https://www.oecd.org/els/family/PH2-2-Tax-relief-for-home-ownership.pdf
   Canada - https://www.canada.ca/en/financial-consumer-agency/services/buying-home.html
   France - https://www.oecd.org/els/family/PH2-2-Tax-relief-for-home-ownership.pdf
   Germany - https://taxsummaries.pwc.com/germany/individual/deductions

India - https://homefirstindia.com/article/loan-against-property-how-can-you-avail-tax-benefits-from-lap/
Italy - https://www.oecd.org/els/family/PH2-2-Tax-relief-for-home-ownership.pdf
Japan - https://www.oecd.org/els/family/PH2-2-Tax-relief-for-home-ownership.pdf
Mexico - https://taxsummaries.pwc.com/mexico/individual/deductions
Singapore - https://taxsummaries.pwc.com/singapore/individual/deductions
South Korea - https://taxsummaries.pwc.com/republic-of-korea/individual/deductions
Spain - https://www.oecd.org/els/family/PH2-2-Tax-relief-for-home-ownership.pdf
Taiwan - https://taxsummaries.pwc.com/taiwan/individual/deductions
United Kingdom - https://www.oecd.org/els/family/PH2-2-Tax-relief-for-home-ownership.pdf
United States - https://www.oecd.org/els/family/PH2-2-Tax-relief-for-home-ownership.pdf

3. Tom Wheelwright, *Tax-Free Wealth,* RDA Press, LLC March 2012
4. Argentina - https://taxsummaries.pwc.com/argentina/corporate/deductions
Australia - https://taxsummaries.pwc.com/australia/corporate/deductions
Canada - https://www.canada.ca/en/revenue-agency/services/tax/businesses/topics/rental-income/capital-cost-allowance-rental-property.html
France - https://taxsummaries.pwc.com/france/corporate/deductions
Germany - https://taxsummaries.pwc.com/germany/corporate/deductions
India - https://taxsummaries.pwc.com/india/corporate/deductions
Italy - https://taxsummaries.pwc.com/italy/corporate/deductions
Japan - https://taxsummaries.pwc.com/japan/corporate/deductions
Mexico - https://taxsummaries.pwc.com/mexico/corporate/deductions
Singapore - https://taxsummaries.pwc.com/singapore/corporate/deductions
South Korea - https://taxsummaries.pwc.com/republic-of-korea/corporate/deductions
Spain - https://taxsummaries.pwc.com/spain/individual/deductions
Taiwan - https://taxsummaries.pwc.com/taiwan/corporate/deductions
United Kingdom - https://taxsummaries.pwc.com/united-kingdom/corporate/deductions
United States - https://taxsummaries.pwc.com/united-states/corporate/deductions
5. Julia Kagan "Bonus Depreciation," Investopedia, April 20, 2021

6.

Cost Segregation Laws			
	Yes	No	Notes
Argentina	✓		In the General Instruction (SDG ASJ-AFIP) 7/2012, the tax authorities expressed that given the lack of particular rules, in order to calculate the tax depreciation of movable assets, it should be understood that the probable useful life refers to a reasonable estimation, and in this regard, the concepts of obsolescence and efficient useful life should be considered when making the calculation.
Australia	✓		Australia allows for diminishing value method to accelerate depreciation. An immediate write-off is available for depreciating assets costing less than AUD1,000 (low-cost assets) (this was reduced from AUD6,500, effective 1 January 2014) for small businesses.
Canada	✓		Assets that are purchased solely in support of equipment may be considered to be a part of that equipment and classified as such (e.g., heating, ventilation and air conditioning (HVAC); plumbing; electrical). This is not required but typically results in significantly more advantageous depreciation rates for the particular assets.
France	✓		The depreciation of fixed assets must be carried out component by component if these components have different lifetimes or if they provide economic benefits to the owner over different time scales. In this situation, they have to be depreciated separately, according to the lifetime of each of them, e.g., heating system or roofing, which are by nature and their use intended to be replaced at regular intervals.
Germany		✓	When determining the depreciation amount for a building, the calculation is based on the total amount of acquisition costs or production costs of the whole building. The valuation of depreciation on individual parts, such as heating systems, windows, or walls is normally not permitted. However, using different useful lives for different parts is permitted in special cases – for example, where solar panels have been placed on the top of buildings or if a specific part of a building was built separately.

Cost Segregation Laws			
	Yes	No	Notes
India		✓	Assets are classified as tangible or intangible. The classification is further divided into different categories. Accordingly, rates applicable to the relevant category shall be applied to claim depreciation.
Italy	✓		For assets that consist of several items, the taxpayer will have to determine the cost of each component. Assets with different useful estimated lives have to be recorded and tracked individually.
Japan	✓		Companies are required to break assets down by the following categories for Japanese tax purposes: buildings, building improvements, other structures, machinery, equipment, vessels, aircraft, and vehicles.
Mexico	✓		Varied lives/rates can be applied to different assets depending on the limits and percentages mentioned in tax law. Although it is not required to do so, it is possible to separate parts of a building.
Singapore		✓	Capital allowances can be claimed on plant or machinery. The parts of a building that are plant or machinery are eligible for capital allowance claims.
South Korea		✓	In general, corporations may depreciate tangible fixed assets using the straight-line, declining-balance, or unit-of-production (output) depreciation methods. However, buildings and structures must be depreciated using the straight-line method.
Spain	✓		Tax depreciation should be applied element by element, i.e., companies are required to distinguish between parts of the building and apply different lives and rates to each part (e.g., furniture, air conditioning units).
Taiwan	✓		Law allows depreciation on buildings, fixtures, machinery, equipment, tools, appliances, apparatus, vessels, and other fixed assets. In effect, practically all personal and real property (except land) used in the business enterprise is depreciable. Each asset must be listed in the schedule of properties and depreciated separately.

Cost Segregation Laws			
	Yes	No	Notes
United Kingdom	✓		Claimants are required to break down assets into individual items to allow them to be categorized for capital allowances. It is necessary, therefore, to have a detailed cost breakdown of all capital expenditures incurred, particularly with respect to buildings.
United States	✓		Generally, a property is required to be broken down (even though it's not enforced) into components for purposes of computing tax depreciation. There are special rules however. For example, when a building is acquired, it is common to identify property items within the building that are separate assets from the building and may be required to be depreciated differently.

7. Argentina - https://assets.ey.com/content/dam/ey-sites/ey-com/en_gl/topics/tax/tax-guides/2021/ey-worldwide-capital-and-fixed-assets-guide-2021.pdf?download

   Australia - https://www.bmtqs.com.au/tax-depreciation/education/depreciation-methods

   Canada - https://assets.ey.com/content/dam/ey-sites/ey-com/en_gl/topics/tax/tax-guides/2021/ey-worldwide-capital-and-fixed-assets-guide-2021.pdf?download

   France - https://assets.ey.com/content/dam/ey-sites/ey-com/en_gl/topics/tax/tax-guides/2021/ey-worldwide-capital-and-fixed-assets-guide-2021.pdf?download

   Germany - https://assets.ey.com/content/dam/ey-sites/ey-com/en_gl/topics/tax/tax-guides/2021/ey-worldwide-capital-and-fixed-assets-guide-2021.pdf?download

   India - https://assets.ey.com/content/dam/ey-sites/ey-com/en_gl/topics/tax/tax-guides/2021/ey-worldwide-capital-and-fixed-assets-guide-2021.pdf?download

   Italy - https://assets.ey.com/content/dam/ey-sites/ey-com/en_gl/topics/tax/tax-guides/2021/ey-worldwide-capital-and-fixed-assets-guide-2021.pdf?download

   Japan - https://assets.ey.com/content/dam/ey-sites/ey-com/en_gl/topics/tax/tax-guides/2021/ey-worldwide-capital-and-fixed-assets-guide-2021.pdf?download

Mexico - https://assets.ey.com/content/dam/ey-sites/ey-com/en_gl/topics/tax/tax-guides/2021/ey-worldwide-capital-and-fixed-assets-guide-2021.pdf?download

Singapore - https://assets.ey.com/content/dam/ey-sites/ey-com/en_gl/topics/tax/tax-guides/2021/ey-worldwide-capital-and-fixed-assets-guide-2021.pdf?download

South Korea - https://assets.ey.com/content/dam/ey-sites/ey-com/en_gl/topics/tax/tax-guides/2021/ey-worldwide-capital-and-fixed-assets-guide-2021.pdf?download

Spain - https://assets.ey.com/content/dam/ey-sites/ey-com/en_gl/topics/tax/tax-guides/2021/ey-worldwide-capital-and-fixed-assets-guide-2021.pdf?download

Taiwan - https://egrove.olemiss.edu/cgi/viewcontent.cgi?article=1021&context=dl_dhs

United Kingdom - https://assets.ey.com/content/dam/ey-sites/ey-com/en_gl/topics/tax/tax-guides/2021/ey-worldwide-capital-and-fixed-assets-guide-2021.pdf?download

United States - https://assets.ey.com/content/dam/ey-sites/ey-com/en_gl/topics/tax/tax-guides/2021/ey-worldwide-capital-and-fixed-assets-guide-2021.pdf?download

8. Argentina - https://assets.ey.com/content/dam/ey-sites/ey-com/en_gl/topics/tax/tax-guides/2021/ey-worldwide-capital-and-fixed-assets-guide-2021.pdf?download

Australia - https://assets.ey.com/content/dam/ey-sites/ey-com/en_gl/topics/tax/tax-guides/2021/ey-worldwide-capital-and-fixed-assets-guide-2021.pdf?download

Canada - https://assets.ey.com/content/dam/ey-sites/ey-com/en_gl/topics/tax/tax-guides/2021/ey-worldwide-capital-and-fixed-assets-guide-2021.pdf?download

France - https://assets.ey.com/content/dam/ey-sites/ey-com/en_gl/topics/tax/tax-guides/2021/ey-worldwide-capital-and-fixed-assets-guide-2021.pdf?download

Germany - https://assets.ey.com/content/dam/ey-sites/ey-com/en_gl/topics/tax/tax-guides/2021/ey-worldwide-capital-and-fixed-assets-guide-2021.pdf?download

India - https://assets.ey.com/content/dam/ey-sites/ey-com/en_gl/topics/tax/tax-guides/2021/ey-worldwide-capital-and-fixed-assets-guide-2021.pdf?download

Italy - https://assets.ey.com/content/dam/ey-sites/ey-com/en_gl/topics/tax/tax-guides/2021/ey-worldwide-capital-and-fixed-assets-guide-2021.pdf?download

Japan - https://taxsummaries.pwc.com/japan/corporate/deductions

Mexico - https://assets.ey.com/content/dam/ey-sites/ey-com/en_gl/topics/tax/tax-guides/2021/ey-worldwide-capital-and-fixed-assets-guide-2021.pdf?download

Singapore - https://assets.ey.com/content/dam/ey-sites/ey-com/en_gl/topics/tax/tax-guides/2021/ey-worldwide-capital-and-fixed-assets-guide-2021.pdf?download

South Korea - https://taxsummaries.pwc.com/republic-of-korea/corporate/deductions

Spain - https://assets.ey.com/content/dam/ey-sites/ey-com/en_gl/topics/tax/tax-guides/2021/ey-worldwide-capital-and-fixed-assets-guide-2021.pdf?download

Taiwan - https://taxsummaries.pwc.com/taiwan/corporate/deductions

United Kingdom - https://assets.ey.com/content/dam/ey-sites/ey-com/en_gl/topics/tax/tax-guides/2021/ey-worldwide-capital-and-fixed-assets-guide-2021.pdf?download

United States - https://assets.ey.com/content/dam/ey-sites/ey-com/en_gl/topics/tax/tax-guides/2021/ey-worldwide-capital-and-fixed-assets-guide-2021.pdf?download

9. Argentina - https://assets.ey.com/content/dam/ey-sites/ey-com/en_gl/topics/tax/tax-guides/2021/ey-worldwide-capital-and-fixed-assets-guide-2021.pdf?download

Australia - https://assets.ey.com/content/dam/ey-sites/ey-com/en_gl/topics/tax/tax-guides/2021/ey-worldwide-capital-and-fixed-assets-guide-2021.pdf?download

Canada - https://assets.ey.com/content/dam/ey-sites/ey-com/en_gl/topics/tax/tax-guides/2021/ey-worldwide-capital-and-fixed-assets-guide-2021.pdf?download

France - https://assets.ey.com/content/dam/ey-sites/ey-com/en_gl/topics/tax/tax-guides/2021/ey-worldwide-capital-and-fixed-assets-guide-2021.pdf?download

Germany - https://assets.ey.com/content/dam/ey-sites/ey-com/en_gl/topics/tax/tax-guides/2021/ey-worldwide-capital-and-fixed-assets-guide-2021.pdf?download

India - https://assets.ey.com/content/dam/ey-sites/ey-com/en_gl/topics/tax/tax-guides/2021/ey-worldwide-capital-and-fixed-assets-guide-2021.pdf?download

Italy - https://assets.ey.com/content/dam/ey-sites/ey-com/en_gl/topics/tax/tax-guides/2021/ey-worldwide-capital-and-fixed-assets-guide-2021.pdf?download

Japan - https://assets.ey.com/content/dam/ey-sites/ey-com/en_gl/topics/tax/tax-guides/2021/ey-worldwide-capital-and-fixed-assets-guide-2021.pdf?download

Mexico - https://assets.ey.com/content/dam/ey-sites/ey-com/en_gl/topics/tax/tax-guides/2021/ey-worldwide-capital-and-fixed-assets-guide-2021.pdf?download

Singapore - https://assets.ey.com/content/dam/ey-sites/ey-com/en_gl/topics/tax/tax-guides/2021/ey-worldwide-capital-and-fixed-assets-guide-2021.pdf?download

South Korea - https://assets.ey.com/content/dam/ey-sites/ey-com/en_gl/topics/tax/tax-guides/2021/ey-worldwide-capital-and-fixed-assets-guide-2021.pdf?download

Spain - https://assets.ey.com/content/dam/ey-sites/ey-com/en_gl/topics/tax/tax-guides/2021/ey-worldwide-capital-and-fixed-assets-guide-2021.pdf?download

Taiwan - https://taxsummaries.pwc.com/taiwan/corporate/deductions

United Kingdom - https://assets.ey.com/content/dam/ey-sites/ey-com/en_gl/topics/tax/tax-guides/2021/ey-worldwide-capital-and-fixed-assets-guide-2021.pdf?download

United States - https://assets.ey.com/content/dam/ey-sites/ey-com/en_gl/topics/tax/tax-guides/2021/ey-worldwide-capital-and-fixed-assets-guide-2021.pdf?download

10. Argentina - https://assets.ey.com/content/dam/ey-sites/ey-com/en_gl/topics/tax/tax-guides/2021/ey-worldwide-capital-and-fixed-assets-guide-2021.pdf?download

Australia - https://assets.ey.com/content/dam/ey-sites/ey-com/en_gl/topics/tax/tax-guides/2021/ey-worldwide-capital-and-fixed-assets-guide-2021.pdf?download

Canada - https://assets.ey.com/content/dam/ey-sites/ey-com/en_gl/topics/tax/tax-guides/2021/ey-worldwide-capital-and-fixed-assets-guide-2021.pdf?download

France - https://assets.ey.com/content/dam/ey-sites/ey-com/en_gl/topics/tax/tax-guides/2021/ey-worldwide-capital-and-fixed-assets-guide-2021.pdf?download

Germany - https://assets.ey.com/content/dam/ey-sites/ey-com/en_gl/topics/tax/tax-guides/2021/ey-worldwide-capital-and-fixed-assets-guide-2021.pdf?download

India - https://assets.ey.com/content/dam/ey-sites/ey-com/en_gl/topics/tax/tax-guides/2021/ey-worldwide-capital-and-fixed-assets-guide-2021.pdf?download

Italy - https://assets.ey.com/content/dam/ey-sites/ey-com/en_gl/topics/tax/tax-guides/2021/ey-worldwide-capital-and-fixed-assets-guide-2021.pdf?download

Japan - https://assets.ey.com/content/dam/ey-sites/ey-com/en_gl/topics/tax/tax-guides/2021/ey-worldwide-capital-and-fixed-assets-guide-2021.pdf?download

Mexico - https://assets.ey.com/content/dam/ey-sites/ey-com/en_gl/topics/tax/tax-guides/2021/ey-worldwide-capital-and-fixed-assets-guide-2021.pdf?download

Singapore - https://assets.ey.com/content/dam/ey-sites/ey-com/en_gl/topics/tax/tax-guides/2021/ey-worldwide-capital-and-fixed-assets-guide-2021.pdf?download

South Korea - https://assets.ey.com/content/dam/ey-sites/ey-com/en_gl/topics/tax/tax-guides/2021/ey-worldwide-capital-and-fixed-assets-guide-2021.pdf?download

Spain - https://assets.ey.com/content/dam/ey-sites/ey-com/en_gl/topics/tax/tax-guides/2021/ey-worldwide-capital-and-fixed-assets-guide-2021.pdf?download

Taiwan - https://taxsummaries.pwc.com/taiwan/corporate/deductions

United Kingdom - https://assets.ey.com/content/dam/ey-sites/ey-com/en_gl/topics/tax/tax-guides/2021/ey-worldwide-capital-and-fixed-assets-guide-2021.pdf?download

United States - https://taxsummaries.pwc.com/united-states/corporate/deductions

11. Argentina - https://taxsummaries.pwc.com/argentina/corporate/deductions

Australia - https://taxsummaries.pwc.com/australia/corporate/deductions

Canada - https://taxsummaries.pwc.com/canada/corporate/deductions

France - https://taxsummaries.pwc.com/france/corporate/deductions

Germany - https://taxsummaries.pwc.com/germany/corporate/deductions

India - https://taxsummaries.pwc.com/india/corporate/deductions

Italy - https://taxsummaries.pwc.com/italy/corporate/deductions

Japan - https://taxsummaries.pwc.com/japan/corporate/deductions

Mexico - https://taxsummaries.pwc.com/mexico/corporate/deductions

Singapore - https://taxsummaries.pwc.com/singapore/corporate/deductions

South Korea - https://taxsummaries.pwc.com/republic-of-korea/corporate/deductions

Spain - https://taxsummaries.pwc.com/spain/corporate/deductions

Taiwan - https://taxsummaries.pwc.com/taiwan/corporate/deductions

United Kingdom - https://taxsummaries.pwc.com/united-kingdom/corporate/deductions

United States - https://taxsummaries.pwc.com/united-states/corporate/deductions

12. There is frequent confusion among taxpayers and their accountants about the role of depreciation recapture in the tax benefits of real estate. This confusion leads to some accountants advising against bonus depreciation. Big mistake. First, the negative effects of recapture only occur when the property is sold, and then only if the proceeds are not quickly reinvested into more real estate. Second, the recapture tax on contents only applies when the property is sold prior to the end of the useful life of the contents (typically five to seven years). Recapture on the land improvements is taxed at a lower maximum rate (25 percent) than the deduction for the depreciation (up to 37 percent or more). And with proper planning, there never has to be recapture. See Chapter 7 of *Tax-Free Wealth*.
13. Tax Policy Center Briefing Book *Key Elements of the U.S. Tax System,* Tax Policy Center
14. Argentina - https://taxsummaries.pwc.com/argentina/corporate/tax-credits-and-incentives

    Australia - https://taxsummaries.pwc.com/australia/corporate/tax-credits-and-incentives

    Canada - https://www.bloomberglaw.com/product/tax/document/XQIACL18#section(4)(4)(b)

    France - https://www.impots.gouv.fr/portail/internationalenbusiness/tax-incentives

    Germany - https://taxsummaries.pwc.com/germany/corporate/tax-credits-and-incentives

    India - https://taxsummaries.pwc.com/india/corporate/tax-credits-and-incentives

    Italy - https://taxsummaries.pwc.com/italy/corporate/tax-credits-and-incentives

    Japan - https://taxsummaries.pwc.com/japan/corporate/tax-credits-and-incentives

    Mexico - https://www.taxathand.com/article/16050/Mexico/2021/Tax-incentives-granted-in-northern-and-southern-border-regions

    Singapore - https://taxsummaries.pwc.com/singapore/corporate/tax-credits-and-incentives

    South Korea - https://taxsummaries.pwc.com/republic-of-korea/corporate/tax-credits-and-incentives

    Spain - https://taxsummaries.pwc.com/spain/corporate/tax-credits-and-incentives

Taiwan - https://investtaiwan.nat.gov.tw/showPage?lang=eng&search=reward

United Kingdom - https://taxsummaries.pwc.com/united-kingdom/corporate/tax-credits-and-incentives

United States - https://taxfoundation.org/low-income-housing-tax-credit-lihtc/

15. Argentina - https://www.bloomberglaw.com/product/tax/document/XPV1GV18#section(4)_0

Australia - https://www.ato.gov.au/Individuals/Capital-gains-tax/Calculating-your-cgt/

Canada - https://www.bloomberglaw.com/product/tax/document/XQIACM18#section(3)(3)(b)_0

France - https://taxsummaries.pwc.com/france/individual/other-taxes

Germany - https://taxsummaries.pwc.com/germany/individual/income-determination

India - https://taxsummaries.pwc.com/india/corporate/income-determination

Italy - https://taxsummaries.pwc.com/italy/individual/income-determination#:~:text=Capital%20gains%20made%20between%201,the%20whole%20capital%20gains%20amount

Japan - https://www.bloomberglaw.com/product/tax/document/XPV2EB18#section(2)(2)(c)_0

Mexico - https://www.bloomberglaw.com/product/tax/document/XPV1OVH8#section(2)_0

Singapore - https://www.bloomberglaw.com/product/tax/document/27886617640

South Korea - https://taxsummaries.pwc.com/republic-of-korea/individual/income-determination

Spain - https://www.bloomberglaw.com/product/tax/document/XPV2L918#section(3)(3)(g)(3)(g)(2)_0

Taiwan - https://www.ey.com/en_gl/tax-alerts/taiwan-amends-capital-gains-tax-law-for-transfers-of-real-property

United Kingdom - https://www.bloomberglaw.com/product/tax/document/XPV1QNH8?bc=W1siU2VhcmNoIFJlc3VsdHMiLCIvcHJvZHVjdC90YXgvc2VhcmNoL3Jlc3VsdHMvMzU4ZDEzOTUwNThiOTE2ODQ3NzVlNDJiZDBlOGNjYzciXV0--5cb465fc15af1debd7cc1d936a0b128a4e4bc785&guid=b646babc-f005-4511-a8c0-65361f536fbf&search32=_0XAZN4lA8OI3Tviln1sUg%3D%3D8DeU0WJk3R0QkTwMjdE5lYIV0G-XhDTTVkVItJAF0_Wm0q7V4M-4cYFatfLfDwMaFBkfoKTqC6wmXai80nSC8tNrg0Vz8Y9MqKO-3NPkGpr48_06lsWb1hGKEVBLbvKaD6BMIrwi75rAWrwi-uV_fe2n4vK1RqlMMBNlg93P

GyE0vVlTRFXLhr0RCI8XpVGRU0GwYIktw8pl2rVKWCSlFq0NZyzf nZKKO67LLwqe3-DUPkSOqLiV4-7WkY63E9TWps65Gmt IWIyVTjXtD-hSdOonTXF13AvHS-hKekfNE_G07OYu_ qvRA7xopYL3GuUYc20RUEHBkzuyASeOI69aVV_r8HXT_ JoOdZ3EI-2lp5494DCCkh31MP6o90c1HjyqPqioyqwcidUugW7NaZ QmQ0wCsZkW2N4Dtw_hCGL3t8DWuOqj7dM0-E7JQcMv7KVXD Z2mvpmXJR3eZTryRyEBzA%3D%3D

United States - https://www.irs.gov/taxtopics/tc409

16. Argentina - https://www.taxand.com/wp-content/uploads/2017/09/605_taxand-ma_guide-argentina-1.pdf

    Australia - https://www.ato.gov.au/Individuals/Capital-gains-tax/CGT-events/Involuntary-disposal-of-a-CGT-asset/

    Canada - https://agtax.ca/canadian-replacement-property-rules/

    France - https://www.blevinsfranks.com/france-capital-gains-tax-property/

    Germany - https://www.rsm.de/en/what-we-offer/industry-experience/real-estate-construction/real-estate-tax-guide/selling-and-transferring-german-real-estate

    India - https://uk.practicallaw.thomsonreuters.com/7-598-4529?transitionType=Default&contextData=(sc.Default)&firstPage=true

    Italy - https://uk.practicallaw.thomsonreuters.com/7-515-3348?transitionType=Default&contextData=(sc.Default)#co_anchor_a339186

    Japan - https://assets.kpmg/content/dam/kpmg/jp/pdf/2018/jp-en-taxation-in-japan-201811.pdf

    Mexico - https://assets.kpmg/content/dam/kpmg/mx/pdf/2020/03/Investment-in-Mexico-2020.pdf

    Singapore - https://www.iras.gov.sg/irashome/Individuals/Locals/Working-Out-Your-Taxes/What-is-Taxable-What-is-Not/Gains-from-Sale-of-Property--Shares-and-Financial-Instruments/

    South Korea - https://assets.kpmg/content/dam/kpmg/xx/pdf/2018/08/south-korea-2018.pdf

    Spain - https://www.spanishpropertyinsight.com/2019/04/24/capital-gains-tax-mitigation-on-selling-property-in-spain/

    Taiwan - https://assets.kpmg/content/dam/kpmg/xx/pdf/2018/08/taiwan-2018.pdf

    United Kingdom - https://www.gov.uk/business-asset-rollover-relief

    United States - https://www.irs.gov/businesses/small-businesses-self-employed/like-kind-exchanges-real-estate-tax-tips

17. Argentina - https://www2.deloitte.com/content/dam/Deloitte/global/Documents/Tax/dttl-tax-argentinahighlights-2021.pdf?nc=1

Australia - https://www.ato.gov.au/Individuals/Capital-gains-tax/Property-and-capital-gains-tax/Your-main-residence-(home)/

Canada - https://www.canada.ca/en/revenue-agency/services/tax/individuals/topics/about-your-tax-return/tax-return/completing-a-tax-return/personal-income/line-12700-capital-gains/principal-residence-other-real-estate/sale-your-principal-residence.html

France - https://www.bloomberglaw.com/product/tax/document/XPV1UG18#section(2)(2)(h)(2)(h)(1)(2)(h)(1)(d)_0

Germany - https://www.german-probate-lawyer.com/en/glossary/def/capital-gains-tax-on-gains-from-sale-of-property-in-germany.html#:~:text=There%20is%20no%20special%20or%20separate%20capital%20gains%20tax%20in%20Germany.&text=Capital%20gains%20derived%20from%20private,gains%20are%20tax%20exempt%20exempt.

India - https://incometaxindia.gov.in/tutorials/16.%20exemption%20under%2054.pdf

Italy - https://home.kpmg/xx/en/home/insights/2011/12/italy-income-tax.html

Japan - https://japanpropertycentral.com/real-estate-faq/capital-gains-tax/

Mexico - https://www.mexperience.com/the-costs-and-taxes-of-selling-property-in-mexico/

Singapore - https://www.iras.gov.sg/irashome/Property/Property-owners/Selling-renting-out-carrying-out-works/Selling-your-Property/

South Korea - https://www.bloomberglaw.com/product/tax/bloombergtaxnews/daily-tax-report-international/XEUK6FDC000000?bna_news_filter=daily-tax-report-international#jcite

Spain - https://tejadasolicitors.com/tax-spain/capital-gains-tax-spain/

Taiwan - https://www.grantthornton.tw/globalassets/1.-member-firms/taiwan/media/tw_images/publication-pdf/miscellaneous/2017-05.pdf

United Kingdom - https://www.gov.uk/tax-sell-home

United States - https://www.irs.gov/taxtopics/tc701

18. Jenny Schuetz and Sarah Crump, *What the U.S. can learn from rental housing markets across the globe*, Brookings, April 20,2021
19. Argentina - https://www.ey.com/en_gl/tax-alerts/argentina-enacts-tax-incentives-and-voluntary-disclosure-program-to-promote-construction-and-access-to-housing

Australia - https://www.dss.gov.au/housing-support-programs-services-housing-national-rental-affordability-scheme/about-the-national-rental-affordability-scheme-nras#incentive

Canada - https://www.oecd.org/els/family/PH5-1-Measures-financing-affordable-housing-development.pdf

France - https://www.oecd.org/els/family/PH5-1-Measures-financing-affordable-housing-development.pdf

Germany - https://www.oecd.org/els/family/PH5-1-Measures-financing-affordable-housing-development.pdf

India - https://housing.com/news/gst-real-estate-will-impact-home-buyers-industry/

Italy - https://www.blog.usimmigrationadvisor.com/tax-incentives-for-investing-and-renting-residential-properties-in-italy/

Japan - https://www.jetro.go.jp/en/invest/support_programs/incentive/

Mexico - https://assets.kpmg/content/dam/kpmg/mx/pdf/2020/04/Investment-in-Mexico-2020-final.pdf

Singapore - Survey of Global Investment and Innovation Incentives - Singapore - 2020 (deloitte.com)

South Korea - https://taxsummaries.pwc.com/republic-of-korea/corporate/tax-credits-and-incentives

Spain - https://www.oecd.org/els/family/PH5-1-Measures-financing-affordable-housing-development.pdf

Taiwan - https://assets.kpmg/content/dam/kpmg/tw/pdf/2018/08/tw-kpmg-invetment-in-tw-2018.pdf

United Kingdom - https://www.oecd.org/els/family/PH5-1-Measures-financing-affordable-housing-development.pdf

United States - https://www.oecd.org/els/family/PH5-1-Measures-financing-affordable-housing-development.pdf

20. Office of Policy Development and Research, "Low-Income Housing Tax Credit (LIHTC)," Huduser.gov
21. Homesnow.org, "Short History of Public Housing in the US (1930's – Present)," April 3, 2018
22. Nor'Aini Yusof, Ismeal Younis Abu-Jarad, and Hohd Hasanal Badree, "The Effectiveness of Government Incentives to Facilitate an Innovative Housing Delivery System: the Perspective of Housing Developers," Theoretical and Empirical Researches in Urban Management, Volume 7 Issue 1, Feb 2012
23. Omar Havana, "This is Europe: An image of homelessness in Paris, Aljazeera," Dec 23, 2018
24. Megan Janetsky, "Lima's 'Wall of Shame' and the Art of Building Barriers," *The Atlantic*, Sep 7, 2019

25. Argentina - https://taxsummaries.pwc.com/argentina/corporate/deductions
Australia - https://taxsummaries.pwc.com/australia/corporate/deductions
Canada - https://www.canada.ca/en/revenue-agency/services/tax/businesses/topics/rental-income/capital-cost-allowance-rental-property.html
France - https://taxsummaries.pwc.com/france/corporate/deductions
Germany - https://taxsummaries.pwc.com/germany/corporate/deductions
India - https://taxsummaries.pwc.com/india/corporate/deductions
Italy - https://taxsummaries.pwc.com/italy/corporate/deductions
Japan - https://taxsummaries.pwc.com/japan/corporate/deductions
Mexico - https://taxsummaries.pwc.com/mexico/corporate/deductions
Singapore - https://taxsummaries.pwc.com/singapore/corporate/deductions
South Korea - https://taxsummaries.pwc.com/republic-of-korea/corporate/deductions
Spain - https://taxsummaries.pwc.com/spain/corporate/deductions
Taiwan - https://taxsummaries.pwc.com/taiwan/corporate/deductions
United Kingdom - https://taxsummaries.pwc.com/united-kingdom/corporate/deductions
United States - https://taxsummaries.pwc.com/united-states/corporate/deductions

Chapter 5, Investment #4: Energy

1. Argentina - https://iclg.com/practice-areas/oil-and-gas-laws-and-regulations/argentina
Australia - https://uk.practicallaw.thomsonreuters.com/w-011-0184?transitionType=Default&contextData=(sc.Default)&firstPage=true
Canada - https://iclg.com/practice-areas/oil-and-gas-laws-and-regulations/canada
France - https://iclg.com/practice-areas/oil-and-gas-laws-and-regulations/france
Germany - https://uk.practicallaw.thomsonreuters.com/w-029-7186?originationContext=document&transitionType=DocumentItem&contextData=(sc.Default)&firstPage=true
India - https://thelawreviews.co.uk/title/the-oil-and-gas-law-review/india
Italy - https://iclg.com/practice-areas/oil-and-gas-laws-and-regulations/italy
Japan - https://uk.practicallaw.thomsonreuters.com/w-029-5502?originationContext=document&transitionType=DocumentItem&contextData=(sc.Default)&firstPage=true

Mexico - https://uk.practicallaw.thomsonreuters.com/6-524-0285?transitionType=Default&contextData=(sc.Default)&firstPage=true

Singapore - https://www.eia.gov/international/analysis/country/SGP

South Korea - https://www.oecd.org/fossil-fuels/KOR.pdf

Spain - https://www.oecd.org/fossil-fuels/ESP.pdf

Taiwan - http://www.geni.org/globalenergy/library/national_energy_grid/taiwan/TaiwanCountryAnalysisBrief.shtml

United Kingdom - https://www2.bgs.ac.uk/mineralsuk/planning/legislation/mineralOwnership.html

United States - https://revenuedata.doi.gov/how-revenue-works/ownership/

2. Argentina - https://assets.kpmg/content/dam/kpmg/pdf/2015/09/taxes-and-incentives-2015-web-v2.pdf

Australia - https://assets.kpmg/content/dam/kpmg/pdf/2015/09/taxes-and-incentives-2015-web-v2.pdf

Canada - https://assets.kpmg/content/dam/kpmg/pdf/2015/09/taxes-and-incentives-2015-web-v2.pdf

France - https://assets.kpmg/content/dam/kpmg/pdf/2015/09/taxes-and-incentives-2015-web-v2.pdf

Germany - https://assets.kpmg/content/dam/kpmg/pdf/2015/09/taxes-and-incentives-2015-web-v2.pdf

India - https://assets.kpmg/content/dam/kpmg/pdf/2015/09/taxes-and-incentives-2015-web-v2.pdf

Italy - https://assets.kpmg/content/dam/kpmg/pdf/2015/09/taxes-and-incentives-2015-web-v2.pdf

Japan - https://assets.kpmg/content/dam/kpmg/pdf/2015/09/taxes-and-incentives-2015-web-v2.pdf

Mexico - https://assets.kpmg/content/dam/kpmg/pdf/2015/09/taxes-and-incentives-2015-web-v2.pdf

Singapore - dttl-tax-global-rd-survey-aug-2014.pdf (deloitte.com)

South Korea - https://assets.kpmg/content/dam/kpmg/pdf/2015/09/taxes-and-incentives-2015-web-v2.pdf

Spain - https://assets.kpmg/content/dam/kpmg/pdf/2015/09/taxes-and-incentives-2015-web-v2.pdf

Taiwan - https://assets.kpmg/content/dam/kpmg/no/pdf/2020/12/The_Power_Of_Nature_Taxation_Of_Wind_Power_2020.pdf

United Kingdom - https://assets.kpmg/content/dam/kpmg/pdf/2015/09/taxes-and-incentives-2015-web-v2.pdf

United States - https://assets.kpmg/content/dam/kpmg/pdf/2015/09/taxes-and-incentives-2015-web-v2.pdf

3. Argentina - https://www.bnamericas.com/en/news/argentina-offers-tax-incentive-for-distributed-generation

Australia - https://www.energy.gov.au/rebates/renewable-power-incentives

Canada - https://www.energyhub.org/incentives/

France - https://taxsummaries.pwc.com/France/Individual/Other-tax-credits-and-incentives

Germany - https://taxsummaries.pwc.com/germany/individual/other-tax-credits-and-incentives

India - https://taxsummaries.pwc.com/india/individual/other-tax-credits-and-incentives

Italy - https://taxsummaries.pwc.com/italy/individual/other-tax-credits-and-incentives

Japan - https://www.env.go.jp/en/policy/tax/auto/ch3.html

Mexico - https://taxsummaries.pwc.com/mexico/individual/other-tax-credits-and-incentives

Singapore - https://taxsummaries.pwc.com/singapore/individual/other-tax-credits-and-incentives

South Korea - https://taxsummaries.pwc.com/republic-of-korea/individual/other-tax-credits-and-incentives

Spain - https://taxsummaries.pwc.com/spain/individual/other-tax-credits-and-incentives

Taiwan - https://taxsummaries.pwc.com/taiwan/individual/other-tax-credits-and-incentives

United Kingdom - https://taxsummaries.pwc.com/united-kingdom/individual/other-tax-credits-and-incentives

United States - https://www.energy.gov/eere/solar/homeowners-guide-federal-tax-credit-solar-photovoltaics

4. James Newton, *Uncommon Friends: Life with Thomas Edison, Henry Ford, Harvey Firestone, Alexis Carrel, and Charles Lindbergh*, Houghton Mifflin Harcourt, May 1987
5. Edward Tenner, "Abraham Lincoln, Technologist-in-Chief," *The Atlantic*, March 5, 2012
6. Associated Press, "Elon Musk Unveils Tesla's Ambitious New Home Battery System," *Inc*. May 1, 2015
7. Khan Academy, "The Industrial Revolution," The Khan Academy, N.D.
8. History.com Editors "United States freezes Japanese assets," History .com, Nov 16, 2009
9. Oliver Gliech, "Petroleum," Encyclopedia 1914 – 1918, Jan 7, 2015
10. JoeBiden.com, "9 Key Elements of Joe Biden's Plan for a Clean Energy Revolution," https://joebiden.com/9-key-elements-of-joe-bidens-plan-for-a-clean-energy-revolution/
11. Bate Felix and Geert De Clercq, "France Raises carbon taxes, to repay EDF renewables debt," Reuters, Sep 27, 2017

12. Reuters Staff, "France to uphold ban on sale of fossil fuel cars by 2040," Reuters June 11, 2019. https://www.reuters.com/article/us-france-autos-idUSKCN1TC1CU
13. Michel Rose, "Macron wants France to be Europe's top clean car producer," Reuters May 26, 2020. https://www.reuters.com/article/us-health-coronavirus-france-autos-idUSKBN2322D6
14. Roger Harrabin, "Boris Johnson: Wind farms could power every home by 2030," BBC News, Oct 6, 2020. https://www.bbc.com/news/uk-politics-54421489
15. Junichi Sugihara, "Japan minister: Renewable energy to be 'major power source'," Nikkei Asia, Oct 13, 2020. https://asia.nikkei.com/Editor-s-Picks/Interview/Japan-minister-Renewable-energy-to-be-major-power-source
16. EIA, Energy Information Administration (US DOE), "How much carbon dioxide is produced per kilowatt hour of U.S. electricity generation," https://www.eia.gov/tools/faqs/faq.php?id=74&t=11

CO_2 reduction Per kWH	
Coal CO_2 produced per kWH	2.23LB
Solar CO_2 produced per kWH	50 grams
Gram to Lbs conversion	
1Lb = 453.592 grams	
Lbs. to Ton Conversion	
2000lb = 1 Ton	
Total kWH	144,000
Coal CO_2	2.23
Total CO_2	321,120.00
Solar Co_2 (Per gram)	7,200,000
Co_2 LB conversion	15,873
Difference (in Lbs.)	305,247
Total reduction (in Tons)	153

17. National Renewable Energey Laboratory (NREL), "Life Cycle Greenhouse Gas Emissions from Solar Photovoltaics," National Renewable Energy Laboratory, N.D.
18. IRC Section 30C(e)(1)
19. Joel Brown, "101 Robert Kiyosaki Quotes That WILL Inspire You," Addicted2 Success, May 24, 2014

Chapter 6, Investment #5: Agriculture

1. Argentina - https://assets.ey.com/content/dam/ey-sites/ey-com/en_am/tax-and-law/ey-worldwide-corporate-tax-guide-20-july-2020.pdf

   Australia - https://www.ato.gov.au/Business/Primary-producers/In-detail/Tree-farming-(forestry-operations)/?page=1#Expenses_you_can_claim

   Canada - https://www.oecd.org/officialdocuments/publicdisplaydocumentpdf/?cote=TAD/CA/APM/WP(2018)30/%20FINAL&docLanguage=En

   France - https://www.oecd.org/officialdocuments/publicdisplaydocumentpdf/?cote=TAD/CA/APM/WP(2018)30/FINAL&docLanguage=En

   Germany - https://www.oecd.org/officialdocuments/publicdisplaydocumentpdf/?cote=TAD/CA/APM/WP(2018)30/%20FINAL&docLanguage=En

   India - https://www.incometaxindia.gov.in/Tutorials/11.Tax%20free%20incomes%20final.pdf

   Italy - https://www.oecd-ilibrary.org/sites/4d0e258a-en/index.html?itemId=/content/component/4d0e258a-en

   Japan - https://www.oecd-ilibrary.org/sites/bee9b8cb-en/index.html?itemId=/content/component/bee9b8cb-en

   Mexico - https://www.oecd-ilibrary.org/sites/8c6ab47b-en/index.html?itemId=/content/component/8c6ab47b-en

   Singapore - https://assets.ey.com/content/dam/ey-sites/ey-com/en_am/tax-and-law/ey-worldwide-corporate-tax-guide-20-july-2020.pdf

   South Korea - https://www.oecd-ilibrary.org/sites/1bba4166-en/index.html?itemId=/content/component/1bba4166-en

   Spain - https://www.oecd-ilibrary.org/sites/641fe862-en/index.html?itemId=/content/component/641fe862-en

   Taiwan - https://law.moj.gov.tw/ENG/LawClass/LawAll.aspx?pcode=G0340003

   United Kingdom - https://www.gov.uk/government/publications/how-to-calculate-your-taxable-profits-hs222-self-assessment-helpsheet/hs222-how-to-calculate-your-taxable-profits-2021

United States - https://www.oecd.org/officialdocuments/publicdisplaydocumentpdf/?cote=TAD/CA/APM/WP(2018)30/%20FINAL&docLanguage=En

2. Dan Carmody, "A Growing City: Detroit's Rich Tradition of Urban Gardens Plays an Important Role in the City's Resurgence," Urbandland, Mar 19, 2018
3. Australia - https://www.ato.gov.au/Business/Primary-producers/Managing-varying-income/If-your-business-runs-at-a-loss/#Specialexemptionforprimaryproducers

   Canada - https://fbc.ca/blog/facts-about-full-time-part-time-and-hobby-farming-taxes/

   France - https://books.google.com/books?id=Qu8RlyHtYxAC&pg=PA269&lpg=PA269&dq=%22Hobby%22+laws+for+losses+in+%22France%22+for+farmers&source=bl&ots=tVTFsDhw8c&sig=ACfU3U3ryNnVcmUpdnqbXvXMAC2FSMmiXw&hl=en&sa=X&ved=2ahUKEwiU_6CFtPryAhVpFjQIHdj7AP0Q6AF6BAgxEAM#v=snippet&q=%22France%22%20%22Hobby%22&f=false

   Germany - https://edepot.wur.nl/23200 page 142

   India - https://www.incometaxindia.gov.in/Tutorials/11.Tax%20free%20incomes%20final.pdf

   Italy - https://www.oecd-ilibrary.org/sites/4d0e258a-en/index.html?itemId=/content/component/4d0e258a-en page 42

   Japan - https://www.taxathand.com/article/14978/Japan/2020/Overview-of-opportunities-for-utilization-of-tax-losses-

   Singapore - https://www.iras.gov.sg/taxes/individual-income-tax/self-employed-and-partnerships/business-expenses-and-deductions/business-making-losses-and-unabsorbed-capital-allowances

   United Kingdom - https://www.oecd.org/officialdocuments/publicdisplaydocumentpdf/?cote=TAD/CA/APM/WP(2018)30/%20FINAL&docLanguage=En

   United States - https://www.law.cornell.edu/uscode/text/26/183
4. Australia - https://www.awe.gov.au/agriculture-land/farm-food-drought/drought/assistance/tax-relief

   United Kingdom - https://www.gov.uk/capital-allowances/annual-investment-allowance

   United States - https://www.irs.gov/newsroom/tax-reform-changes-to-depreciation-deduction-affect-farmers-bottom-line
5. Argentina - https://coops4dev.coop/en/4devamericas/argentina

   Australia - https://www.oecd.org/officialdocuments/publicdisplaydocumentpdf/?cote=TAD/CA/APM/WP(2018)30/%20FINAL&docLanguage=En

Canada - https://laws-lois.justice.gc.ca/eng/regulations/SOR-99-256/page-1.html

France - http://www.recma.org/sites/default/files/101102.pdf

Germany - https://www.degruyter.com/document/doi/10.1515/jbwg-2020-0016/html

India - https://mscs.dac.gov.in/Guidelines/GuidelineAct2002.pdf

Italy - https://www.oecd.org/officialdocuments/publicdisplaydocumentpdf/?cote=TAD/CA/APM/WP(2018)30/%20FINAL&docLanguage=En

Japan - https://www.oecd.org/officialdocuments/publicdisplaydocumentpdf/?cote=TAD/CA/APM/WP(2018)30/%20FINAL&docLanguage=En

Mexico - https://www.oecd-ilibrary.org/sites/8c6ab47b-en/index.html?itemId=/content/component/8c6ab47b-en

Singapore - https://sso.agc.gov.sg/SL-Supp/S349-2009/Published/20090730?DocDate=20090730

South Korea - https://www.ilo.org/dyn/natlex/natlex4.detail?p_lang=en&p_isn=93311&p_country=KOR&p_count=145

South Korea - https://coops4dev.coop/sites/default/files/2021-06/Republic%20of%20Korea%20Legal%20Framework%20Analysis%20National%20Report.pdf

Spain - https://www.sciencedirect.com/science/article/pii/S2444883420303016

Taiwan - https://law.moj.gov.tw/ENG/LawClass/LawAll.aspx?pcode=G0340003

United Kingdom - https://www.fca.org.uk/firms/registered-societies-introduction/co-operative-community-benefit-societies-act-2014

United States - https://u.osu.edu/coopmastery/taxation/section-521/

6. Chuck Abbott, "World Farm Subsidies Hit $2 billion a Day," Successful Farming, Jun 30, 2020
7. https://www.ers.usda.gov/publications/pub-details/?pubid=102075
8. https://ec.europa.eu/info/food-farming-fisheries/key-policies/common-agricultural-policy/cap-glance_en
9. https://www.agriculture.gov.au/ag-farm-food/ag2030
10. Craig McAngus and Simon Usherwood, "British fishermen want out of the EU-here's why," the Conversation, Jun 10, 2016
11. The Economist, "British Farming after the common agricultural policy," *The Economist,* Nov 28, 2020
12. Global Ag Media, "UK Government unveils sustainable farming policy," The Pig Site, Nov 30, 2020
13. USDA, "Trip Report – "Japan Agricultural Situation," USDA Foreign Agricultural Service, Aug 17, 2012

Chapter 7, Investment #6: Insurance

1. Sylvia Plath: *Method & Madness*, Edward Butscher 1976, 2003
2. Argentina - https://www.globalexpansion.com/hubfs/Country%20Guides/In%20Use/Argentina+–+Global+Employer+Guide.pdf

   Australia - https://taxsummaries.pwc.com/Austria/Individual/Deductions

   Canada - https://www.sbis.ca/are-health-insurance-premiums-tax-deductible-in-canada-for-the-self-employed.html

   France - https://www.pwc.com/sg/en/international-comparison-of-insurance-taxation-2007/assets/icit2007-france.pdf

   Germany - https://taxsummaries.pwc.com/germany/individual/deductions

   India - https://taxsummaries.pwc.com/India/Individual/Deductions

   Italy - https://home.kpmg/xx/en/home/insights/2011/12/italy-income-tax.html

   Japan - https://home.kpmg/xx/en/home/insights/2011/12/japan-other-taxes-levies.html

   Mexico - https://www.oecd-ilibrary.org/sites/3c92e215-en/index.html?itemId=/content/component/3c92e215-en

   Singapore - https://www.iras.gov.sg/irashome/Businesses/Companies/Working-out-Corporate-Income-Taxes/Specific-topics/Tax-Treatment-of-Insurance-Policy-Premium/

   South Korea - https://taxsummaries.pwc.com/republic-of-korea/corporate/deductions

   Spain - https://www.swisslife.com/en/home/media/media-releases/news-archiv/spain__vidacaixa_salud.html

   Taiwan - https://www.nhi.gov.tw/english/Content_List.aspx?n=599B8630AF05C3CE&topn=46FA76EB55BC2CB8

   United Kingdom - https://www.gov.uk/tax-company-benefits/other-company-benefits-youll-pay-tax-on

   United States - https://www.hioscar.com/blog/small-business-owner-here-are-the-tax-benefits-of-offering-health-insurance#:~:text=Health%20insurance%20is%20one%20of,not%20break%20your%20bottom%20line.
3. Scott Eastman, "The 'Cadillac' Tax and the Income Tax Exclusion for Employer-Sponsored Insurance," The Tax Foundation, June 19, 2019
4. United States Department of Treasury, "Tax Expenditures - FY 2020," Pg. 25 Line 130 Column 2020 https://home.treasury.gov/system/files/131/Tax-Expenditures-FY2020.pdf
5. Argentina - https://www.swisslife.com/content/dam/id_corporateclients/downloads/ebrm/Argentina.pdf

Australia - https://www.ato.gov.au/individuals/income-and-deductions/in-detail/structured-settlements/?page=3

Canada - https://www.canada.ca/en/revenue-agency/services/forms-publications/publications/it365r2/archived-damages-settlements-similar-receipts.html

France - http://www.jus.unitn.it/cardozo/review/2002/cannarsa.pdf

Germany - § 2 EStG

India - Section 2(24) in The Income – Tax Act, 1995

Italy - https://taxsummaries.pwc.com/Italy/Individual/Income-determination

Japan - http://www.japaneselawtranslation.go.jp/common/data/notice/jt.pdf page 50

Mexico - https://www.swisslife.com/content/dam/id_corporateclients/downloads/ebrm/Mexico.pdf

Singapore - https://www.iras.gov.sg/irashome/Businesses/Employers/Tax-Treatment-of-Employee-Remuneration/Lump-Sum-Payments/

South Korea - https://www.ilo.org/dyn/natlex/docs/ELECTRONIC/50778/74102/F1386854528/KOR50778%202015.pdf

South Korea - https://www.oecd-ilibrary.org/sites/b5aacd2e-en/index.html?itemId=/content/component/b5aacd2e-en

Spain - https://www.boe.es/buscar/act.php?id=BOE-A-2006-20764 Law 35/2006, of November 28, Article 7

Taiwan - https://law.moj.gov.tw/ENG/LawClass/LawAll.aspx?pcode=G0340003 Income Tax Act, Article 4

United Kingdom - https://www.gov.uk/hmrc-internal-manuals/insurance-policyholder-taxation-manual/iptm5010

United States - https://www.law.cornell.edu/uscode/text/26/105

6. Argentina - https://www.jebsen.com.ar/en/new-releases/taxation-in-argentina/

Australia - https://taxsummaries.pwc.com/Australia/Individual/Deductions

Canada - https://www.canada.ca/en/revenue-agency/services/forms-publications/publications/it309r2/archived-premiums-on-life-insurance-used-collateral.html

France - https://frenchbusinessadvice.com/Deductible-Expenses-Of-Benefits-Of-Companies-In-France

Germany - https://wealins.com/sites/default/files/Wealins-Life-Germany-Tax_Info_EN_2017-12.pdf

India - https://www.incometaxindia.gov.in/tutorials/20.%20tax%20benefits%20due%20to%20health%20insurance.pdf

Japan - https://www.nta.go.jp/english/taxes/individual/pdf/a-17.pdf

Mexico - https://www.oecd.org/finance/insurance/1815326.pdf

Spain - https://www.oecd.org/finance/insurance/1815326.pdf

Singapore - https://taxsg.com/2019/03/06/deductibility-of-life-or-personal-accident-insurance-premiums/

South Korea - https://taxsummaries.pwc.com/republic-of-korea/corporate/deductions

United Kingdom - https://www.aviva.co.uk/adviser/documents/view/al15007c.pdf

United States - https://www.journalofaccountancy.com/issues/2000/jan/companyownedlifeinsurance.html

7. Argentina - https://www.pwc.com/sg/en/international-comparison-of-insurance-taxation-2009/assets/icit2009-argentina.pdf

Australia - https://www.comparingexpert.com.au/life-insurance/tax/

Canada - https://www.canada.ca/en/financial-consumer-agency/services/insurance/life.html

France - http://publications.ruchelaw.com/news/2016-06/French_Life_Insurance.pdf

Germany - https://www.oecd.org/finance/insurance/1815326.pdf

India - https://www.incometaxindia.gov.in/_layouts/15/dit/pages/viewer.aspx?grp=act&cname=cmsid&cval=102120000000093000&searchfilter=%5B%7B%22crawledpropertykey%22:1,%22value%22:%22act%22,%22searchoperand%22:2%7D,%7B%22crawledpropertykey%22:0,%22value%22:%22income-tax+act,+1961%22,%22searchoperand%22:2%7D,%7B%22crawledpropertykey%22:29,%22value%22:%222019%22,%22searchoperand%22:2%7D%5D&filterby=s&optionalfilter=&k=10(10d)&isdlg=1 (10D)

Italy-https://www.pwc.com/sg/en/international-comparison-of-insurance-taxation-2009/assets/icit2009-italy.pdf

Japan - https://www.oecd.org/finance/insurance/1815326.pdf

Mexico - https://thelawreviews.co.uk/title/the-private-wealth-and-private-client-review/mexico#:~:text=For%20income%20tax%20purposes%2C%20any,company%20is%20a%20Mexican%20insurer.

Singapore - https://www.pwc.com/sg/en/international-comparison-of-insurance-taxation-2009/assets/icit2009-singapore.pdf

South Korea - https://www.pwc.com/sg/en/international-comparison-of-insurance-taxation-2009/assets/icit2009-korea.pdf

Spain - https://www.oecd.org/finance/insurance/1815326.pdf

Taiwan - https://www.pwc.com/sg/en/international-comparison-of-insurance-taxation-2009/assets/icit2009-taiwan.pdf

United Kingdom - https://www.oecd.org/finance/insurance/1815326.pdf

United States - https://www.irs.gov/faqs/interest-dividends-other-types-of-income/life-insurance-disability-insurance-proceeds#:~:text=Answer%3A,t%20have%20to%20report%20them

8. Argentina - https://taxsummaries.pwc.com/argentina/corporate/deductions
   Australia - https://taxsummaries.pwc.com/Australia/Corporate/Deductions
   Canada - https://taxsummaries.pwc.com/canada/corporate/deductions
   France - https://taxsummaries.pwc.com/france/corporate/deductions
   Germany - https://taxsummaries.pwc.com/germany/corporate/deductions
   India - https://taxsummaries.pwc.com/india/corporate/deductions
   Italy - https://taxsummaries.pwc.com/italy/corporate/deductions
   Japan - https://taxsummaries.pwc.com/japan/corporate/deductions
   Mexico - https://taxsummaries.pwc.com/mexico/corporate/deductions
   Singapore - https://taxsummaries.pwc.com/singapore/corporate/deductions
   South Korea - https://taxsummaries.pwc.com/republic-of-korea/corporate/deductions
   Spain - https://www.dentons.com/en/issues-and-opportunities/global-tax-guide-to-doing-business-in/spain
   Taiwan - https://taxsummaries.pwc.com/taiwan/corporate/deductions
   United Kingdom - https://taxsummaries.pwc.com/United-Kingdom/Corporate/Deductions
   United States - https://www.law.cornell.edu/cfr/text/26/1.163-8T
9. David Cummins, Michael Cragg, Bin Zhou, and Jehan deFonseka, "The Social Economic Contributions of the Life Insurance Industry," The Brattle Group, Sep. 2018
10. Cummins, *ibid*
11. Notice that I never do an opportunity cost analysis for the government. This is because the government does not directly have control over how residents or citizens use their money. It cannot be assumed that residents or citizens will put the money to productive use, thereby producing taxable income in which the government would naturally share. Without incentive, the individual would more likely spend their money on items that produce little or no benefit to the government. If the individual puts their money into a bank account, there likely would be little or no earnings to tax. If the individual spends their money on consumable items, then while the expenditure becomes taxable income to the business receiving it, there is no guarantee that the business will make a profit on the money.

12.

Level Premium Whole Life Insurance Policy Tabular Detail

Male 40 Year Old
Male Age 40 Standard No Tobacco Div Opt: PUA
Riders: 7YT LPUA ADBR+ PDF

Initial Annual Premium: $39,999.99
Initial Face Amount: $249,373

		Guaranteed			Non-Guaranteed Assumptions 100% of Current Dividend Scale					
Age	Year	Contract Premium	Net Cash Value	Death Benefit	Contract Premium	Cumulative Premium	Annual Dividend	Increase in Net Cash Value	Net Cash Value	Death Benefit
41	1	40,000	33,532	1,163,230	40,000	40,000	2,165	35,697	35,697	1,165,395
42	2	40,000	69,316	1,297,464	40,000	80,000	2,360	38,219	73,915	1,309,730
43	3	40,000	106,171	1,427,239	40,000	120,000	2,567	39,581	113,496	1,450,152
44	4	40,000	144,127	1,552,714	40,000	160,000	2,990	41,195	154,691	1,587,030
45	5	40,000	183,237	1,674,044	40,000	200,000	3,028	42,500	197,191	1,720,762
46	6	40,000	223,552	1,791,355	40,000	240,000	3,896	44,689	241,881	1,851,048
47	7	40,000	265,103	1,904,774	40,000	280,000	4,726	46,907	288,787	1,980,360
48	8	8,000	277,608	1,129,774	8,000	288,000	5,524	18,844	307,631	1,223,823
49	9	8,000	290,395	1,129,774	8,000	296,000	6,159	19,980	327,611	1,244,418
50	10	8,000	303,472	1,129,774	8,000	304,000	6,337	20,696	348,307	1,266,111
51	11	8,000	316,828	1,129,774	8,000	312,000	6,527	21,425	369,732	1,287,701
52	12	8,000	330,451	1,129,774	8,000	320,000	7,344	22,777	392,509	1,309,825
53	13	8,000	344,321	1,129,774	8,000	328,000	7,585	23,562	416,071	1,333,247
54	14	8,000	358,455	1,129,774	8,000	336,000	7,823	24,379	440,450	1,356,640

This is an illustration only, not an offer, policy, contract, or promise of future policy performance. Coverage is subject to the terms and conditions of the policy.

Level Premium Whole Life Insurance Policy Tabular Detail (Continued)

Male 40 Year Old

Male Age 40 Standard No Tobacco Div Opt: PUA

Riders: 7YT LPUA ADBR+ PDF

Initial Annual Premium: $39,999.99

Initial Face Amount: $249,373

		Guaranteed			Non-Guaranteed Assumptions 100% of Current Dividend Scale					
Age	Year	Contract Premium	Net Cash Value	Death Benefit	Contract Premium	Cumulative Premium	Annual Dividend	Increase in Net Cash Value	Net Cash Value	Death Benefit
55	15	8,000	372,844	1,129,774	8,000	344,000	8,085	25,222	465,672	1,380,004
56	16	8,000	387,523	1,129,774	8,000	352,000	8,335	26,112	491,784	1,403,355
57	17	8,000	402,517	1,129,774	8,000	360,000	8,577	27,042	518,826	1,426,643
58	18	8,000	417,848	1,129,774	8,000	368,000	8,824	28,021	546,847	1,449,842
59	19	8,000	433,523	1,129,774	8,000	376,000	9,070	29,024	575,871	1,472,942
60	20	8,000	449,523	1,129,774	8,000	384,000	9,390	30,093	605,964	1,495,999
61	21	8,000	467,749	1,129,774	8,000	392,000	9,717	33,080	639,044	1,519,112
62	22	8,000	486,441	1,129,774	8,000	400,000	10,107	34,365	673,409	1,542,332
63	23	8,000	505,595	1,129,774	8,000	408,000	10,499	35,661	709,069	1,565,722
64	24	8,000	525,197	1,129,774	8,000	416,000	10,903	36,959	746,029	1,589,273
65	25	8,000	545,251	1,129,774	8,000	424,000	11,325	38,293	784,322	1,612,993
66	26	0	562,108	1,129,774	0	424,000	7,609	31,856	816,178	1,632,742
67	27	0	579,292	1,129,774	0	424,000	7,932	32,883	849,061	1,648,358
68	28	0	596,780	1,129,774	0	424,000	8,288	33,921	882,982	1,664,184
69	29	0	614,586	1,129,774	0	424,000	8,657	35,001	917,983	1,680,243
70	30	0	632,651	1,129,774	0	424,000	9,060	36,043	954,026	1,696,560
71	31	0	650,942	1,129,774	0	424,000	9,477	37,060	991,086	1,713,157
72	32	0	669,380	1,129,774	0	424,000	9,919	37,991	1,029,077	1,730,047
73	33	0	687,897	1,129,774	0	424,000	10,391	38,858	1,067,935	1,747,260

This is an illustration only, not an offer, policy, contract, or promise of future policy performance. Coverage is subject to the terms and conditions of the policy.

Level Premium Whole Life Insurance Policy Tabular Detail (Continued)

Male 40 Year Old — Initial Annual Premium: $39,999.99

Male Age 40 Standard No Tobacco Div Opt: PUA — Initial Face Amount: $249,373

Riders: 7YT LPUA ADBR+ PDF

		Guaranteed			Non-Guaranteed Assumptions 100% of Current Dividend Scale					
Age	Year	Contract Premium	Net Cash Value	Death Benefit	Contract Premium	Cumulative Premium	Annual Dividend	Increase in Net Cash Value	Net Cash Value	Death Benefit
74	34	0	706,425	1,129,774	0	424,000	10,874	39,639	1,107,574	1,764,809
75	35	0	724,931	1,129,774	0	424,000	11,394	40,409	1,147,983	1,782,720
76	36	0	743,403	1,129,774	0	424,000	11,920	41,171	1,189,154	1,801,003
77	37	0	761,818	1,129,774	0	424,000	12,479	41,937	1,231,091	1,819,677
78	38	0	780,177	1,129,774	0	424,000	13,046	42,713	1,273,804	1,838,750
79	39	0	798,445	1,129,774	0	424,000	13,638	43,465	1,317,269	1,858,234
80	40	0	816,567	1,129,774	0	424,000	14,264	44,160	1,361,430	1,878,157
81	41	0	834,451	1,129,774	0	424,000	14,896	44,714	1,406,143	1,898,524
82	42	0	852,042	1,129,774	0	424,000	15,523	45,165	1,451,309	1,919,319
83	43	0	869,259	1,129,774	0	424,000	16,203	45,530	1,496,839	1,940,581
84	44	0	886,014	1,129,774	0	424,000	16,909	45,760	1,542,598	1,962,346
85	45	0	902,181	1,129,774	0	424,000	17,679	45,827	1,588,425	1,984,677
86	46	0	917,625	1,129,774	0	424,000	18,477	45,668	1,634,094	2,007,614
87	47	0	932,222	1,129,774	0	424,000	19,227	45,221	1,679,314	2,031,113
88	48	0	945,802	1,129,774	0	424,000	20,016	44,479	1,723,793	2,055,203

This is an illustration only, not an offer, policy, contract, or promise of future policy performance.
Coverage is subject to the terms and conditions of the policy.

Level Premium Whole Life Insurance Policy Tabular Detail (Continued)

Male 40 Year Old — Initial Annual Premium: $39,999.99

Male Age 40 Standard No Tobacco Div Opt: PUA — Initial Face Amount: $249,373

Riders: 7YT LPUA ADBR+ PDF

		Guaranteed			Non-Guaranteed Assumptions 100% of Current Dividend Scale					
Age	Year	Contract Premium	Net Cash Value	Death Benefit	Contract Premium	Cumulative Premium	Annual Dividend	Increase in Net Cash Value	Net Cash Value	Death Benefit
89	49	0	958,297	1,129,774	0	424,000	20,841	43,615	1,767,407	2,079,937
90	50	0	969,674	1,129,774	0	424,000	21,703	42,685	1,810,093	2,105,369
91	51	0	979,955	1,129,774	0	424,000	22,605	41,797	1,851,889	2,131,557
92	52	0	989,241	1,129,774	0	424,000	23,559	41,108	1,892,998	2,158,572
93	53	0	997,658	1,129,774	0	424,000	24,503	40,609	1,933,607	2,186,422
94	54	0	1,005,420	1,129,774	0	424,000	25,418	40,461	1,974,068	2,215,085
95	55	0	1,012,921	1,129,774	0	424,000	26,257	40,986	2,015,054	2,244,485
96	56	0	1,020,220	1,129,774	0	424,000	26,920	41,439	2,056,493	2,274,434
97	57	0	1,027,134	1,129,774	0	424,000	27,335	41,272	2,097,765	2,304,660
98	58	0	1,033,585	1,129,774	0	424,000	27,738	40,913	2,138,678	2,335,129
99	59	0	1,039,505	1,129,774	0	424,000	28,161	40,410	2,179,088	2,365,871
100	60	0	1,044,826	1,129,774	0	424,000	28,571	39,726	2,218,814	2,396,888
101	61	0	1,049,571	1,129,774	0	424,000	28,912	38,989	2,257,802	2,428,122
102	62	0	1,053,887	1,129,774	0	424,000	29,161	38,445	2,296,247	2,459,493
103	63	0	1,057,796	1,129,774	0	424,000	29,392	37,909	2,334,156	2,490,984
104	64	0	1,061,377	1,129,774	0	424,000	29,608	37,511	2,371,668	2,522,593
105	65	0	1,064,755	1,129,774	0	424,000	29,771	37,319	2,408,987	2,554,272
106	66	0	1,068,235	1,129,774	0	424,000	29,901	37,774	2,446,760	2,585,991

This is an illustration only, not an offer, policy, contract, or promise of future policy performance. Coverage is subject to the terms and conditions of the policy.

Level Premium Whole Life Insurance Policy Tabular Detail (Continued)

Male 40 Year Old — Initial Annual Premium: $39,999.99

Male Age 40 Standard No Tobacco Div Opt: PUA — Initial Face Amount: $249,373

Riders: 7YT LPUA ADBR+ PDF

		Guaranteed			Non-Guaranteed Assumptions 100% of Current Dividend Scale					
Age	Year	Contract Premium	Net Cash Value	Death Benefit	Contract Premium	Cumulative Premium	Annual Dividend	Increase in Net Cash Value	Net Cash Value	Death Benefit
107	67	0	1,071,896	1,129,774	0	424,000	30,153	38,538	2,485,298	2,617,867
108	68	0	1,075,420	1,129,774	0	424,000	30,785	38,957	2,524,255	2,650,279
109	69	0	1,078,810	1,129,774	0	424,000	31,526	39,481	2,563,736	2,683,361
110	70	0	1,082,052	1,129,774	0	424,000	32,403	40,109	2,603,845	2,717,253
111	71	0	1,085,182	1,129,774	0	424,000	33,379	40,910	2,644,755	2,752,062
112	72	0	1,088,164	1,129,774	0	424,000	34,817	42,086	2,686,841	2,788,250
113	73	0	1,091,034	1,129,774	0	424,000	36,420	43,505	2,730,346	2,826,001
114	74	0	1,093,791	1,129,774	0	424,000	38,194	45,093	2,775,439	2,865,489
115	75	0	1,096,412	1,129,774	0	424,000	39,854	46,505	2,821,944	2,906,599
116	76	0	1,098,931	1,129,774	0	424,000	41,398	47,883	2,869,826	2,949,210
117	77	0	1,101,337	1,129,774	0	424,000	42,804	49,088	2,918,915	2,993,176
118	78	0	1,103,631	1,129,774	0	424,000	44,066	50,144	2,969,059	3,038,346
119	79	0	1,105,823	1,129,774	0	424,000	45,189	51,086	3,020,145	3,084,580
120	80	0	1,107,901	1,129,774	0	424,000	46,144	51,821	3,071,966	3,131,702
121	81	0	1,129,774	1,129,774	0	424,000	26,978	87,625	3,159,591	3,159,591

The benefits and values are not guaranteed. The assumptions on which they are based are subject to change by the insurer. Actual results may be more or less favorable.

This is an illustration only, not an offer, policy, contract, or promise of future policy performance.
Coverage is subject to the terms and conditions of the policy.

13. The face value of the policy net of loans is only $1,100,000; presumably the other $500,000 is still owned as equity in the real estate investments. The gross face value is still $1,600,000.

Chapter 8, Investment #7: Retirement Savings

1. Argentina - https://www.reuters.com/article/us-argentina-pensions-facts-1/factbox-argentinas-private-pension-funds-system-idUSTRE49L5ER20081022

   Australia - https://money.usnews.com/money/retirement/articles/2012/05/29/4-countries-with-better-401k-plans-than-the-united-states

   Canada - https://www.swanwealthcoaching.com/knowledge-centre/401k-in-canada

   France - https://ec.europa.eu/social/main.jsp?catId=1110&langId=en&intPageId=4539

   Germany - https://www.lexology.com/library/detail.aspx?g=4d73e768-7b37-4cdb-aad9-188243dc0243

   India - https://www.oecd.org/els/public-pensions/PAG2019-country-profile-India.pdf

   Italy - https://www.oecd.org/els/public-pensions/PAG2019-country-profile-Italy.pdf

   Japan - https://www.oecd.org/els/public-pensions/PAG2019-country-profile-Japan.pdf

   Mexico - https://www.oecd.org/els/public-pensions/PAG2017-country-profile-Mexico.pdf

   Singapore - https://www.investopedia.com/financial-edge/0412/retirement-plans-from-around-the-world.aspx#singapore

   South Korea - https://www.oecd.org/els/public-pensions/PAG2017-country-profile-korea.pdf

   Spain - https://www.oecd.org/els/public-pensions/PAG2019-country-profile-Spain.pdf

   Taiwan - https://www.pensionfundsonline.co.uk/content/country-profiles/taiwan

   United Kingdom - https://money.usnews.com/money/retirement/articles/2012/05/29/4-countries-with-better-401k-plans-than-the-united-states

   United States - https://money.usnews.com/money/retirement/articles/retirement-accounts-you-should-consider

2. Argentina - https://content.next.westlaw.com/9-547-9765?__lrTS=20210214082052909&transitionType=Default&contextData=(sc.Default)&firstPage=true

Argentina - https://www.oecd.org/els/public-pensions/PAG2019-country-profile-Argentina.pdf

Australia - https://www.ato.gov.au/business/super-for-employers/paying-super-contributions/how-much-super-to-pay/

https://www.oecd.org/els/public-pensions/PAG2017-country-profile-Australia.pdf

Canada-https://www.canada.ca/en/revenue-agency/services/tax/registered-plans-administrators/pspa/mp-rrsp-dpsp-tfsa-limits-ympe.html

France - https://www.oecd.org/finance/private-pensions/42565911.pdf

Germany - https://www.oecd.org/finance/private-pensions/42565755.pdf

India - https://www.oecd.org/els/public-pensions/PAG2019-country-profile-India.pdf

Italy - https://www.oecd.org/finance/private-pensions/42566263.pdf

Japan - https://www.oecd.org/els/public-pensions/PAG2019-country-profile-Japan.pdf

Mexico - https://www.oecd.org/els/public-pensions/PAG2017-country-profile-Mexico.pdf

Singapore - https://www.oecd.org/finance/private-pensions/46260911.pdf

South Korea - https://taxsummaries.pwc.com/republic-of-korea/individual/other-taxes

Spain - https://mbwl-int.com/insights/spain-new-pension-contribution-limits/

Taiwan - https://www.pensionfundsonline.co.uk/content/country-profiles/taiwan#:~:text=Employees%20can%20voluntarily%20contribute%20up%20to%206%25%20of%20their%20salary

United Kingdom - https://www.oecd.org/finance/private-pensions/42566007.pdf

United States - https://www.irs.gov/retirement-plans/plan-participant-employee/retirement-topics-401k-and-profit-sharing-plan-contribution-limits

United States - https://www.irs.gov/retirement-plans/plan-participant-employee/retirement-topics-ira-contribution-limits

United States - https://www.irs.gov/retirement-plans/plan-participant-employee/retirement-topics-simple-ira-contribution-limits#:~:text=The%20amount%20an%20employee%20contributes,%2412%2C500%20in%202015%20%E2%80%93%202018

United States - https://www.irs.gov/retirement-plans/plan-participant-employee/retirement-topics-defined-benefit-plan-benefit-limits#:~:text=More%20In%20Retirement%20Plans&text=In%20

general%2C%20the%20annual%20benefit,and%202020%3B%20%24225%2C000%20for%202019)

United States - https://www.irs.gov/retirement-plans/choosing-a-retirement-plan-profit-sharing-plan

3. https://www.canada.ca/en/revenue-agency/services/tax/individuals/topics/rrsps-related-plans/making-withdrawals.html
4. Australian Taxation Office, *Self-managed Super funds*, Australian Government https://www.ato.gov.au/Super/Self-managed-super-funds/
5. Tom Wheelwright, *The Stock Market Is a (Legal) Ponzi Scheme,* Entrepreneur, Sept 25, 2020
6. Argentina - https://www.oecd.org/finance/private-pensions/41408080.pdf

Australia - https://www.oecd.org/daf/fin/private-pensions/2401405.pdf

Canada - https://www.canada.ca/en/revenue-agency/services/tax/technical-information/income-tax/income-tax-folios-index/series-3-property-investments-savings-plans/series-3-property-investments-savings-plan-folio-10-registered-plans-individuals/income-tax-folio-s3-f10-c1-qualified-investments-rrsps-resps-rrifs-rdsps-tfsas.html#toc0

France - https://www.oecd.org/daf/fin/private-pensions/2401405.pdf

Germany - https://www.oecd.org/daf/fin/private-pensions/2401405.pdf

India - https://www.researchgate.net/profile/Shivam-Mca/publication/350846952_NPS_and_NSSF_A_Comparative_Analysis_of_Pension_Schemes_in_India_China/links/6075c39a4585151ce182d14c/NPS-and-NSSF-A-Comparative-Analysis-of-Pension-Schemes-in-India-China.pdf

Italy - https://www.oecd.org/daf/fin/private-pensions/2401405.pdf

Japan - https://www.oecd.org/daf/fin/private-pensions/2401405.pdf

Mexico - https://www.oecd.org/daf/fin/private-pensions/2401405.pdf

Singapore - http://www.nomurafoundation.or.jp/en/wordpress/wp-content/uploads/2019/03/NJACM3-2SP19-06.pdf

South Korea - https://www.oecd.org/daf/fin/private-pensions/2401405.pdf

Spain - https://www.oecd.org/daf/fin/private-pensions/2401405.pdf

Taiwan - https://www.blf.gov.tw/8821/8844/8913/14388/

United Kingdom - https://www.oecd.org/daf/fin/private-pensions/2401405.pdf

United States - https://www.irs.gov/retirement-plans/plan-participant-employee/retirement-topics-plan-assets

7.

Year	Investment Amount	Tax	Interest	Tax on Interest
		32%	6%	32%
1	$ 25,000	$ 8,000	$ 1,020	$ 326
2	$ 25,000	$ 8,000	$ 2,581	$ 826
3	$ 25,000	$ 8,000	$ 3,707	$ 1,186
4	$ 25,000	$ 8,000	$ 4,878	$ 1,561
5	$ 25,000	$ 8,000	$ 6,097	$ 1,951
6	$ 25,000	$ 8,000	$ 7,365	$ 2,357
7	$ 25,000	$ 8,000	$ 8,686	$ 2,780
8	$ 25,000	$ 8,000	$ 10,060	$ 3,219
9	$ 25,000	$ 8,000	$ 11,491	$ 3,677
10	$ 25,000	$ 8,000	$ 12,980	$ 4,154
11	$ 25,000	$ 8,000	$ 14,529	$ 4,649
12	$ 25,000	$ 8,000	$ 16,142	$ 5,165
13	$ 25,000	$ 8,000	$ 17,821	$ 5,703
14	$ 25,000	$ 8,000	$ 19,568	$ 6,262
15	$ 25,000	$ 8,000	$ 21,386	$ 6,844
16	$ 25,000	$ 8,000	$ 23,279	$ 7,449
17	$ 25,000	$ 8,000	$ 25,248	$ 8,079
18	$ 25,000	$ 8,000	$ 27,299	$ 8,736
19	$ 25,000	$ 8,000	$ 29,432	$ 9,418
20	$ 25,000	$ 8,000	$ 31,653	$ 10,129
21	$ 25,000	$ 8,000	$ 33,965	$ 10,869
22	$ 25,000	$ 8,000	$ 36,370	$ 11,639
23	$ 25,000	$ 8,000	$ 38,874	$ 12,440
24	$ 25,000	$ 8,000	$ 41,480	$ 13,274
25	$ 25,000	$ 8,000	$ 44,193	$ 14,142
26	$ 25,000	$ 8,000	$ 47,016	$ 15,045
27	$ 25,000	$ 8,000	$ 49,954	$ 15,985
28	$ 25,000	$ 8,000	$ 53,012	$ 16,964
29	$ 25,000	$ 8,000	$ 56,195	$ 17,982
30	$ 25,000	$ 8,000	$ 59,508	$ 19,043
Total Tax		**$ 240,000**		**$ 241,853**

8.

Year	Investment Amount	Interest	No Tax
		6%	Without Tax @ 6% Return
1	$ 25,000	$ 1,500	$ 26,500
2	$ 25,000	$ 3,090	$ 54,590
3	$ 25,000	$ 4,775	$ 84,365
4	$ 25,000	$ 6,562	$ 115,927
5	$ 25,000	$ 8,456	$ 149,383
6	$ 25,000	$ 10,463	$ 184,846
7	$ 25,000	$ 12,591	$ 222,437
8	$ 25,000	$ 14,846	$ 262,283
9	$ 25,000	$ 17,237	$ 304,520
10	$ 25,000	$ 19,771	$ 349,291
11	$ 25,000	$ 22,457	$ 396,749
12	$ 25,000	$ 25,305	$ 447,053
13	$ 25,000	$ 28,323	$ 500,377
14	$ 25,000	$ 31,523	$ 556,899
15	$ 25,000	$ 34,914	$ 616,813
16	$ 25,000	$ 38,509	$ 680,322
17	$ 25,000	$ 42,319	$ 747,641
18	$ 25,000	$ 46,358	$ 819,000
19	$ 25,000	$ 50,640	$ 894,640
20	$ 25,000	$ 55,178	$ 974,818
21	$ 25,000	$ 59,989	$ 1,059,807
22	$ 25,000	$ 65,088	$ 1,149,896
23	$ 25,000	$ 70,494	$ 1,245,389
24	$ 25,000	$ 76,223	$ 1,346,613
25	$ 25,000	$ 82,297	$ 1,453,910
26	$ 25,000	$ 88,735	$ 1,567,644
27	$ 25,000	$ 95,559	$ 1,688,203
28	$ 25,000	$ 102,792	$ 1,815,995
29	$ 25,000	$ 110,460	$ 1,951,455
30	$ 25,000	$ 118,587	$ 2,095,042

9. When the amount was contributed, the deduction was at the taxpayer's highest margin tax bracket (32%). When the money is withdrawn, assuming no other income, the taxpayer will receive the benefit of the lower tax brackets so the money is, in fact, taxed at a lower rate.
10. J. VanDerhei, S. Holden, L Alonso, and S. Bass, "What Does Consistent Participation in 401(k) Plans Generate?" Changes in 401(k) Account Balances, 2007–2012
11.

Year	Pay Tax		No Tax	
	With 32% Tax @ 6% return		Without Tax @ 6% Return	
1	$	18,020	$	26,500
2	$	36,775	$	54,590
3	$	56,296	$	84,365
4	$	76,613	$	115,927
5	$	97,758	$	149,383
6	$	119,767	$	184,846
7	$	142,673	$	222,437
8	$	166,514	$	262,283
9	$	191,328	$	304,520
10	$	217,154	$	349,291
11	$	244,034	$	396,749
12	$	272,011	$	447,053
13	$	301,129	$	500,377
14	$	331,435	$	556,899
15	$	362,978	$	616,813
16	$	395,807	$	680,322
17	$	429,976	$	747,641
18	$	465,539	$	819,000
19	$	502,553	$	894,640
20	$	541,077	$	974,818
21	$	581,173	$	1,059,807
22	$	622,905	$	1,149,896
23	$	666,339	$	1,245,389
24	$	711,546	$	1,346,613

Year	Pay Tax	No Tax
	With 32% Tax @ 6% return	Without Tax @ 6% Return
25	$ 758,597	$ 1,453,910
26	$ 807,568	$ 1,567,644
27	$ 858,537	$ 1,688,203
28	$ 911,585	$ 1,815,995
29	$ 966,798	$ 1,951,455
30	$ 1,024,263	$ 2,095,042

12. Of course, all this assumes no inflation, raises, and fluctuations in the market. All of which happen in real life. This is why constant monitoring of your investments along with an advisor is so important.
13.

Depreciation over 50 years			
Year	Year 1 Bonus Depreciation	Subsequent Year Depreciation 27.5 year	Total Depreciation
1	$ 25,000	$ 2,727	$ 27,727
2	$ 25,000	$ 5,455	$ 30,455
3	$ 25,000	$ 8,182	$ 33,182
4	$ 25,000	$ 10,909	$ 35,909
5	$ 45,000	$ 15,818	$ 60,818
6	$ 25,000	$ 18,545	$ 43,545
7	$ 25,000	$ 21,273	$ 46,273
8	$ 25,000	$ 26,182	$ 51,182
9	$ 25,000	$ 28,909	$ 53,909
10	**$ 45,000**	$ 31,636	$ 76,636
11	$ 25,000	$ 34,364	$ 59,364
12	$ 25,000	$ 39,273	$ 64,273
13	$ 25,000	$ 42,000	$ 67,000
14	$ 25,000	$ 44,727	$ 69,727
15	**$ 45,000**	$ 47,455	$ 92,455
16	$ 25,000	$ 52,364	$ 77,364
17	$ 25,000	$ 55,091	$ 80,091
18	$ 25,000	$ 57,818	$ 82,818

Depreciation over 50 years			
Year	Year 1 Bonus Depreciation	Subsequent Year Depreciation 27.5 year	Total Depreciation
19	$ 25,000	$ 60,545	$ 85,545
20	$ 45,000	$ 65,455	$ 110,455
21	$ 25,000	$ 68,182	$ 93,182
22	$ 25,000	$ 70,909	$ 95,909
23	$ 25,000	$ 73,636	$ 98,636
24	$ 25,000	$ 76,364	$ 101,364
25	**$ 45,000**	$ 81,273	$ 126,273
26	$ 25,000	$ 84,000	$ 109,000
27	$ 25,000	$ 86,727	$ 111,727
28	$ 25,000	$ 86,727	$ 111,727
29	$ 25,000	$ 86,727	$ 111,727
30	**$ 45,000**	$ 86,727	$ 131,727
31	$ –	$ 84,000	$ 84,000
32	$ –	$ 79,091	$ 79,091
33	$ –	$ 76,364	$ 76,364
34	$ –	$ 73,636	$ 73,636
35	$ –	$ 70,909	$ 70,909
36	$ –	$ 68,182	$ 68,182
37	$ –	$ 63,273	$ 63,273
38	$ –	$ 60,545	$ 60,545
39	$ –	$ 57,818	$ 57,818
40	$ –	$ 55,091	$ 55,091
41	$ –	$ 52,364	$ 52,364
42	$ –	$ 47,455	$ 47,455
43	$ –	$ 44,727	$ 44,727
44	$ –	$ 42,000	$ 42,000
45	$ –	$ 39,273	$ 39,273
46	$ –	$ 36,545	$ 36,545
47	$ –	$ 31,636	$ 31,636
48	$ –	$ 28,909	$ 28,909
49	$ –	$ 26,182	$ 26,182
50	$ –	$ 23,455	$ 23,455

About the Author

Tom Wheelwright, CPA

Tom Wheelwright, CPA, is the creative force behind WealthAbility®, the world's premier Tax-Free Wealth movement serving entrepreneurs and investors worldwide. As the founder and CEO, Tom has been responsible for innovating new tax, business, and wealth consulting, and strategy services for premium clientele for more than 25 years.

Tom is a leading expert and published author on partnerships and corporation tax strategies, a well-known platform speaker and a wealth education innovator. Robert Kiyosaki, bestselling author of *Rich Dad Poor Dad*, calls Tom "... a team player that anyone who wants to be rich needs to add to his team." In Kiyosaki's book, *The Real Book of Real Estate*, Tom, himself, authored Chapters 1 and 18 of this book. Tom also contributed to Robert Kiyosaki's *Rich Dad's Success Stories. Who Took My Money?, Unfair Advantage* and was Robert's adjuvant for *Why the Rich Are Getting Richer.*

Tom has written articles for publication in major professional journals and online resources and has spoken to thousands throughout the United States, Canada, Mexico, Asia, South America, Africa, Europe, and Australia.

For more than 40 years, Tom has devised innovative tax, business, and wealth strategies for sophisticated investors and business owners in the manufacturing, real estate, and high-tech fields. His passion is teaching these innovative strategies to the thousands who come to hear him speak. He has participated as a keynote speaker and panelist in multiple roundtables, and led ground-breaking tax discussions challenging the status quo in terms of tax strategies.

Tom has a wide variety of professional experience, ranging from Big 4 accounting, where he managed and led professional training for thousands of CPAs at Ernst & Young's National Tax Department in Washington, DC, to in-house tax advisor for Pinnacle West Capital Corporation, at the time a Fortune 1000 company. Tom also served as an adjunct professor in the Masters of Tax program at Arizona State University for 14 years where he created the course for teaching multi-state tax planning techniques and taught hundreds of graduate students.

Tom has his Master of Professional Accounting degree from the University of Texas at Austin and his Bachelor of Arts degree from the University of Utah.

Index

f
401(k)aos (Tanner), 136
401(k) plan, 130, 131
borrowing, 119
contributions ceiling, 135
defined contribution plan, 136, 140

A
Accounting methods, 23–29
Accrual method, usage, 26
Agriculture
credits, 102–104
debt, 108–109
deductions, 98–102
farm building purchase, bonus depreciation (usage), 102
government strategies, impact, 105
hobby loss rules, application, 100
investment, 97
impact, policies, 104
incentives, 98–104
non-taxed income, 102–104
tax benefits, offsets, 106
taxpayer strategy, payoff, 106–108
technology, impact, 51–52
Arab Spring, 7
Asset, purpose, 22
Automobiles
acquisition
example, 157f
real estate, combination, 158f
deductions, 155–160
taxation, 159f, 160f

B
Biden, Joe
clean energy investment, 90
presidential preferences, 151
Bonus depreciation/cost allowance, 66
Bonus depreciation, usage, 102, 107–108
Brexit, impact, 104
Bright-line test (IRS), 101
Buildings
appreciation, 148–149
business expense deductions, 76–77
contents, depreciation, 65
cost, segregation, 63
depreciation deduction, investment costs (government rate of return), 78–79
life, 63–64
purchase
building sale, 81
business use, tax savings, 67
example, 73
government costs, 78
residential housing, government responsibility, 76
sale, example, 79
Business
advantage, tax incentives (impact), 14–29
auto calculation, 40
auto deduction, calculation, 41
bright-line test, 101
building use, tax savings, 67

Business (*Continued*)
component, identification, 50
creation, tax incentives, 42
deductions, 49, 116–117
expenses, 49
business purpose, requirement, 18
deductibility tests, 16–17
deductions, 76, 77
tests, 16f
flexibility, increase, 28
growth, encouragement, 20
investment, 13
government payment, 41
money, reinvestment (tax deductibility), 15
owners
expenses, deductions, 41
income postponement, 38
purchase (business use), tax savings, 67
purpose
deductibility, 16
rental real estate deductions test, 61
small business stock (sale), gain (exclusions), 25
starting, incentives, 29–31
tax incentives, 37
policy considerations, 29–34
total home office expenses, allocation, 39
Business Asset Rollover Relief, 72
Business use building, purchase (tax savings), 80
"Buy, borrow, die," 73

C

Capital cost allowance, 62
Capital expenditures, 21–22
country allowance, 21
Capital gains
benefits, 71
rates, 69–71
taxes, impact, 54
Captive insurance, 103, 119
Carbon dioxide reduction per KWH, 203
Cars. *See* Automobiles
depreciation, 40
Cash-based accounting, usage, 98–99
Cash flow, management (importance), 109
Cash method
change, business choice, 27
country allowance, 26–27
usage, 26
Cash surrender value (CSV), 118, 123–124
Central Provident Fund, 130
Certified Professional Accountants (CPAs), importance, 60
Chatzky, Jean, 141
Climate change, impact, 90
Commercial building, purchase (example), 66–67
Commercial development, investment, 59–60
Commercial/industrial construction, government encouragement, 76
Commercial properties, development/ownership, 74
Common Agricultural Policy (CAP), impact, 104
Contribution retirement limits, country analysis, 133–135
Co-operative and Community Benefit Societies Act (2014), 103
Cooperatives Act (1883), 103
Corporate reorganizations, tax-free ability, 171–173
Corporate tax rates, 22f
Cost segregation, 66, 107
laws, 188–190
usage, 107–108

COVID-19 vaccines, government incentives, 53
Credits, 46–48
Cyber-security, importance, 7

D

Debt (agriculture), 108–109
Deductible business interest expense, 18f
Deductions, 45–46
  allowance, 38
  documentation, country approval, 17
  energy deductions, 85–87
  government usage, 15
  tests, 16–20
Defense, aspects, 6–7
Defined benefit retirement plan, 135–136
Defined contribution retirement plan, 135–136
Democratic governments, direct subsidies avoidance, 5–6
Depletion, depreciation (comparison), 85–86
Depreciable asset, sale, 71
Depreciation, 81
  acceleration, 86
  building contents depreciation, 65
  calculation, 63–64, 222–223
  deduction
    investment costs, government rate of return, 78–79
    receiving, 93
    tax benefits/realized investment amounts, 68
  recapture, role (confusion), 195
Depreciation/capital cost allowance, 62
Disney, Walt, 44
Dividend received deduction (DRD), 19
Documentation deductions, rental real estate deductions test, 62
Documented expense, deductibility, 17
Double taxation
  avoidance, 139
    flow-through entities (offering), 20
  single taxation, contrast, 19
Duplex purchase/cost segregation, 125

E

Earnings, double taxation (avoidance), 139
Eco-car tax reduction, 89
Economy, growth (consideration), 34
Edison, Thomas, 44, 89
Education, importance, 8
Elderly, care, 129
Electric charging station, service station example, 94–95
Employee Retirement Income Security Act of 1974 (ERISA), 142
Employees, hiring incentives, 31–32
Employees Provident Fund Organization & New Pension System, 130
Employment, numbers (comparison), 6
Energy, 52–53
  cooperative rules/regimes, 103
  credits, 87–89
  deductions, 85–87
  electric charging station, service station example, 94–95
  equipment, purchase
    government benefit, solar credit benefit, 91
    solar credit benefit, 88
  government purpose, 83
  government strategy, success, 90–91
  investment, 59–60, 83

Energy (*Continued*)
spurring, policies, 89–90
tax incentives, 84–89
natural resources private ownership, 84
production/consumption, 52f
production/independence, 6–7
renewable energy credits, 88–89
taxpayer strategy, payoff, 92–95
US production costs, 85
Entrepreneur, business income (example), 80
Environment, energy investment, 83
Equipment, business expense deductions, 76–77
Estate taxation, proceeds, 118
Excise taxes, exemption, 29
Expense, deductions (tests), 17
Experimentation, process, 50–51
Exports, government purpose, 97

F

Farm building purchase, bonus depreciation (usage), 102
Farming businesses, deduction claim, 98
Federal tax rate, example, 55
Financial goals, example, 156–157
Financial statements, understanding (importance), 109
Flow-through entities, 19
offering, 20
Food
government purpose, 97
importance, 7
Framework Act on Cooperatives, 103
Free-Trade Zones, income tax exemption application, 31

G

Global ramifications, impact, 55
Government Pension System, 130
Governments
funds, leverage, 10
goals, 5–8, 33
government-sponsored activities, wealth (usage), 5
incentivized activities, investments (value), 152
jobs, inefficiency, 6
life insurance tax benefits, 122–123
partnering, 3
reward, 155–160
purpose, 13–14, 43–44
strategy, impact, 35–37, 53–55
taxes
gain, 37
incentives, 2, 44
receipt, example, 36–37
taxpayer, partnership, 153–154
technology developments incentives, 54
Gross income taxes, basis, 1

H

Harris, Kamala, 7
Healthcare, government tax purposes, 43–44
Health, government incentives, 53
Health insurance
deductibility, 113–114
premiums, Tax Foundation estimates, 115
Hobby loss rules, application, 100
HOME Investment Partnerships Program, 75
Home office
allowance, 181–182
depreciation, 39
education, 35, 37–38
expenses, apportionment, 39
total deductions, 42
total home office expenses, allocation, 39
Home ownership, 74
tax incentives, 60–61

Housing
available, government strategy, 77–79
duplex purchase/cost segregation, 125
investment, 59–60
Huawei hardware, US ban, 51
Hydrocarbons, ownership, 84

I

Income, 116–119
generation, 76–77
taxation, proceeds, 118
Incoming tax revenue, 35–36
Individual Retirement Account (IRA), 130
investment, absence, 142
Individual tax rates, 23f
Injury, compensation, 115–116
Innovation, 13–14
government tax purposes, 43–44
Insurance
agent, importance, 60
captive insurance, 103, 119
cash surrender value (CSV), 118, 123–124
deductions, 113–116
government
insurance tax benefits, 122–123
purpose, 111–112
strategy, payoff, 121–123
health insurance deductibility, 113–114
incentives, policies (impact), 120–121
income, 116–119
injury, compensation, 115–116
interest expense, 120
investment, 111
incentives, 113–120
return on investment (ROI), 126
life insurance premiums, 116–117
loan/loan expense, 124
policy, face value (growth), 125–126
tax benefits, 125
tax incentives, 113
taxpayer strategy, payoff, 123–127
total assets/tax benefit, 126f
Intangible drilling costs (IDC), 85
Interest expense, 120
Interest Tracing rules, 120
Internal Revenue Code (IRC)
business applications, 42
Section 183(d), 100
Section 448, 27
International tax incentives, 32–33
Investment
amount, example, 219–220
cash flow, 147
costs, government rate of return, 78–79
incentivization, tax law categories, 9–11
property, example, 146
tax credit (Kennedy proposal), 1
Investor contribution, 106
Italian National Medical Service Funds (Fondi Integrative al Servizio Sanitario Nazionale) contributions, 114

J

JobMaker Hiring Credit, 31
Jobs
creation, 13–14, 34
investment, 59–60
Jobs, Steve, 44
Johnson, Boris, 90
Junior Minerals Exploration Incentives, tax credits, 29

K

Kennedy, John (investment tax credit proposal), 1
Key-man life insurance premiums, 117
Kiyosaki, Robert, 155–156

L

Labor Pension Scheme, salary contribution, 134
Land
  improvements, 64–65
  purchase, 105
Law of Cooperatives (LC), 103
Level premium whole life insurance policy (tabular detail), 211–215
Life insurance
  benefits, payment, 121
  companies, long-term horizon, 121
  premiums, 116–117
  proceeds, taxability, 117–118
Like-kind exchanges, 71–73
  allowance, 71–72
Lincoln, Abraham, 89
Long-term contracts, revenue, 27
Loophole, impact, 9
Loss carryforward, country allowance, 28
Low-income housing
  credit, 68
  tax credit, 75–76
Low-Income Housing Tax Credit (LIHTC) program, 75

M

Macron, Emmanuel, 90
Malware, impact, 51
Manufacturing, investment, 59–60
Marginal tax rate, 137, 142, 144
Mexican Real Estate Investment Trust, real estate contribution, 72
Minimum viable product (MVP), 44
Money reinvestment, tax deductibility, 15
Monsanto, impact, 51
Mortgage interest, deductibility, 74
Multi-State Co-operative Societies Act, 103
Musk, Elon, 44, 89

N

National defense, 6–7
National Employment Savings Trust & Private Pensions, 130
National Rental Affordability Scheme contribution, 75
National security
  government tax purposes, 43–44
  investment, 83
National Socialists, rise, 7
National Strategic Special Area, investment (income deduction), 30
Natural resources private ownership, 84
Necessary deductions, rental real estate deductions test, 62
Necessary expense, deductibility, 16–17
Net income taxes, 15
  assessment, 1
Net Investment Income Tax (NIIT), 92
Net operating losses, 28–29
Non-business income, taxation, 23
  rate, contrast, 24
Non-qualified retirement plan, 131–133
  incentivization, absence, 132
Non-taxed income, 102–104

O

Oil/gas revenues, economies (relationship), 90
Online business, starting, 38
Operator return, irrelevance, 55
Ordinary deductions, rental real estate deductions test, 61
Ordinary expense, deductibility, 16
Ordinary income, 70
Ordinary income/expenses, example, 18
Organization for Economic Co-operation and Development (OECD), 2

P
Paper assets, pension investments (government requirements), 141–142
Pass-through business entity, formation, 23
Pass-through income, taxation, 23
  contrast, 24
Payouts, postponement, 35–36
Pay tax, QRP tax (contrast), 137, 221–222
Pension Fund Regulatory and Development Authority (PFRDA), fund investment, 141
Pension investments, government requirements, 141–142
Pension plan, borrowing, 119
Percentage depletion, 85–86
Permanent gain elimination, 73
Personal residence exemption, sale, 74
PLA Software, 14
Playworx, 14
Pod techniques, 52
PPP loans, impact, 14
Premature death, risk (spread), 120
Private businesses, job creation, 34
Private enterprises, local/federal government leverage, 9
Private-industry labor, output production, 34
Production, 13–14
Productive competitiveness, energy investment, 83
Profit-Sharing Plans, 130
Public Service Pension Fund, 130
Purchases, calculation (example), 39

Q
Qualified Opportunity Zones (QOZ), 72–73
Qualified retirement plan (QRP), 131, 133
  double taxation, avoidance, 139
  example, 143
  government regulation, 132
  investment
    contrast, 138
    tax benefits, 144
  tax, pay tax (contrast), 137, 221–222
  types, 135–136
  usage, benefit, 144–145
Qualified small business corporation shares (QSBCS), disposal, 25

R
Real estate
  bonus depreciation/cost allowance, 66
  capital gains, country differences, 70
  deductions, 61–68
  depreciation, 62
    deduction, tax benefits/realized investment amounts, 68
    recapture, role (confusion), 195
  development credits, 69
  investment, 59
    government purposes, 59–60
    incentives, 60–69
    spurring, policy, 74–77
  land improvements, 64–65
  low-income housing credit, 68
  low-taxed transactions benefit, 69
  non-taxed transactions benefit, 69
  professionals, 60
  rental real estate deductions, tests, 61–62
  sale
    capital gains rates, 69–70
    home ownership, 74
    like-kind exchanges, 71–73
    permanent gain elimination, 73
    tax benefits, 69–74
  segregated components, 63
  syndicators, capital (raising), 95

Real estate (*Continued*)
  tax credits, 68–69
  tax incentives, 61
  taxpayer strategy, process, 79–82
  total tax benefits, 81
  usage, retirement example, 145–149
Registered Retirement Savings Plan (RRSP), early withdrawal penalty, 140
Renewable energy
  credits, 88–89
  deductions, 86–87
  depletion, absence, 85
  technologies, impact, 53
Rental property
  development/ownership, incentives, 75
  useful life, 63
Rental real estate deductions, tests, 61–62
Rent, business expense deductions, 76–77
Research and Development (R&D), 29–30, 66
  business expense, 49
  costs (payment), government money (usage), 56
  credit percentages
    country ranking, 46
    state ranking, 47–48
  credits, 86
  deduction percentages, country ranking, 45
  investment, 43
    example, 55
  tax benefits, qualification, 57
  tax incentive, 56–57
  unused research tax benefits, 56–57
Residential properties, development/ ownership, 74
Retirement, 111
  benefits, government strategy, 142–143
  contribution limits, country analysis, 133–135
  deductions, 133–136
  deferral, 136–139
  financial statement, example, 145f
  incentives, policies (impact), 140–142
  income, analysis, 148–149
  investing, incentives (usage), 132–139
  investment
    cash flow, 147
    property, example, 146
  non-qualified retirement plan, 131–133
  outside of plan, investment (contrast), 138
  plans, government preference, 143
  programs
    country listing, 130–131
    types, 131–132
  qualified retirement plan (QRP), 131, 133
    contribution, example, 137–139
    types, 135–136
  savings, investment/government purpose, 129
  taxation, contrast, 139
  taxpayer strategy, payoff, 143–149
Return on investment (ROI), 126
Revenue, receipt (claim), 177
Risk, spread, 120–121
Rollover Relief, 71
Roth 401(k), tax benefit/liability (absence), 131
Roth IRA
  contributions ceiling, 135
  tax benefit/liability, absence, 131

S

Safe harbor, 100
Sales taxes, basis, 1
Scientific/engineering research, requirement, 50
Security, 111
Segregated components (real estate), 63
Self-undertaking, income, 99
Shelter
  government purpose, 97
  human needs, 76
  providing, 7–8
  technology, impact, 51–52
SIMPLE Plans, contributions ceiling, 135
Single taxation, double taxation (contrast), 19
Small and medium enterprises (SMEs), corporate tax deduction, 24, 30
Small Business Income Tax offset, 24
Small business stock (sale), gain (exclusions), 25
Solar panels
  installation, depreciation deduction, 87–88
  return on investment, 92
  service station, example, 94–95
  tax credit, 91, 93
SolarWinds, hack, 51
Special Singapore Government Securities (SSGS), pension scheme gains, 142
Stamp Duty Land Tax, exemption, 61
State tax rate, example, 55
Store/restaurant building (addition), cost segregation/bonus depreciation (usage), 107–108
Subscription revenue, 27
Substantial holding, 25
Superannuation, 131
Superannuation guarantee (SG), 130
Super funds, investment/usage/ withdrawal laws, 140

T

Taiwan National Health Insurance, deductibility, 114
Tanner, Andy, 136
Taxable income, government share, 35
Tax Cuts and Jobs Act (TCJA), 63, 65–66, 72
Taxes
  benefits, 56–57, 151
    differences, 37
    requirements, 49–51
  bracket, example, 53–54
  corporate tax rates, 22f
  credits, 45, 46
    tax deductions, contrast, 49
  credits/benefits, combination (impact), 56
  deductions, 45, 74
    example, 35–36
    government allowance, 38–39
  deferral, government gain, 36
  elimination strategy, 73
  game, 3–4
    object, 4–5
  incentives, 84–85, 151
    government strategy, impact, 35
    impact, 14–29
    importance, 8, 10
    strategy use, 79–80
    types, 45
  individual tax rates, 23f
  laws
    establishment, 2
    fairness, 152–153
    impact, 8

Taxes (*Continued*)
liability (offsetting), tax incentives (impact), 1
loophole, impact, 9
payment
avoidance, 152
methods, 29
rates, reduction, 22–23
rules, understanding, 4
Tax-Free Wealth (Wheelwright), 73, 80
Taxpayer
government partnership, 153–154
strategy, payoff process, 37–42, 55–57
Technological development
incentives, impact, 44–51
tax incentives, policy considerations, 51–53
Technological warfare, 51
Technology
developments incentives, 54
investment, 43, 59–60
example, 55
Three-out-of-five-year rule, 101
Timber, purchase, 105
Total deductions, calculation, 40–41
Trade, 13–14
Trump, Donald (election preference), 151

U

United States
credit, amount, 87
production costs, 85
Universal Basic Income, 7
Universal life policy, investment value, 118
Unused research tax benefits, 56–57

V

Value Added Tax (VAT), exemption, 29
Vehicles, depreciation limitations, 182–183
Vineyard
building/equipment (purchase), bonus depreciation (usage), 107
development, 106

W

Wealth
building, 4
technologies, impact, 44
increase, 9
WealthAbility®, 14, 55
software, example, 56
WealthAbility® Network, 44
WealthAbility Roadmap™, 44
Welfare, 111
Wheelwright Manahan, 14
Whole life insurance policy, 119
investment value, 118
level premium whole life insurance policy (tabular detail), 211–215
security, 112
Worldwide cereal production growth, 52f

Y

Yang, Andrew, 7